THE
NEW YORK CITY
ARTISAN
1789–1825

Frontispiece: New York in 1807, NYHS

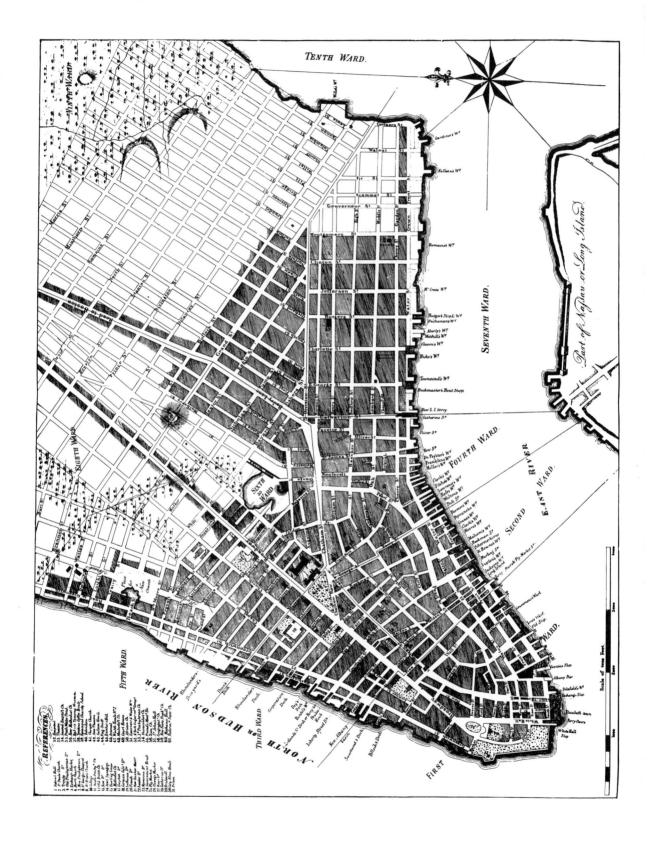

THE NEW YORK CITY ARTISAN

1789–1825

A Documentary History

Edited by
HOWARD B. ROCK

State University of New York Press

SUNY Series in American Labor History
Robert Asher and Charles Stephenson, Editors

Published by
State University of New York Press, Albany

Printed in the United States of America

For information, address State University of New York Press
State University Plaza, Albany, NY 12246

Library of Congress Cataloging-in Publication Data

The New York City artisan: a documentary history, 1789-1825 / Howard B.
  Rock, editor.
          p.   cm. — (SUNY series in American labor history)
    Bibliography: p.
    Includes index.
    ISBN 0-7914-0096-4. — ISBN 0-7914-0097-2 (pbk.)
    1. Artisans—New York (N.Y.)—History. 2. Entrepreneurship—New
York (N.Y.)—History. 3. Small Business—New York (N.Y.)—History.
4. Labor and laboring classes—New York (N.Y.)—History.   I. Rock,
Howard B., 1944-   II. Series.
HD2346.U52N546   1989
331.7'94—dc19   88-32412
                                                             CIP

10 9 8 7 6 5 4 3 2 1

For David and Daniel
Two Aspiring Apprentices

CONTENTS

PART TWO *Politics*

PART THREE *The Marketplace*

PART FOUR *Masters and Journeymen*

Collective Action 215

The Masters' Response 243

LIST OF ILLUSTRATIONS

ABBREVIATIONS

MCNY	Museum of the City of New York
MMNY	Metropolitan Museum of New York
NYCMA	New York City Municipal Archives
NYHS	New-York Historical Society
NYPL	New York Public Library

PREFACE

The early republic, the period covered in this volume, was in many ways the golden age of American artisans. Their craft, represented in New York by such monuments as New York's elegant City Hall or the graceful furniture of Duncan Phyfe, was of the highest order. Politically, their numbers positioned them as one of the critical factors in the monumental struggle for control of the destiny of the new nation. Their shift from the Hamiltonian Federalists to the Jeffersonian Democratic-Republicans was vital to the election of Jefferson in 1800. It also meant that the artisans' vision of republicanism would remain at the forefront of American culture and policy. Economically, craftsmen composed the heart of the urban work force. They were at the center of the transformation of metropolitan production from bespoken or personally ordered goods to large-scale production intended to compete in expanding national and international markets. Journeymen-master labor disputes arising from this transformation provided the seedbed of the American labor movement.

The importance of the American artisan has been recognized in recent years in a number of important monographs. However, to this date there has been no parallel documentary collection. This became most apparent to me a number of years ago while I was on sabbatical at Northwestern University. Spending my days housed in a library carrel close by the multi-volume editions of the works of the founding fathers of the American republic, I often reflected on the lack of such a collection for the men and women who supported and elected these heroic figures. There was, of course, the obvious difficulty that most mechanics left no or few written records. However, in working on my monograph on New York City artisans, I discovered documents that, taken together, provided a direct window into the life and work of this critical segment of American urban society. With the publication of this volume, the mechanic now has the opportunity to be recorded with his words as well as with the many fine craft items that yet grace homes and museums.

In selecting documents for inclusion, I have striven to identify the most representative, most significant, and most colorful of the material available. Original spelling and punctuation are retained. I have provided introductions and, where appropriate, annotation. As much as possible, however, my intention is to allow the space available to remain with the central figure: the craftsman. Thus, endnotes are generally limited, brief, and to the point. In addition to the written material, this collection contains nearly one hundred illustrations. I have sifted through the holdings of many pictorial collections looking for appropriate drawings, paintings, posters, handbills, etc. These constitute important documents themselves.

🙖 🙖 🙖

In putting together this work I have been assisted by a number of institutions and individuals. The New-York Historical Society, one of this country's great repositories, has been most helpful, particularly James A. Mooney, the librarian, and Wendy Shadwell, Curator of Maps and Illustrations. The staffs of the New York Public Library, the New York City Municipal Archives, the Museum of the City of New York, and the Metropolitan Museum of Art offered valuable assistance. In addition, a number of scholars tendered helpful advice, including Graham Hodges, Thomas Schlereth, Sean Wilentz, and the dean and mentor of American artisan studies, Alfred F. Young. My colleagues at Florida International University as well lent much appreciated counsel and encouragement. The difficult compilation and preparation of text owes much to the efforts of Judy Green and Elena Maubrey. The sponsorship and encouragement of Dean James A. Mau and Provost Judith Hicks Stiehm is also deeply appreciated. Finally, my sons David and Daniel, to whom this book is dedicated, and my wife Ellen, whose support is all important, are part of any and all of my achievements.

INTRODUCTION

T hen as today, New York City in the early national era was the most dynamic
urban center in the United States. In 1790 New York, only seven years
removed from British occupation, had but 33,131 residents. By 1800, with
some 60,515 inhabitants, it had surpassed Philadelphia in population and, of
course, has never since been equalled. By 1810 the metropolis housed 96,373
and, by 1825, 166,086 inhabitants. Thus the population quintupled in these
thirty-five years.[1] Physically too, the city grew rapidly. At Washington's inaugu-
ration in 1789 a resident could have walked from one corner of the city to
·another in a half hour or less. A mile's stroll north of the Battery would bring
him to Mr. Rutger's farm in the East followed by a swamp, or to the Collect
Pond in the North surrounded by open fields or, to the West, to the Bulls Head
Tavern and the inception of rural countryside. By 1825, the city was a much
different place, reaching beyond the present Washington Square in the West
and just beyond the present Houston (then North) Street in the East. Too, the
city's streets were constant scenes of construction, trade, exchange, and manufacture; nothing in the country compared to the entrepreneurial spirit of Gotham.

A traveler arriving in New York at almost any time during the early national
era except during war and embargo, would have been awed with the sights.
The elegance of St. Paul's and Trinity Church, both recently constructed, the
austere stature of the Bank of New York, the new City Hall (1815), and the
prominence and bustle of the Tontine Coffee House and Fraunces Tavern
surely would have left strong impressions. A visitor who possessed entry into
the Georgian townhouses of the city's gentry would have held in wonder the
graceful furniture of Duncan Phyfe's shop as well as the many imported pieces
of china, glass, and assorted decor. Too, the sumptuous mid-day meal—courses
of fish and poultry, topped by wine and cigars—would perhaps have struck the
visitor as it did one British traveler, as "more luxurious than that of the same
description of people found in England." Other evidence of the burgeoning
wealth of New York and the willingness of New Yorkers to display it could be
seen in the polished carriages with livery that crowded the streets, in the carefully tailored waistcoats and breeches for men and the resplendent gowns for
ladies, and in the carefully prepared hair and headware of both sexes. The

Broad Street, 1797. GEORGE HOLLAND, WATERCOLOR, STOKES COLLECTION, NYPL

New York housed a mercantile and professional class possessing elegant coaches and distinguished townhouses. Broadway from Bowling Green, 1826. W.J. BENNETT, AQUATINT, ENO COLLECTION, NYPL

many drawing and music schools for young women and the frequent cotillions, assemblies, concerts, and theatrical performances paid tribute to the refined life and culture available to New York's elite.[2]

Even while admiring the wealth and elegance of New York City, our visitor could not have missed the ample evidence of poverty and distress. The city and state had the highest number of slaves in the North, most of them working as domestic servants. They could be observed in the homes and on the carriages of the mercantile gentry. So too New York was the center for Irish immigration—7,000 arrived in 1817—many of whom settled in the sixth ward. These poor migrants joined the free blacks and unskilled laborers who found shelter in two- to three-story homes in which up to sixty souls crowded together. In periods of epidemic, severe weather, or economic recession, large numbers depended on relief. During the yellow fever epidemic of 1798, the city maintained 2,400 impoverished citizens as the majority of wealthy citizens fled the city; during the cold wave of 1805, Mayor Dewitt Clinton was concerned over the survival of 10,000 New Yorkers; and during the economic dislocations in 1814 caused by the war with Britain, 19,078 people, or more than one-fifth of the city's population, were assisted by public agencies.[3]

Between the lower-class population—slaves, the destitute and the unskilled—who clung to a bare subsistence and the wealthy stood the artisan classes. To find their residences and workshops our out-of-town visitor would have had to wander past the shops and offices on Pearl and Broad Street toward the outer wards of the city. Here there was a marked contrast in the setting. The expertly built brick buildings gave way to two- and three-story wooden constructions, some of them hastily erected, varying greatly in size and style. Behind these shelters would be sheds and yards and alleys filled with assorted livestock and piles of wood. The streets, often unpaved and with perilous footing, were filled with wandering animals, particularly pigs (17,000 in 1817), that were allowed to scavenge at large. Occasional empty fields were littered with the fetid remains of decaying animals and vegetable matter. Near the docks sewage was piled in unseemly fashion.

These were the mechanic wards, home of the great majority of the city's artisan population. While the poor also lived in pockets within these areas, for the most part these mechanic wards, though in striking contrast to the more genteel areas, were not slums but rather modest and respectable sections of the city. If up early, perhaps at six, our visitor would see many craftsmen, dressed in leather pantaloons and jackets, on their way to work, many to the shipyards near the docks or to construction sites throughout the city; others to workshops located in every ward. Some areas were known for the presence of specific craftsmen. In the sixth ward, for example, scores of craftsmen would be saddling their horses and driving off to fill the city's streets with vehicles of every shape imaginable as they transported the wares of the bustling port. Our visitor would also have been advised to keep careful lookout for racing drivers. In the fourth ward, his sense of smell would surely locate the enterprises of the city's tan-

A cartman delivering tea-water (drinking water) in the mechanic wards. Generally, two to three artisan families rented space in a dwelling. These often had alleys running between them and pens in back in which animals were kept. William Chappel, a tinsmith, painted scenes of early nineteenth-century New York from memory in the 1850s and 1860s. OIL ON CARDBOARD, EDWARD ARNOLD COLLECTION, MMNY

ners. The garrets of many of these dwellings contained shoemakers with their awls and lasts or tailors with needles, patterns and wool.

In any of the wards, our traveler would seldom see these craftsmen returning home for a leisurely afternoon dinner. While they did take a number of breaks, mechanics generally remained on the job until sundown. Some lived behind their shop in their own home, but most rented crowded space in one of the wooden houses. While their residences were not as crowded as those of immigrants and unskilled laborers, still a number of families, totalling twenty-five to thirty residents, generally lived in four- or five-room dwellings, while single journeymen tended to lodge in boarding houses close to the waterfront.[4]

The term "mechanic," the most common word used to depict artisans in this era, generally referred to skilled handicraftsmen who owned their own tools. Master craftsmen worked either for themselves or as foremen for con-tractors and merchants; journeymen worked for a daily and weekly wage or for a piece rate. Unlike the rural craftsman who often was a 'jack of all trades,' urban artisans worked in a large number of specific trades ranging from intricate gold- and silversmithing to the refined labor of cabinetwork, to the hard chores of black-smithing and the demanding routines of baking and butchering.[5]

A shoemaker stitching in his shop. ANDERSON COLLECTION, NYPL

Many of these crafts required complex skills that could be acquired only after many years of training and refinement. Shoemaking, for example, involved a number of separate tasks. Working in a shop or at home, the craftsman cut the leather to the needed shape, then hammered it on a lapstone, sized it on a last, and sewed on the heel. The shoemaker then carefully fastened the shoe through stitching and the use of a leather welt, and, finally, trimmed and polished it. Each of these procedures could be done crudely or carefully, and the result was either rough footwear conforming very loosely to a size or a precisely fitted shoe and boot carefully sewn and designed. Cabinetmaking, one of the most demanding of the mechanic trades, required knowledge of drawing, proportion, current styles, wood texture and adaptability, as well as expert skill in such processes as veneering, gluing, varnishing and joint construction. Here again, the quality of the work could vary immensely, as the large-scale production of windsor chairs required far less artful skill than the erection of a piano forte or a specially designed bureau.

The artisan population of New York that worked at these many crafts was large, composing between 50 and 60 percent of the city's occupational force. This ranged from 4,000 working tradesmen in a population of 33,031 in 1790 to approximately 14,000 craftsmen in a population of 123,706 in 1820.[6] There were, of course, many subcommunities; mechanics divided according to religious preference, ethnic background, individual craft, neighborhood, political affiliation, and journeyman or master craftsman status.

Beyond all of these differences, however, New York's artisans clearly remained a community, a social group with a common heritage and common

Pedestal End Sideboard of Duncan Phyfe (1825).
Notice the intricate carving and finishing. MCNY

interests and characteristics. It perceived itself and was perceived as distinct in some respects from the rest of society. The primary determinant of this uniqueness was unquestionably professional skills. It was the association with skilled manual labor that allowed poor craftsmen to differentiate themselves from unskilled laborers, while the same association with artisan production separated more eminent mechanics from the city's gentry. Other characteristics such as common dress and similar housing and place of residence also contributed to this mutual identity, as did continuing historic traditions such as the apprenticeship required to learn the mystery of a craft. Also affirming and fostering a sense of community were the fraternal associations that mechanics joined for social and recreational outlets. Politics as well was a significant forum for separate community involvement, coming to a height in the Revolutionary era but continuing throughout the early national era. The greatest evidence of this sense of common identity was that artisans were the single group to whom most election appeals were addressed. No ethnic or religious group rivalled them.

An ancient final bond that united artisans was the historic perception of craftsmen as men of inferior status and lesser ability. Definitions taken from Samuel Johnson's noted *Dictionary of the English Language* reveal the standing that craftsmen occupied. Johnson terms a mechanic as "mean, servile; of mean occupation," while quotations in the *Oxford English Dictionary* reinforce this point. A study of colonial printers found that they, like their counterparts in England, "had to face the hard, discouraging fact that in the eyes of their neighbors they were by training mechanics, without full legitimacy as men of independent intellect and creed." A biographer of Alexander McDougall, a milkman who rose to become a leader of the Sons of Liberty and later a general in the Continental Army, noted the strong influence of a "deference-based" society on his character.[7]

This legacy of deference and deferential expectations was, however, offset by a colonial experience that, based upon widespread land availability and a shortage of labor, allowed craftsmen greater possibilities for economic advancement than was commonly available in England. Lower suffrage requirements in New York also permitted increased political participation, at least to the extent of choosing among the elite groups that vied for power in eighteenth-century New York.

With the coming of the Revolution, artisans took on an active political and military role that resulted in a new sense of pride and dignity in being part of the birth of a republic. Sean Wilentz, in his recent book, *Chants Democratic: New York City and The Rise of the American Working Class,* describes the ideology of the artisan community as one of "artisan republicanism." The Revolution molded a spirit of solidarity within the artisan community. Artisans' reading of Thomas Paine and participation in the crowds of the Stamp Act and the Mechanics committee that shared governance in New York resulted in the integration of a political philosophy based upon longstanding republican traditions. To artisans republicanism meant that society was best governed by those who were most critical to its well-being: the producers. Those who accumulated property without a productive trade—mercantile speculators, bankers, lawyers— were politically suspect. As Jefferson idealized the independent yeoman, republicanism idealized the small, independently owned artisan shop. The workshop was a place of harmony where masters and journeymen worked cooperatively to produce the vital goods necessary for the economic welfare of the new nation. Under this ideal there was no conflict within mechanic ranks, as journeyman standing was to be only a temporary stop on the road to full proprietorship. Moreover, the collective craft spirit of the shop was reflected outside the workplace in a sense of public service that held the needs of the body politic of higher importance than those of individual gain. Indeed, the useful harmony of the workshop was the ideal that the nation as a whole ought to strive for if the new republic was to succeed.[8]

Equally prominent as this public spirit of republicanism was a more individualist and Lockean sense of the meaning of the new nation. As Joyce Appleby has pointed out, the American Revolution ignited a spirit of expectant capitalism within the ranks of Jeffersonian partisans, including much of the artisan community. At last free of British mercantile restrictions, artisans understood the Revolution to mean unlimited economic horizons. Republicanism and capitalism went hand in hand as the spirit of freedom, the end of deference and aristocracy, and the new meaning of equality demanded a truly open marketplace.[9]

These two forms of republicanism—one based on the civic humanism of Machiavelli's Florence and the other on the individualism and contractual society of Locke—form the basis of the current debate over the meaning of republicanism in early national America. Both strains were clearly present among the mechanic community. Both were useful in attacking the lingering remnants of a deferential society. Both had contradictions. How, for example, could a sense of public spirit, of civic humanism, of a harmonious workshop, survive as fewer and fewer journeymen became able to attain the standing of independent proprietor? Or, how could the free market guarantee republican society as the gap between the wealthy and the middling artisan classes increased and the influx of capital only made economic independence and advancement less common?[10]

Ultimately, neither in politics nor in the marketplace could artisans control their fate, and republican ideals would falter in the wake of the rise of new national political parties while economic aspirations would eventually yield to the forces of what Wilentz terms "metropolitan industrialization."[11] Yet the sweatshops and impoverishment that overtook much of the artisan community in the 1830s could not be foreseen in the age of Jefferson. This was an age of optimism among both major segments of the craftsman population: journeyman and master. The documents within this collection illustrate the expectations spawned by the American Revolution within this sector of American society and their efforts—successful and unsuccessful—to shape the nation to its ideals. It is a colorful, dramatic, hopeful if ultimately disappointing effort, one that played a vital part in the shaping of American social and labor history.

PART ONE

Citizenship

The impact of the American Revolution markedly affected all aspects of a crafts-man's life. At work, in politics and at home, he lived in a new republican world, one much altered from that of his colonial predecessor. Since the new country was one of his making and not one that he had found himself in by chance of fate, the artisan in early national New York was actively and constantly conscious of his new status as a free citizen of a republic.

THE LEGACY OF '76

On no occasion did mechanics more proudly declare and exhibit their sense of nationalism and republicanism than at celebrations of national holidays, particularly the Fourth of July. On that day, various artisan societies, composed of masters, journeymen or on some occasions both, would assemble, march in procession, listen to an oration (often given by a member of one of the associations), and then partake in a festive dinner climaxed by round after round of patriotic and congratulatory toasts (Document 1). Holiday sermons and toasts are particularly insightful for their expression of the particular meaning of republicanism to mechanics. Common were vivid recollections of the tyranny of British rule; exaltation of the new age of American freedom, preserved by democracy and civil liberties; and declarations of the need for citizens to exercise their political rights within a framework of self-sacrifice and virtue. There was no room in America for pretensions of aristocracy or expectations of deference. No hereditary holding unwarranted by merit should hinder craftsmen from their place in the market and their due share in government. The possession of wealth did not imply any particularly genius or ability. Many of these themes—encompassing the proud ideals of civic humanism on this day of remembrance of common good and collective sacrifice—are to be found in the important oration of sailmaker James Warner in 1797 (Document 2). Warner, along with John T. Irving (Document 3) placed particular emphasis on the centrality of the artisan to the well being of the republic. It was he (with the yeoman) who would maintain the virtue and sensibility necessary to keep the ship of state on course.[1]

Patriotism, love for and identity with the new country, was deeply felt within the artisan community. Celebrations of the various craft societies, such as the cordwainers, commonly intertwined in their toasts images of the craft with praise of the nation (Document 4). So, too, major national events such as the ratification of the Constitution (1788) and the completion of the Erie Canal (1825) saw long parades in which artisan societies marched proudly, emblems flying, once again expressing the importance of the crafts to the republic (Document 5). War or threat of war too saw artisans rally by trade to volunteer their labor, while victories or peace also saw elegant displays (Documents 6-7).[2]

National pride and celebration extended to the French Revolution; most craftsmen viewed this momentous event as an affirmation and continuation of the American cause. Artisans were strong supporters of the new government in Paris and proudly wore French emblems, sang French songs, and some even took to calling themselves "citizen." They composed the core of the membership of the Democratic Societies which openly supported the French cause. The Preamble and a section of one of its public statements illuminate the spirit and hope that the Revolution kindled in patriotic mechanics as well as other citizens (Documents 8-9).[3]

1. Fourth of July Celebration, 1810

REPUBLICAN JUBILEE

ARRANGEMENTS for celebrating the commencement of the Thirty Fifth year of American Independence.

At sun rise the National Flag will be displayed at the places of meeting of the different Societies.

The different Societies will march from their respective places of meeting, and assemble in the Park, at 9 o'clock precisely, where, under the direction of Robert Townsend, Jun., Grand Marshall of the day, they will be formed in the following order:

1st   Tammany Society, or Colombian Order
2d   Taylor's do.
3d   Hatter's do.
4th   Hibernian Provident do.
      Grand Standard of the Union, supported by the
      Genius of America, and Music
5th   Mason's Society
6th   Carpenter's do.
7th   Shipwright's do.
8th   Columbian do.
9th   Military Officers (off-duty)
10th Naval Officers (off-duty)
11th The Corps of Veterans bring up the rear

When the Societies are formed a National Salute will be fired in the Park by the corps of Veterans, commanded by Capt. John McLean, after which the procession, preceded by a Herald on Horseback, sounding a trumpet, will immediately proceed from the Park to Beekman street, down Beekman street to Pearl street, through Pearl to Cherry street, thro' Cherry to East Rutgers, up

The Tammany society celebrating the Fourth of July, 1812. Tammany, which counted many aspiring artisans within its membership, was originally a fraternal society, but became both political and Jeffersonian in the 1790s. Known for its Indian costumes and Tammany Hall (left) it marched with other artisan and fraternal societies on the Fourth. This scene is on Park Row looking south toward the brick Presbyterian church with City Hall Park to the west. WILLIAM CHAPPEL, OIL ON CARD-BOARD, NYHS

East Rutgers to the Presbyterian Church, the procession will halt, and open from right to left, the Genius of America then descending from the pedestal will receive Tammany and Columbus, when followed by the supporters and the music, and headed by the Grand Marshal will proceed up the line into the Church; the Naval and Military Officers and Societies will immediately follow in reversed order.

The Societies being seated, the Grand Marshal will call the whole to order, and then announce the ceremonies of the day to be as follows, viz.:

1st An Address to the *Throne* of Grace by the Rev. Mr. Muldoller.

2nd An Appropriate piece of Music, by the Band

3rd The Declaration of Independence will be read by Citizen George Harson, Junr. from the Carpenter's Society

4th Music will again perform while a collection is made

5th An oration will be delivered by Doctor Cumming from the Hibernian Provident Society

6th Music Again

7th To be concluded with prayer, by the Rev. Doctor Kuyper

The ceremonies of the Church being concluded, the Societies &c. will return under the Grand Marshal, in the same order from the church, through Essex street to Hester street, through Hester street to Bowery Lane, down Bowery Lane to Chatham street, through Chatham street to the Park, when the Grand Marshal will form the Societies in a circle, in the centre of which will be placed the Grand Standard and Music, inclosed by the Standards and Banners of the different Societies. The Band will perform some appropriate airs; after which the Standards and Banners will be borne to their respective Societies, a signal will then be given by the Grand Marshal for nine cheers, accompanied with music by the Band, which on the discharge of a gun by the Veteran Corps, the Societies will return to their respective places of meeting.

American Citizen, July 4, 1810

2. Fourth of July Oration, 1797

MEANS FOR THE PRESERVATION OF PUBLIC LIBERTY
GEORGE JAMES WARNER

Fellow Citizens,

Again we are met to celebrate the Birthday of OUR NATION. One, untaught in the Schools of Science, is deputed to address you on the great, the interesting event. In undertaking the task, he trusts that your candor will accompany him, and that you will not be disappointed by the absence of talents which his situation in life has prevented him from acquiring. He does not aspire to lead the judgement, or to rouse the passions by any elocutive strains—the display of Ciceronian oratory or of Demosthenian eloquence; he will be amply gratified, if he can only command your attention while he delivers a few plain sentiments, expressed in the sincerity of patriotism.

The Historians of our country have acquainted us with the rise, progress, and establishment of her freedom and independence. They have told us, and many here *this day* well remember, how the earnest petitions of the people for a redress of grievances were disregarded; every new supplication producing some new outrage, or some severer act of oppression. A mere posture of defence was at length deemed a signal for the spilling of blood, and at Lexington it first streamed, in the glorious cause of Freedom and our Country. Thus rendered hopeless of gaining by submission, and left without prospect of any reasonable accommodation; finding our Country invaded, our Towns fired, and our Citizens inhumanly butchered, the delegates from the then provinces, solemnly appealing to Heaven for the rectitude of their intentions, declared America emancipated from the yoke of Monarchic Sovereignty, and freed from any dependence on BRITAIN.

The language of that celebrated declaration we have just heard. It was the voice of an oppressed people exclaiming against the assumptions of a Government, which while it was arrogating every thing to itself, contemplated to leave us nothing. The sentiments contained in it, ought to be deeply engraven on every heart—they point out the true condition of man—they speak the language of a bold resistance to tyranny, and we may indeed expect that Liberty herself will expire, when they shall cease to be longer respected among us.

This, however, we have reason to hope will not be the case. We trust that the same American spirit and virtue which animated to the contest the Heroes of the Revolution, and induced them to refer toil, and poverty, and suffering, and death to the slavery of their Country, will still predominate in every breast. It was gloriously triumphant over the proud legions of DESPOTIC BRITAIN; and it has subsequently prevailed in directing the National Convention of '87, to the Constitutional establishment of the liberty we at this day enjoy. May it ever continue the safeguard of Republican virtue, the scourge of anarchy, and our guide to the summit of political happiness!

To those who faithfully accomplished these events, we shall *ever* feel ourselves *greatly* indebted, while a sense of LIBERTY and JUSTICE prevails among us. The glory which as a people we have acquired by the Revolution, and the prosperity and happiness we have experienced since that period, have amply repaid us for all the hardships endured, and all the dangers encountered in its accomplishment. To PERPETUATE the advantages we possess unimpaired to the latest posterity, is now a duty incumbent on us, as the original actors are daily passing away from this stage of human things, and as they vanish are seeming to say to their posterity, "improve on what we have done, and let not our labours be lost to the future benefit of Mankind."

Perhaps the present opportunity cannot be better employed, than by calling your attention for a few moments, to some of the means necessary to effect this desirable end.

And *first*, in addition to the sound system of Legislative policy which has been GENERALLY adopted in our country, and has grown out of the principles of our Revolution, we must individually encourage by example and by precept, the practice of all the *moral virtues*. Without *these* no free government can long exist. That they are the only true sources of individual happiness is generally conceded, though unfortunately they are but little practised.

The Bible, a venerable old book, now too often laid by on the shelf, dusty and neglected, contains an ample enumeration of them, and a glorious promise of the advantages resulting from their general application and use. This leading principle in the composition of a free government, "Do unto others as you would have others do unto you," is derived from that invaluable source; and were all our actions performed under the influence of this principle, union, equal liberty, and the steady administration of justice might certainly be expected as the happy result. We should then become better men, more disinterested patriots and honester politicans. For what man is there who possesses virtuous sentiments himself, and would not *cherish* and approve of them in others? Who that sincerely loves liberty, would not conscientiously wish its enjoyment to all the members of the community, and join in every proper measure necessary to its preservation?

The principle contended for, is so plain in itself, that it would scarcely have been deemed necessary to call it into view, on this occasion, were it not, that many at the present time shew themselves willing to evade every injunction to the strict observance of the duties of morality, as bordering too much on the principles of the Christian Religion, a remnant of superstition, which the *superior light* of the present day has rendered *quite* unfashionable.

Secondly. We must guard as a most invaluable privilege, the freedom and rights of election. WHEREVER the wealthy by the influence of riches, are enabled to direct the choice of public officers, *there* the downfall of liberty cannot be very remote. It is our own fault if an influence so dangerous, has become in any measure prevalent among us. It would not be the case if the people did not consent to become the dupes of design. It is because tradesmen, mechanics, and the industrious classes of society consider themselves of TOO LITTLE CONSEQUENCE to the body politic that *any thing* belonging to the system of oppression at all obtains. We ought to spurn from us with disdain, the individual who would solicit our vote, from motives of personal consideration. He ought not to be listened to, who would *demand* it as the price of friendship, or who would *expect* it from regard to his superior riches. It too often happens that men only capable of attracting public notice by an ostentatious display of their wealth, are deemed best qualified to protect the rights of the people, and consequently receive their suffrages; while our choice ought only to be directed to men of TALENTS and VIRTUE whatever their situation in life may be. The *possession* of riches is not necessarily accompanied by superior understanding or goodness of heart. On the contrary, the experience of ages confirms this opinion, that a state of mediocrity is more favorable to them both.

If, instead of improving on its original plan, our government, at any future period, should be irresistably impelled in an unalterable course toward despotism, the dividing line between the *rich* and the *poor* will be distinctly marked, and the *latter* will be found in a state of vassallage and dependence on the former.

Be it your care then, my fellow-citizens, to guard with unceasing vigilance against the growth of this evil; assume the native dignity of your character and maintain with a modest but determined spirit, the liberty of opinion. Suffer no one to DICTATE imperiously what line of conduct you are to pursue; but at the same time let no one be sacrificed at the alter of public vengeance, for a candid and liberal expression of his sentiments.

Thirdly. We must endeavor to acquaint ourselves with the political situation and relative interests of our country. Without this information, we shall either be unable to form an accurate opinion of our own, or often become the dupes of the designing. The PUBLIC PRINTS naturally present themselves as the vehicles of this necessary knowledge. Those conducted in a spirit of liberality, yet altogether consonant to the principles on which our revolution was achieved, should employ the public attention and meet its decided support. It will be found, that a JUST and EQUAL GOVERNMENT will ever derive additional stability, as the PEOPLE obtain a more general knowledge of its principles and operations. The result is, that every sincere friend to our NATIONAL CONSTITUTION, ought sedulously to promote the dissemination of this knowledge, as a barrier to the risings of sedition, as well as to the encroachments of arbitrary power.

Fourthly. Be solicitous that your children are properly educated. "Education," says the celebrated Godwin,[4] "has the advantage of taking MIND in its original state, a soil prepared for culture, and as yet uninfested with weeds: certainly the task is much easier, to plant right and virtuous dispositions in unprejudiced understandings, than to root up errors that have already, as it were, become a part of ourselves." Give your children, then, as your ability may permit, the opportunity of receiving instruction in the commonest branches; and if possible, instruct them yourselves, as to the RIGHTS which they possess, and the DUTIES which they owe society. Teach them to love their country; to contend for liberty; to despise monarchy:—That while constitutions and written forms are susceptible of improvement, the principles of TRUTH and of JUSTICE are eternal and imprescriptible. Learn them, as their political creed, that immortal declaration of our rights and emancipation, the promulgation of which, we have *this day* met to celebrate. Encourage them to the reverence of the aged; to the exercise of candor, sincerity, and universal benevolence; and in general to the practice of every social and moral virtue.

Thus will the increase of knowledge and patriotism be promoted, as we shall have far less reason to fear the PREDICTED reign of VICE and TYRANNY. How often have we been told, that our government, fast following in the footsteps of the ancient establishments of Europe, will *soon* overtake them in a career of despotism? Have we not heard the language of complaint resounding through the nation—the sword of the REVOLUTION long since returned to its scabbard, is buried in rust; the rights which it maintained, and the principles which it defended, are nearly forgotten. A FATAL SECURITY, while it obliterates and cancels what is past, opens an ample field for the sports of TYRANNY and the arts of CORRUPTION! Reflection, the nurse of manly and heroic sentiments, the guardian, life, and protector of public freedom, is extinguished! The hoary WARRIOR feels our ingratitude and laments our weakness. The tear of regret steals down his channeled cheek. On the precipice of the grave, he sighs for the misfortunes and the servitude of future generations. Seven LONG YEARS have I toiled in vain—the principles for which I struggled, are withering away—the rising generation are forgetting their rights, and neglecting the duties of freemen. I rejoice that I cannot live, to be a witness of the shame and enthralment of my country. It wounds me to the heart, to see some of those who gallantly fought by my side—who swore never to survive the disgrace of their country, the determined advocates of measures that are pregnant with public ruin. With indignation I see them pursuing maxims of government, that lead to the misery and degradation of mankind. BUT, I see them through the veil of years, and feel myself incapable of arresting their progress. Yet a *little* time and I am no more—a perversion of principle and a corruption of heart, will insult my memory, and triumph o'er my grave!' Who can view *without emotion*, this interesting picture of our situation, which the imagination has drawn? Who is there, that would *designedly* render it just? If none of us would, then ought we to endeavor to preserve the purity of public morals, and to keep a watchful eye over the *conduct* of our public officers: for whatever their political sentiment may be, we ought never to forget that they are MEN.

MEANS

FOR THE

PRESERVATION

OF

𝔭𝔲𝔟𝔩𝔦𝔠 𝔩𝔦𝔟𝔢𝔯𝔱𝔶.

—

ORATION

DELIVERED IN THE NEW DUTCH CHURCH,

ON THE

FOURTH OF JULY, 1797.

BEING THE TWENTY-FIRST

ANNIVERSARY OF OUR INDEPENDENCE,

By *G. J. WARNER.*

"COLUMBIA, Hail! immortal be thy Reign,
Without a king, we till the smiling Plain :
Without a king, the Laws maintain their Sway,
While Honor bids each generous Heart obey,
Be OURS the Task, the Ambitious to reftrain,
And this great Leffon teach---that kings are vain ;
That warring Realms to certain Ruin hafte,
That kings fubfift by War ; and Wars are Wafte :
So fhall OUR NATION, form'd on VIRTUE's Plan,
Remain the GUARDIAN of the RIGHTS OF MAN."
Freneau.

NEW-YORK :
PRINTED AT THE ARGUS OFFICE,
FOR
THOMAS GREENLEAF AND NAPHTALI JUDAH.
==
1797.

Title Page of Warner, Means for the Preservation of Public Liberty. *Most Fourth of July orations were printed and sold publicly.* NYHS

Well aware of the rocks, on which so many have been dashed to pieces, let us by a sacred regard to social duty, endeavor to preserve our POLITICAL BARQUE safe, in her progress on the OCEAN OF TIME.

MY COUNTRYMEN! You have been famed for the accomplishment of a glorious revolution, and for the establishment of an excellent form of government; preserve with the most scrupulous attention the great advantages you possess. By your all-important exertions the progress of mind has been greatly accelerated; and the HUMAN RACE must ultimately be benefited by them. The long enslaved nations of EUROPE, have caught the blaze of freedom, and are following your example, in adopting the principles of self-government: The hydra of despotism will THERE soon be subdued, and order and fair liberty, will arise out of the confusion dismay, and carnage in which the nations are involved. Already the mild lights of reason and philosophy become *superior* to the scepticism and delusion, of the ignorant and designing. Behold! the era of GENERAL VIRTUE, LIBERTY, and HAPPINESS is at hand, may our endeavors be united to hasten its approach!

George James Warner, *Means for the Preservation of Public Liberty* (New York, 1797), pp. 7–19

3. Fourth of July Oration, 1809

JOHN T. IRVING

. . . .

On this August anniversary of our independence, therefore, it becomes us to resolve these things seriously in our minds, and to renew the watchword of our liberties. To whom in such reflection be addressed with more propriety than to you, who compose, in a manner, the sinews and muscles of our country. Men who form the centre of population, the very axis of society: whose interests and affections are reposed at home; whose hearts, I trust, are bound and linked with adamantine bands to the welfare of our country. In your hands must the palladium of our liberty rest. You cannot be inflated by the dangerous cravings for aristocratic distinction; you do not float like the ephemeral bubbles of pride and fashion, on the surface of society; nor are you of that uninformed class, too low to be agitated with the current of events, and who, like dull weeds, sleep secure at the bottom of the stream. To you, therefore, must we look for the protection of our national advantages. It behooves you, vigilantly to guard every avenue by which the vitals of your country may be assailed.

John Treat Irving, *An Oration* (New York, 1809), p. 20

4. Anniversary Meeting of the Cordwainers Society, 1809

NEW YORK CORDWAINERS BENEFIT
SOCIETY.

Monday last being the anniversary meeting of this Institution, the following gentlemen took their seats as officers for the ensuing year:

William Jones, President
David Law, Vice President
James Norris, Secretary
Ralph Archibald, Treasurer
John Jacobs } Trustees
John Bennet, }
Stephen Meally } Stewards
John I. Vanderpool, }

The usual business of the Society having been transacted, the members sat down to an excellent entertainment prepared by Mr. Meally, the pleasure of which was greatly heightened by reflecting on the relief which they had heretofore been able to administer to their distressed brethren, and the exhilarating prospect of the utility which was likely to accrue in future from this truly benevolent association. The cloth being removed, the following Toasts were drank and interspersed with appropriate Songs.

1st   The day, and those who honour it—May our posterity, feeling the happy effects of the institution, meet to celebrate its anniversary with the same heartfelt satisfaction which we at present experience.

2   The New York Cordwainers Benefit Society—May their funds be always commensurate with the benevolent designs of the institution.

3   The infant manufactures of America—May no mistaken policy, like the cold blasts of winter, nip them in the bud.

4   Crispin's Fire side—the seat of hospitality, all reality, and no formality—no good craft will ever abuse it.

5   The sons of St. Crispin—May they all be blest with good wives, and fine children; their daughters amiable and virtuous, and their sons *real flints*.

6   The Sons of St. Crispin—May they never be troubled with *rotten thread*, dull *knives*, nor want of cash.

7   May the enemies of shoemakers be compelled to perform a long journey bare-footed, over rough roads in frosty weather.

8   Faithful Journeymen—May they always find just and generous employers.

9   May the *increase* of this and similar institutions never *decrease* their harmony.

10   Agriculture & Commerce, twin *threads*–May they long continue to be twisted by the hand of industry, *waxed* with the cement of patriotism, and pointed with the *bristle* of enterprize.

11   Industry the handmaid of virtue–May it ever be a distinguishing characteristic of the members of this society.

12   Prosperity to this society–May its members in health long enjoy it, and may those afflicted with disease be speedily restored to their wanted activity and usefulness.

13   The President of the United States–May *wisdom* be his guide in the discharge of the arduous duties of his exalted station.

14   The Vice-President of the United States–May his declining years be happy, and his eminent services held in grateful remembrance by posterity.

15   The Congress of the United States–May their minds be rounded by the *last* of our Constitution; too *compact* for licentiousness, and too *easy* for despotism.

16   The immortal memory of WASHINGTON, the Father of his country and the Friend of man–May his successors in office ever endeavor to follow his *glorious* example.

17   The daughters of Columbia–May they continue to be as distinguished for virtue as for beauty.

Evening Post, March 10, 1809

5. Cordwainers Display: Parade in Celebration of the Completion of the Erie Canal

CORDWAINERS' SOCIETY

Marshalls.
James Lennon, Marcus Rimball.
The PRESIDENT, TREASURER, and SECRETARY of the Society.

The President carried a hammer, curiously wrought, of ebony, curled maple, and ivory, and a scroll with the style of the Society–"Cordwainers of New York." On his right, the Treasurer, carrying a gilt key; on his left, the Secretary, carrying a gilt pen.

A STANDARD six feet square, for blue silk, yellow fringe and tassels, born by James Lawler, wearing a blue sash; his Supporters decorated with blue collars and rosettes. The Standard displayed the Cordwainers' Arms viz. three goats heads in a shield, supported by Journeymen in working dress; one on the right side, holding in his right hand a woman's shoe, the other on the left side, holding a man's boot, representing the two branches of the trade. Crest—A segment of a globe, surmounted by an eagle in a brilliant glory, holding in his talons a scroll with the words "Liberty and Independence." Over the whole the Motto—"United we stand, Divided we fall;" underneath, "Cordwainers of the City of New York." The whole subject included within an oak wreath.

The Marshals were mounted, having an Assistant on foot on each flank of the column.

Four hundred and fifty Employers and Journeymen, with blue badges bearing the Arms of the Trade, appeared on the occasion, having a Band of Music in the centre. Three small Banners, with appropriate devices, were placed at equal distances in the Procession. In the rear Mr. Daniel Reeder, bearing a Standard, displaying in the Arms in a shield. Supporters; on the right side a Cordwainer in working dress, at his feet, and beneath the shield, the cornucopia; on the left side, a female figure in a white dress and purple robe, holding in her left hand a Scroll with the words—"Industry rewarded in America;" oak boughs under her feet. Crest a goats head in a cloud, surrounded by golden rays, in which appears the cherub Liberty in the act of crowning the male figure with a civic wreath. Motto, over the whole—"Union is our strength." Motto underneath—The same as on the first standard.

The Vice-President closed, carrying a hammer and scroll, with the words "Cordwainers of New York."

The President and Vice-President wore blue sashes fringed with gold, and ornamented with gold stars. The Treasurer and Secretary wore blue collars and rosettes. The Standard Bearers wore blue sashes; their Supporters blue collars.

ALEXANDER WADDY, President of the day.
NICHOLAS M. SLIDELL, Vice-President.
ABRAHAM MERRILL, Treasurer.   THOS. BAKER, Secretary.
COMMITTEE
MATHEW ARMSTRONG,   ABRAHAM BECKER,
Wearing blue collars and rosettes.
Delegates to confer with the Corporation.
ABRAHAM MERRILL,   SIMON VAN WINKLE.

Cadwallader Colden, *Memoir Prepared at the Request of a Committee of the Common Council of the City of New York*, (New York, 1828), pp. 220–221.

6. Celebration of Lawrence's Victory: War of 1812

Illuminations—On Saturday evening, the City Hall, agreeably to a vote of the corporation, was most brilliantly and tastefully illuminated, together with all the large public buildings in the neighborhood. We have not time to do justice to particulars. Transparencies were every where seen representing the several naval victories achieved by those American heroes who have so much distinguished themselves on our element, the water. The memorable words of the gallant Lawrence "DON'T GIVE UP THE SHIP" were enscribed on a transparency in front of the City Hall in letters so large that they could easily be distinguished throughout the Park. The number of spectators of all descriptions was immense, and their joyful sensations were kept alive and encouraged by a full band of music in the gallery of the City Hall, playing our most popular airs. At ten the lights were extinguished, and, as if by enchantment, an orderly and scarcely broken silence prevailed, in that place so lately alive with merriment and revelry. It deserves mention that the Butchers of the city distinguished themselves on this occasion, by illuminating their stalls in various markets, with a profusion of lights placed in such a manner as to produce the most striking effect. They too had their transparency with *"Free Trade and Butchers' Rights."*

Evening Post, October 25, 1813

7. Artisan Celebrations of Peace Concluding the War of 1812

Mechanics Bank. "The Hammer and Hand" enwreathed with two oak branches, denoting strength. In the foreground the Cornucopia, as an emblem of plenty, discharging Eagles and Dollars, in anticipation of the speedy recommencement of specie payment, the happy effects of peace. In the background, commerce, represented by an inward-bound ship. Motto "Peace the Mechanic's Friend."

Joseph Frank *gun-maker*, Greenwich Street. Above the door, on the outside of the house, this motto—

Order of Proceſſion,
In Honor of the Conſtitution of the United States.

AT eight o'Clock on Wedneſday Morning the 23d of July, 10 Guns will fire, when the PROCESSION will parade and proceed by the following Route, viz : Down Broad-Way to Great-Dock-Street, thence through Hanover-Square, Queen, Chatham, Diviſion, and Arundel-Streets ; and from thence through Bullock-Street to Bayard's-Houſe.

No. 1.   2 Horſemen with Trumpets.
2.   1 piece of Artillery.

No.	First DIVISION.	No.	
3	4 Foreſters in Frocks, carrying Axes.		
4	Columbus in his Ancient Dreſs—on Horſeback.	12	A Band of Muſic.
5	6 Foreſters, &c.	13	Taylors.
6	A Plough.	14	Meaſurers of Grain.
7	A Sower.	15	Millers.
8	A Harrow.	16	Inſpectors of Flour.
9	Farmers.	17	Bakers.
10	United States Arms, borne by Col. White, ſupported	18	Brewers.
11	Gardeners. [by the Society of the Cincinnati.	19	Diſtillers.

No.	Second DIVISION.	No.	
20	Coopers.	22	Tanners and Curriers.
21	Butchers.	23	Leather Dreſſers.

Third DIVISION.

24. Cord Wainers.

No.	Fourth DIVISION.	No.	
25	Carpenters.	27	Hatters.
26	Furriers.	28	Peruke-Makers and Hair-Dreſſers.

No.	Fifth DIVISION.	No.	
29	White Smiths.	35	Windſor Chair-Makers.
30	Cutlers.	36	Upholſterers.
31	Stone Maſons.	37	Fringe Makers.
32	Brick-Layers.	38	Paper Stainers.
33	Painters and Glaziers.	39	Civil Engineers.
34	Cabinet Makers.		

No.	Sixth DIVISION.	No.	
40	Ship-Wrights.	44	Block and Pump-Makers.
41	Black-Smiths.	45	Sail-Makers, and Rope-Makers.
42	Ship-Joiners.	46	Riggers.
43	Boat-Builders.		

No.	Seventh DIVISION.	No.	
47	Federal Ship Hamilton.	50	Marine Society.
48	Pilot Boat and Barges.	51	Printers, Book-Binders and Stationers.
49	Pilots.		

No.	Eighth DIVISION.	No.	
52	Cartmen.	60	Gold and Silver-Smiths.
53	Mathematical Inſtrument-Makers.	61	Potters.
54	Carvers and Engravers.	62	Chocolate-Makers.
55	Coach-Makers.	63	Tobacconiſts.
56	Coach-Painters.	64	Dyers.
57	Copper-Smiths and Braſs-Founders.	65	Bruſh-Makers.
58	Tin-plate Workers.	66	Tallow-Chandlers.
59	Pewterers.	67	Saddlers, Harneſs and Whip-Makers.

No.	Ninth DIVISION.	No.	
68	Gentlemen of the Bar.	70	Preſident and Students of the College.
69	Philological Society.	71	Merchants and Traders.

Tenth DIVISION.

No.	
72	Clergy.
73	Phyſicians.
74	Strangers.
75	Militia Officers.
76	1 piece of Artillery.

By Order of the Committee of Arrangements,
RICHARD PLATT, Chairman.

That artisans composed the bulk of New York's work force and that they were behind the Constitution is evident in this Order of Procession. NYHS

The Federal ship Hamilton *carried as a float in the procession celebrating the ratification of the Constitution.* NYHS

Silk Banner (restored) of Society of Pewterers, July 23, 1788. NYHS

At length the dread clash of arms is o'er
War's dread shot is heard no more!
Our hopes, our fears—our sorrows cease,
Each murmur hush'd, and all is—Peace

An arc was formed from the front door, and with two rows of muskets—the bayonets reversed, each musket having a candle on it; they rose with a regular ascent toward the ceiling; at the end of each row a circle of bayonets was placed reversed, with a candle in each also—immediately back of the whole, was the following verse—

Lo! War with rage and fury burn'd,
Now, Peace, so mild is-conjured turned!
Her magic wand displays such tricks
Ten muskets change to—candlesticks.

Mr. Phyfe,[5] *Partition Street.* Nineteen transparent lamps suspended across the street. In the centre, a portrait of Washington, Ten lamps each a letter forming the word Washington; eight other lamps containing the names of naval heroes. In Mr. Phyfe's centre store Justice and Liberty on a pedestal, Eagle and Lion drinking emblems of commerce; in the foreground, implements of war, destroyed and scattered. In the background, the rising sun with sixteen stars—motto, "Peace."

Columbian, March 14, 1815.

Nearly every mechanical branch constructed a float for the long parade held in celebration of the completion of the Erie Canal. NYPL (CADWALLADER COLDEN, MEMOIR OF . . . CANALS)

8. Preamble of Constitution of the Democratic Society of the City of New-York

THAT all legitimate power resides *in the People*, who have at all times the natural and inherent RIGHT to amend, alter, or abolish the form of Government which they have instituted, is now considered a TRUTH so demonstrable, that to attempt to explain the intuitive principles on which the maxim is founded, might, in this enlightened age and country, be deemed superfluous. Under this conviction, We, whose names are hereunto subscribed, do declare, THAT to support and perpetuate the EQUAL RIGHTS OF MAN, is the great object of this Association: That to this grand point of all our deliberations shall tend; to the furtherance of this glorious and important design, our views and exertions shall be solely directed; and to this end we will, with the moderation and obedience, inseparable from GOOD CITIZENS; in consistency however with the independence and firmness which ever characterize PATRIOTS, constantly express our sentiments as well of our PUBLIC OFFICERS, as their MEASURES . . . .

New York Journal, February 19, 1794

9. Democratic Society of the City of New-York: Address to the Republican Citizens of the United States, May 28, 1794

. . . Yes, fellow-citizens, we take a pleasure in avowing thus publicly to you, that we are lovers of the French nation, that we esteem their cause as our own, and that we are the enemies, the avowed enemies, of him or those who dare to infringe upon the holy law of *Liberty*, the sacred *Rights of Man*, by declaring, that we ought to be strictly neutral, *either in thought or speech*, between a nation fighting for the dearest, the undeniable, the invaluable Rights of Human Nature, and another nation or nations wickedly, but hitherto (we thank God) vainly, endeavoring to oppose her in such a virtuous, such a glorious struggle.

If this is the language of treason, if this is the language of faction and sedition, come forward, ye votaries of opposite principles, ye stoical apathists, who can sit with folded arms, with sullen silence, with unmoved composure, while the house of your next neighbor, your former benefactor, *your only real friend,* is on fire, without affording even one single solitary bucket of water, to aid in quenching the raging, the wide spreading flame; ye secret abettors of tyranny and depotism, ye hermaphroditical politicians, come forward, we call upon you, bring us legal means, if such you can contrive, to the bar of justice, and punish us for these our open, our avowed principles, from which no earthly consideration shall ever tempt us to recede. But, be cautious! Could ye select, in this land of freedom, such an execrable group of judges and jurymen as condemned the innocent, the virtuous, the patriotic MUIR,[6] our brethren, who we now address, would not only rise as one man, and, by every constitutional method, prevent the iniquitous, the unjust sentence from being put into execution, but would, if they failed therein, open the sluices of their justly provoked wrath, and crush forever the nefarious opposers of these principles; principles which they know, we know, and you *ought* to know, brought forth the most glorious epoch in the annals of our country, the ever memorable 4th of July, 1776.

We would not be understood to mean, that every man who opposes our societies, is an enemy to this country, or even an aristocrat in his heart; but we most firmly believe, that he who is an enemy to the French Revolution, cannot be a firm republican; and therefore, though he may be a good citizen in every other respect, ought not to be entrusted with the guidance of any part of the machine of government.

Address to the Republican Citizens of the United States, May 28, 1794, *New York Journal*, May 31, 1794

FRATERNITY

For a source of uncompromised affirmation of their value to society and their place in the republic, and also as a haven of fraternal comfort, the various benevolent societies were unparalleled. Whether it was the venerable Mechanics Society, formally the General Society of Mechanics and Tradesmen, or one of the more ephemeral journeymen societies (many of whom also had economic leverage as a function – see Part IV), or a local volunteer fire company, these associations offered mechanics a chance to meet, wine, and dine in a spirit of mutual adulation and harmony.

The Mechanic's Society was by far the most prominent of the artisan societies. Its founding in 1785 and incorporation in 1792 (despite the fears of merchants that artisans might use the occasion to monopolize their services), were occasions of great celebration for the entire craftsman community.[7] Composed of artisans from the different trades of the city, it soon became a nonpartisan fraternity of the more prominent master craftsmen that lobbied for the interests of mechanic trades, particularly seeking greater protective tariffs and freer access to bank capital. The Society's constitution provided for the democratic election of the president, vice-president, treasurer, and secretary; annual and monthly meetings; and measures to collect fees for allocation to poor members, widows, and orphans. Also in the Constitution are the Society's initiation rites, indicative of the fraternal nature of the organization (Document 10).[8]

The Mechanics Society held monthly meetings where it balloted for new members, granted loans and benefits, attended to the Society's finances, authorized communications with other societies and planned for its two annual celebrations on the anniversary of its founding and the Fourth of July. In 1803 it also constructed a handsome building, Mechanics Hall, in which it held its meetings and which served as a strong symbol of the artisans' presence in the city.

Of great pride to the Society was the opening of a school for members' children in 1813. Education was considered the greatest insurance for the continuance of both republicanism and a secure standing for the artisan in American society. Established with funds from the Mechanics Bank, it offered free education to the sons of disabled or deceased society members, while the children of other members paid tuition. Artisans with somewhat greater income might

send their children to one of the city's common pay schools while poor
mechanics who were not members might choose one of the city's charity
schools. (While there were no compulsory school laws at this time, at any given
day in 1796, 52 percent of children from five to fifteen were attending school.
Many of the rest also attended at one time or another; perhaps 80 or 90 percent
of the population received some formal education.)[9] Students at the Mechanics
School would learn the fundamentals of reading, writing, and arithmetic. Further attendance at another school might lead to knowledge of accounting,
navigation, and possible grammar-school level work in Latin, Greek and
mathematics (Documents 11–12).

Evening schools were available for apprentices. In addition, the Society
offered occasional evening lectures for apprentices (Document 13). Even more
significant was the establishment in 1820 of an Apprentices Library that, according to Society minutes, was widely used (Document 14). The opening of this
institution was a major municipal event attended by the Mayor and other
dignitaries. It featured addresses by baker Thomas Mercein, the President of
the Mechanics Society, and by representatives of the Mechanics School and of
the apprentice community. The holdings of the library were largely technical,
moral, historical, religious and philosophical, reflecting the strict moral and
republican outlook of the society. There were also a few volumes of literature
which, despite occasional protest, the Society allowed to remain in circulation.

Fire companies spread throughout the city. Supervised by the mayor
and Common Council, they were responsible for the protection of the city from
the ever-present danger of a conflagration. These companies also acted as
fraternal societies: they had constitutions not unlike those of the artisan
societies, and they provided members an opportunity for social mixing and
disability and death benefits. Artisans composed the majority of the membership of these associations; they were an important part of life for many craftsmen. In protecting their community from truly mortal danger they fulfilled one
of the highest obligations citizens owed to their community (Document 15).[10]

10. Initiation Rites of the Mechanics Society

CHAPTER VIII. — A LAW REGULATING THE CEREMONY OF THE INITIATION OF MEMBERS.

1. BE IT ORDAINED by the General Society of Mechanics and
Tradesmen of the City of New York, That every person who may here-after be
elected a member of this Society shall, within three meetings thereafter, apply
for the purpose of being initiated; and in case any person so elected shall

neglect to apply within the time aforesaid, his election shall, by such neglect, become void.

2. All members who are waiting for the purpose of being initiated shall be regularly introduced to the Society by two brothers, previously appointed by the President or presiding officer, as masters of ceremonies for that evening. The masters of ceremonies, when arrived at the door of the Hall, accompanied by the persons to be initiated, shall give notice thereof by three distinct raps, which shall be answered by the President with two strokes of his hammer; the brothers at the same time will rise and uncover, while the masters of ceremonies shall approach the chair and present the newly elected members. The presiding officer will then address them as follows. (To be spoken in the plural or singular, as the case may require.)
"FELLOW CITIZENS:

A membership certificate of the Mechanics Society shortly after its formation. Among the engravings can be found representations of liberty and the founding of America; help for those in distress; scenes of artisans at work; and the husbandman clearing the American wilderness and so advancing the republic. At the top stands the arm and hammer, the symbol that all arts and crafts, indeed all of society, rests on the work of the mechanic. WINTERTHUR MUSEUM

By 1822 the Mechanics Society had become a relatively elite organization of prominent master crafts-men, some of whom were men of considerable fortune. The engraving reflects this change. NYPL

"You have been regularly admitted members of this Society. This mark of favor, with which our institution has honored you, is the happy result of those flattering recommendations we have received of your character. Let sobriety, industry, integrity, and uprightness of heart continue the ornaments of your name.

"We now hail you brothers! Delightful union, when the bond of friendship is benevolence! To dry the tear from misery's eye, to succor the afflicted, and to save the sinking is our present aim, and constituted an original and principal object with the founders of our institution.

"You are about to join your efforts to those of your brethren around you: a compliance with the tenor of our laws will entitle you to an equal participation of those privileges and benefits derived from this incorporation. May the interests, harmony, and reputation of this General Association be ever dear to you.

"You will now inscribe your names on the general register of this Society, in whose behalf I tender you the right hand of fellowship."

Minutes of the General Society of Mechanics and Tradesmen, November 3, 1802

The first Mechanics Hall. This building was a source of great pride to the city's mechanics. It was used for meetings of the Mechanics Society and rented out for public use. MAGAZINE OF AMERICAN HISTORY

The 1827 Certificate of Membership in the Coopers Society. The engraving stresses the theme of the centrality of the artisan crafts to the progress of civilization together with the importance of benevolence. NYHS

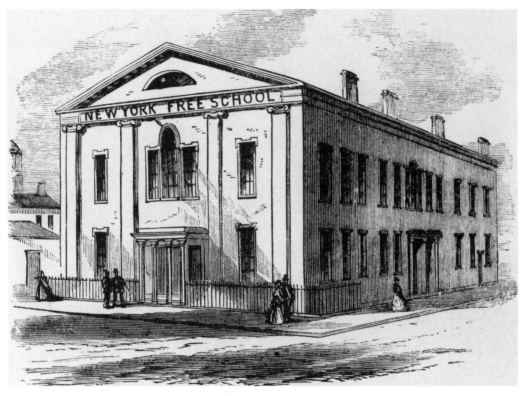

NEW YORK FREE SCHOOL NO. 1.
THE NEW BUILDING OPENED IN 1809 IN TRYON ROW.

Most children attended school in New York, though seldom continuously. The better schools were private during this era, and sons (and some daughters) of the wealthier artisan community often attended them where they learned the fundamentals of reading and arithmetic and occasionally some accounting and measuring skills. Children of poorer mechanics attended either charity schools or those of the Free School Society, the forerunner of the public school. The Mechanics Society operated its own school for members' children, particularly offspring of deceased members. Few continued past the age of twelve or thirteen. Children were generally taught by the Lancasterian Method in which teachers used older students as monitors in very large classes. NYHS

11. Mechanics Society: Report of School Committee, 1824

The School at present consists of 117 scholars of whom 53, embracing every child who is entitled to the bounty of the Society, and for whom application has been made, are taught free of expense.

The number who pay in part is 84, and those who pay full price (5 dollars) is 56.

The branches taught in the School are reading, writing, arithmetic, Grammar, Geography, History, Astronomy, with the use of the globes and Orrery Mensuration, Gauging, Surveying, and Bookkeeping, in most of which the scholars will be examined on the evening of the anniversary, and the following Wednesday evening in this room, at which time the members are respectfully invited to attend, and may obtain tickets for admission from the office of the Society or the members of the School Committee.

Minutes of the General Society of Mechanics and Tradesmen, January 7, 1824

12. Mechanics Society: Report of School Committee, 1827

The School Committee in conformity to the salutary Bye-Laws of the Society respectfully submit to the members the following view of the present state of the School committed to their charge. The boys' school consists at this time of 122 scholars of whom 24 are taught free of expense, the average number of the latter for the past year has been about 30.

The reduction has taken place since November when several boys were put to trades or were employed at home. The School is divided into 6 classes or divisions and the course of studies presented by each class is as much in conformity with the regulations heretofore submitted to the Society as the situation of the School, and the varied talents of the scholars and their opportunities for studying at home will allow. The School is under the immediate care of W. E. Wheaten as Principal, aided by Mr. George Everet as Assistant Teacher.

The whole course of study from the elementary to the higher branches, regular and systematic, and the Committee believe judicious, gradually leading the mind from grade to studies to another, with as much rapidity as due proficiency and a particular regard to the different capacities of the scholars will warrant. The resolution of the Society passed February, 1826, authorized the School Committee to establish a school exclusively for females, and appropriating this room for its accommodation, has been carried into effect, and with a success commensurate with the expectations of its friends.

The School was opened on the First day of May last, and now consists of 95 pupils of whom 19 are taught free of expense, the others the daughters of some of the most respectable and valuable members of the Society, pay the full price of tuition which was fixed as in the boys' school at $5 per quarter.

This school is also under the general superintendence of Mr. Wheaten, who has for Principal, Mrs. Haskell, a lady of competent abilities and well qualified for the important duties. Miss Knapp still acts as Assistant Teacher, and ably fulfills the duties incident to her station.

The same organization and system prevails here as in the boys' school; and the studies are nearly similar, excepting that needle work, both plain and ornamental, and painting and drawing are substituted for mathematics and geometry. The Committee forbear any comments on the progress of the scholars, as a public and particular examination of all the pupils commenced yesterday afternoon, and will be continued daily throughout the week from 2 until 5 o'clock P.M...

Minutes of the General Society of Mechanics and Tradesmen, January 3, 1827

13. Mechanics Society: Motion Regarding Teaching at Mechanics School

. . . WHEREAS, Charles Starr, a member of the Society, has gratuitously taught a course of English Grammar to a class of Apprentice Boys, exhibiting to the world the novel and interesting spectacle of mingling Literature with labor—of a Master Mechanic and a large class of Mechanics' Apprentices, elevating their leisure evenings to literary improvement most creditable to the Teacher, beneficial to the pupils and honorable to the mechanic name; therefore,

RESOLVED: that the thanks of this Society be voted to Mr. Starr and that the Secretary give him notice of the same.

RESOLVED: that Mr. Starr be requested to furnish the Society with a list of the apprentices' names he has so taught.

Minutes of the General Society of Mechanics and Tradesmen, August 7, 1822

14. Mechanics Society: Report of Apprentices' Library Committee

The Committee also reported that there is now on the Register of this Institution, 7,033 volumes; of these 63 have been missing in the last three years, being thirteen in addition to those before reported. Remaining out in the hands of readers, 165. Lost by readers and paid for, 33; mutilated and sold during the time above stated, 273. And there has been added since last report, 529, mostly valuable books, leaving now on the shelves of the Library, 6,487 volumes. The number of readers during the last year have been twelve hundred and eighty-six, and your Committee are much pleased to see that they have taken more history and treatise on the Mechanic Arts than in former years, and as they can accommodate double that number of readers they would urge it on their Brother mechanics to recommend it to their apprentices to become readers at this Institution, as we think it will be the means in the hands of a kind Providence of reforming and keeping them form the haunts of vice and immor-

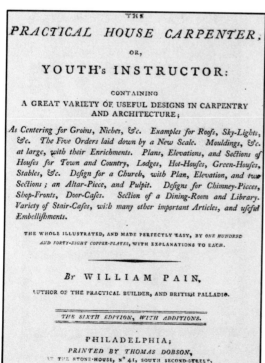

One reason for the decline of apprenticeship in the early national era was the availability of manuals that allowed ambitious youths to learn a trade on their own or, at least, with lesser guidance and lesser need for prolonged training. These popular books were accessible at institutions such as the Apprentices Library. THE PRACTICAL HOUSE CARPENTER, NYHS

ality and of making them more useful members and brighter stars in the great
and growing republic.

And your Committee would earnestly recommend to those members
who sign as approvers to certificates, that they sign for none but responsible
guarantees as the Library has met with considerable losses, by such neglect in
the approvers.

> J. Stephens, Jr.
> P. Young
> A. M. Arcularius
> P. McCarter, Jr.
> E. Arrowsmith

ADJOURNED

Minutes of the General Society of Mechanics and Tradesmen, December 6, 1826

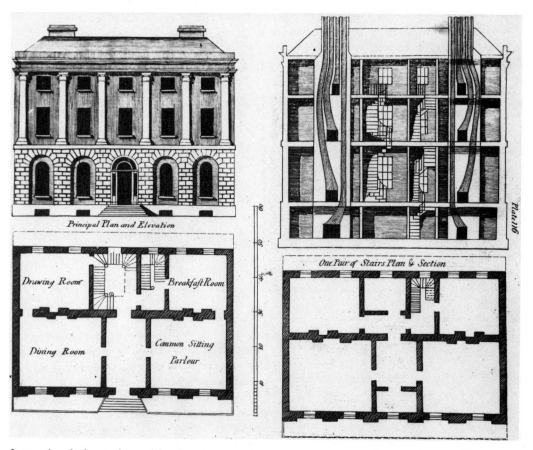

*Instructional plate to be used by those learning the carpentry trade as well as by those wishing to stay
abreast of recent style.* THE PRACTICAL HOUSE CARPENTER, NYHS

15. Fire Company Number 11: Journal (Minutes and By-Laws)

At a meeting of Company No. 11 at the house of Mr. William Bradford, 10th November 1791, Richard Williamson and William Quick were elected members of said company in the room of Jeremy Jessop removed out of the city and Andrew Myer resigned.

At a meeting of Co. No. 11 at the house of Mr. William Bradford 10th, November 1791, the Question being first whether the Chimney Fines should be put in a Fund (for the relief of poor disabled Firemen, Widows and Orphans of firemen who may lose their lives at Fires) and other uses as may be determined by the Trustees of Said Fund; it was agreed to by a Majority of Votes—

At said time the Question was put for Appropriating the Washing fines and other private Fines of Said Company to the Same use. It was negatived by a Majority of said Co.

Alarm of fire 27 April [1797] at three O'clock in the Morning which proved to have been occasioned by the prisoners attempting to make their Escape

Certificate of membership in one of the City's Fire Companies, 1822. NYPL

from Jail. Absent were Joseph George, John Young, Jacob Morris, John King, John Wilkins, Jacob Wagener, Richard Ham, Peter Van Schiver, John Hilyer.
. . . .

Received of New York, June 1806 from Fire Co., No. 11, The Sum of Six 00/600 Dollars in full for liquors &c. this Evening.

Thomas Ingham

By-Laws of the Company Belong to Fire Engine No. 11, Passed 23 December 1807.

Article 1

Whenever there is an alarm of fire it shall be the duty of each member to repair to the the engine house, and if the engine is there to take it out with the materials among thereto, and immediately proceed to the fire and there to be under the direction of the foreman or in his absence the assistant, if both absent then it shall be the duty of the oldest member present to take charge of the Engine.

Article 2

It shall not be lawful for any member to absent himself in time of fires from the engine without permission of the foreman. And after obtaining leave if he should not return at time appointed, He shall forfeit the sum of 1 Dol.

Article 3

After the fire is extinguished no member shall absent himself before the engine and materials belonging thereto are brought to the Engine house well washed and cleaned before they are put up. Any member neglecting their Duty in such a case shall forfeit the sum of One Dol., and it shall be the Duty of each member to Remain at the Engine house after the roll is called until discharg'd by the foreman, under the penalty of paying for every such default, 25 cents.

Article 4

Should any member be absent at an alarm and if he shall at the next regular meeting of the company be asked to an account by the foreman, or in his absence the assistant or Clerk and if his excuse should not appear sufficient to a majority of the Co. then present he shall forfeit the sum of 1 Dol., to be collected by the Treasurer immediately after.

Article 5

That no excuse be taken for a man's nonattendance to a fire except confinement by Sickness or death in the family Without a Majority of the Co. should determine to the contrary.

Article 6

Any member knowing of Chimneys being on fire, And not acquainting the foreman of the place and number within twenty-four hours his knowledge of the same shall pay for every such default the sum of 75 cents.

Article 7

That the days appointed for washing the Engine shall be the first Monday in May at five O'clock PM and the first Monday in October at 5 O'clock PM; and

Engraver Alexander Anderson combines the symbolls of the Mechanics Society and artisan community, the hammer in hand, amidst a fire company battling a conflagration. The majority of firemen were artisans. It is possible that this is the emblem of a fire insurance company either founded by mechanics or intended to serve mechanics. ANDERSON COLLECTION, NYPL

if any member Does not appear and answer to his name at roll call he shall forfeit the Sum of 25 Cents. And if any member Does not appear before the Engine is brought to the place of washing, He shall pay for every such default an Additional Sum of 25 cents; and if any member does not appear before the Engine is filled with water or does not appear at all, He shall For every such Default pay an additional sum of 25 cents. And further, that no excuse by taken of a man's nonattendance at washing except confined by sickness or Some other misfortune or death in his family so as to make it indecent for him to attend.

Article 8

It shall be the duty of the Foreman to call at least a meeting of the Co. in every three months . . . .

Article 9

At every such meeting on the appearance of a majority of the Co. a chairman shall be chosen and as soon as he has taken his seat shall call the members to order and then the minutes of the preceding meeting shall be read . . . . a majority of the Co., shall be competent to transact all business relative thereto . . . .

Article 10

That when a member is wanted, any of the Co. shall have liberty to propose one person, first observing that no person can be admitted unless he resided southward of a line drawn from the N. river through Day Street . . . . Any persons proposed shall be balloted for and a majority of votes shall be finally determined the choice. And, further, the initial fee shall be 5 Dol. untill a majority of the Co. shall otherwise determine.

Chappel described this illustration as the "Firemans Washing Day the Meeting of Two Company, then Sport." This is his description of a hose contest between two companies on the Bowery at the corner of Grand Street. Fire companies inspired strong loyalties among its members. Recreational events such as this were common. WILLIAM CHAPPEL, OIL ON CARDBOARD, MCNY

Article 11

Any person using profane language at any regular meeting of the Co. shall pay the sum of 25 cents for each and every offence.

March 20, 1809

A dispute and Quarrel having occured in the 2 classes while taking care of the Ladders on Friday afternoon the 10th inst. between James Denham, Stephen Minard and James Corwin, which was submitted to the consideration of the Co. by the latter of the above named Members. They were requested to retire, after relating the circumstances whereon the Co. after a patient hearing of them and others in the same class who were present at the time, resolved that James Denham and Stephen Minard have leave to resign previous to the next Quarterly meeting when the Co. would determine on the expediency of expelling both or either of them in case they should not have resigned—James Corwin acquitted.

May 23, 1809

James Denham and Stephen Minard having made satisfactory concessions for the Dispute which occured between them and James Corwin on the 10 Feb. were acquitted and restored to the favour of the Co.

Minutes and By-Laws of Fire Company Number Eleven, NYHS

KEEPING UP THE NEIGHBORHOOD

Like other citizens, artisans were deeply concerned that their neighborhoods, largely the outer wards, have the amenities of other parts of the city and be free of nuisances that would make their lives uncomfortable. All citizens of the republic were owed by society (the city) a respectful and decent living. Over the years, numerous petitions were sent to the Common Council asking for new or improved services. This might include requests for a new pump or public market, or repairs to the street (Documents 16–17). Equally numerous were remonstrances against artisan enterprises that caused residents discomfort from distasteful and even dangerous byproducts, such as a slaughterhouse (Document 18). Too, residents wanted the peace and quiet necessary for those of the producer classes who toiled long hours at work. Black garbage men disrupting the evening quiet were unacceptable, as was the proposed erection of a school for undesirables in their vicinity (Documents 19–20). Many of these petitions contained demands that mechanics be treated with the same dignity and afforded the same rights as residents living in more eminent neighborhoods.

Also common were complaints about the sanitary conditions of the ward. For example, the citizens of the tenth ward were unhappy with the Common Council's decision to allow manure to be stored in their area (Document 21).[11] One of the most interesting of these controversies found the interests of civic leaders and a number of well-to-do artisans pitted against those of poorer mechanics and less skilled near-indigent laborers over the issue of swine. Hogs ran freely through the streets of New York in the early nineteenth century, serving as scavengers and as a source of food for the poor. They also posed a serious threat to pedestrians and an unsightly stigma upon the city's dignity. After an incident involving a prominent soap boiler, John Slidell, the Common Council passed a law requiring all hogs to be confined in closer quarters. This brought strong protests from the residents of the outer wards; they argued that many of the poor would be unable to make it though the winter without their hogs and that the streets in those areas would be without their best means of waste removal (Document 21). Deciding that the poor had the better case (or more votes), the Council repealed the ordinance–to the great dismay of the *Evening Post*, the Federalist newspaper leading the fight for swine regulation (Document 22).[12]

16. Petition of Inhabitants of the Seventh Ward for a New Market

To the Honrable the Mayor, Recorder, Aldermen and Common Council of the City of New York

The Petition of the Inhabitants of the seventh ward of the City of New York

Humbly Sheweth

That your petitioners and a Number of others the Inhabitants of the above mentioned ward labor under a great disadvantage on account of there not

William Chappel's painting of the Fly (formerly the Dutch "Vly") Market. Every neighborhood wanted a market within reasonable walking distance. Women often shopped daily. WILLIAM CHAPPEL, OIL ON CARDBOARD, EDWARD ARNOLD COLLECTION, MMNY

being erected in the said ward a public market. That a number of the Inhabitants of the said Ward are Mechanics and are therefore obliged to attend to their daily employment on account of which most of their wives and children are compelled to do their daily marketting.

That the distance that your petitioners lives from the now established markets makes it very inconvenient.

That most of the said Inhabitants are not in Circumstances to advance money for their daily meat on account of their receiving Wages Weekly and do further set forth that if some persons who are well acquainted amongst the said Inhabitants were Allowed to sell to them meat it would make it much more convenient to them not only on Account of the distance from the said markets but also on the terms of payments.

Your petitioners therefore most Humbly pray that the honorable the common council will pass a law to enable Gilbert Knapp and William Botton to exercise the office of Butchers at their Slaughter house in the said Seventh Ward until a public market is there erected—and that his honor the Mayor will grant a License to them for that purpose in duty bound your petitioners will ever pray—

New York, December 11, 1795
City Clerk Filed Papers, NYCMA

17. Dangerous Street Conditions

To the Honorable the Mayor, Recorder, Aldermen and Common Council of the City of New York

The Petition of the Subscribers Inhabitants of Warren Street, Most Humbley Sheweth

That in the Summer of 1793, the pavement of this Street, was by order of your Board taken up at the expence of the Inhabitants thereof, That in consequence of this We had reason to expect that an order would have Issued directing the repaving of the Same, as soon as the Season became favorable for that purpose; But to our great surprize, the whole of last Summer passed away without anything being done for us, Which has compelled us to endure the Hardships of a Street in the most miserable condition, of any in this city of equal size and number of Inhabitants. Two whole winters have we been dragging through the mud, and almost two Summers when ever it rained heavily the Street in a few hours frequently became almost impassable, excepting for Horses and Carriages, and they have often been in no small danger from the large heaps of stones collected almost before every lot on both sides of the Street. We trust that there are many members of the Corporation, who have had occular demonstrations of, and can bear Testimony to the truth of the above facts.

These are therefore to request your Honorable Board to take our condition into consideration and Grant us that relief, which only can be obtained by your order for commencing the Repavement of this street as early in the Spring as the Weather will permit—which will not only benefit the public at large, but us more particularly, and confer an obligation on the Corporation's friends and humble servants.

[Thirty Signatures]

Warren Street
New York, 18th March 1795
City Clerk Filed Papers, NYCMA

18. Protest Against Slaughter House on Elizabeth Street (Sixth Ward)

To the Honorable the Board of Health of the City of New York.

The Representation of James Phillips of the Sixth ward of the Said City—

That conceiving it necessary at this Season of the year as Much as possible to present the origin of disorders and knowing that it is the wish of the Board to Give their aid on all occasions, he begs leave to inform them that there is a Slaughter house in Elizabeth Street Near Nicholas Street, which is not only Extremely offensive but which at times Renders it almost impossible for the neighbours to Remain in Some parts of the Houses owing to the offals and filth which is Suffered to Remain there, after killing their cattle—and to the best of my knowledge information and beliefe, that they never get the Dung Carried out of their yard only every two weeks—and producing the Most disagreeable Effluvia the Consiquence that must be produced from this in hot weather it is to be feared May Render that part of the City Very Sickly—Messr. Shipp & Applee May inform the Board and the City Inspector, that they wash their Slaughter house every Day after Killing, I will admit of all this that they wash the floor of the Slaughter house after Killing. I do not Expect they will Tell the Board or the City Inspector where the Blood and Water run too—it Runs amongst the Contents of the Entrails of animals with some gutts and Trotters and Every Description of filth, where it Remains for two weeks to putrify—

The Neighborhood begs and pray that the Honorable Board would take Such Steps as in their Power and their wisdom Should Direct to Remove this

Dreadful Nuisance and thereby Render the habitation of Many person who live near to it More Comfortable.–

    The Subscriber to this Narative is Ready and Willing to Attest to the truth of the Same–

    With Great Respect and Esteem Gentlemen–

    I am your Most obedient Humble Servant

James Phillips

June 10th 1806
Referred to Committee to Meet Committee of Butchers
Committee of Butchers will remedy this complaint.

City Clerk Filed Papers, NYCMA

19. Protest Against the Conduct of Nightmen

To the Honorable the Corporation of the City of New York–

    The subscribers inhabitants of the first ward of the said city–Respectfully represent–

    That a practice has modernly prevailed in the part of the city in which your memorialists have their dwellings which would be disgraceful to any community having the least pretentions to be civilized, or even to decency.–

    A number of vagabond negroes who have taken upon themselves the business of nightmen[13] exercise their functions in such a manner as is excessively offensive and outrages all propriety. These persons scream through the streets at all hours of the night with such vociferation as to disturb everyone within reach of their detestable cries–The sick are tormented by their noise, and if any appeal is made to them on this account the evil is only increased by a torrent of clamarous abuse–They transact their business often at a very early hour in the evening while the streets are full of passengers–The first shilling they earn is commonly spent for rum and before their work is over they are very generally in a state of intoxication oweing to this or from carelessness they sometimes drop their loads where it is left over night and for many hours of the morning to poison all in its vicinity–It is not only their savage yells that are offensive but they are in the habit of bawling out such expressions as are most shockingly indecent–They commonly go in pairs and perform a duet of this description, but a person in the neighborhood of Franklin Square may often hear a dozen or twenty of them at once vieing with each other in such noise & indecency as no stranger would believe could be tolerated anywhere but in an encampment of Savages.

    These people do not frequent Broadway, Park Place, State Street or other Genteel parts of the town. If they did your memorialists are confident they would not be endured for a single week.

But your memorialists humbly presume to hope that the industrious part[14] of the community are as much entitled as any other to the interferance of the police to protect them in the enjoyment of their rest, to preserve their health and to prevent their families from being exposed to such violation of decency as are the present subject of complaint.

It is true that these people are employed in a work that cannot be dispenced with. But it is not necessary that it should be performed after their manner—The evidence of this is that till within these three or four summers there has been no ground for complaints on this subject.—

Your memorialists therefore hope that not only in regard to them but for the sake of the *character* of the *city* your honorable body will adopt such regulations as may correct the evils of which they complain.

and your memorialists as in duty bound will always pray that your honors may be

[Thirty-six signatures]

August 12, 1817
Referred to City Inspector
City Clerk Filed Papers, NYCMA

20. Protest Against Erection of School on Augustus Street (Sixth Ward)

The Honorable the Mayor, Alderman and Commonalty of the City of New York in Common Council convened

The Petition of the Subscribers respectfully sheweth, that they have been informed that your Honorable Body contemplate granting a Lot of ground in Augustus Street to the Trustees of the Economical Free School for the purpose of erecting a public school thereon.[15]

That there will be the greatest impropriety in establishing more schools in the neighbourhood of the Subcribers, than those already in operation, has been fully shown in a petition presented by them to your Honorable Body, against the granting a lot in the point of Augustus Street to the Trustees of the African Free school. They believed the prayer of that petition had been granted until very lately—when they were informed that a lot had been granted to the Presbyterian Congregation near the one at the point of Augustus Street, for the purpose of erecting a public School.—This will make an addition of two hundred Scholars, (without accounting the very probable encrease) to the number in the New York Free School which is daily encreasing which they consider no small grievance knowing that two schools near each other that would not amount together to One hundred Scholars, very frequently become an annoyance to the inhabitants residing near them. But when they were informed that your Honorable Body contemplate granting a lot for the purpose of erecting another School in the vicinity of the two already established; it excited the greatest Surprise and anxiety;

They however believe that if your Honorable Body will reflect a moment, they will perceive the confusion that will continually take place where one thousand Scholars composing three different Schools will be let out at the Same time – They therefore hope that your Honl. Body Judging of the evils that will result to your petitioners by the erection of another School so near them, will grant a lot to the Trustees aforesaid in Some other part of the City than the one now in contemplation –

> John Remmey
> Elizabeth Schroader
> Archibald Taylor
> John N. Wethershine
> John Downing
> Caroline Magadlen Farr
> Jno. Fellows
> Wm. Moore
> Peter Lorillard
> George Lorillard
> Clarkson Crolius
> George Cuming

July 24, 1810
City Clerk Filed Papers, NYCMA

21. Petition for Allowance of Swine in the Streets

To the Honourable the Mayors, Aldermen and Commonalty of the City of New York,

The petition of the subscribers most respectfully sheweth,

That Your petitioners have heard with much concern that Your Honorable Body have it in contemplation to pass a law for the purpose of preventing swine from running in the streets; but for the reasons, which they

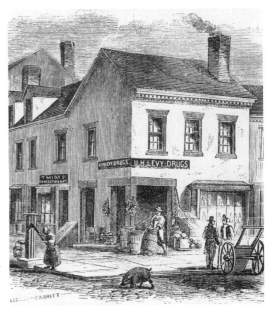

CORNER OF BROADWAY AND MURRAY STREET, 1820.

A hog removing garbage from the streets of New York without charge to the city. The allowance of hogs loose in the city streets remained a subject of fierce political debate until they were finally removed prior to the Civil War. NYHS

now take the liberty of suggesting with the greatest deference to your superiour wisdom, they trust, that it will not be enacted.

Your petitioners are so far from considering the running of swine in the streets as a nuisance, that they rather think it may be deemed a public benefit; for they are in fact our best scavengers, as they instantly devour all fish-guts, garbage and offals of every kind, which if suffered to remain, during the summer months, would be very offensive & might very probably be injurious to the health of the inhabitants.

We beg leave to represent, that by the keeping of swine, there are many poor persons, who are thereby enabled, to pay their rents and to supply their families with animal foods during the winter and likewise, by the sale of some of the pigs, to procure some other articles necessary for their comfort and convenience.

Your petitioners need not remind Your Honourable Board of the great distress of the poor, during the last winter, nor of the large expenditures, which, from motives of humanity, you were induced to make, on their account; but your petitioners most respectfully beg leave to present it as their opinion, that if you should pass a law to prevent the running of swine in the streets, several hundreds will be a public burden during the ensuing winter, who not-withstanding the excessive severity of the weather during the last, contrived to maintain themselves.

From these considerations and others, which will naturally occur to the minds of your Honourable Board, they are convinced, that you will have pity

on the poor. They, therefore earnestly pray, that the law now in contemplation
may not be passed, and as in duty bound &c.
New York 19th May 1817

Adam Marshall	Henry Lawson
Daniel Aldridge	Jacob Tomas
Edward Hains	Benjamin Ami
John Patterson	Elizabeth Brown
William Brown	James Moore
John Hunt	Charles Cavallier
Henry Williams	Samuel Lewis
Richard S. Chase	George Johnson

[And thirty-five other signatures]
Laid on table.

City Clerk Filed Papers, NYCMA

22. The *Evening Post* on Swine in the Streets

Swine once more. – We are sorry indeed that there should still be occasion to
bring up once more this intolerable nuisance before the public. We have
understood that the late repeal of the law restricting hogs from running at large,
was not the voice of the majority of the Board, but that advantage was taken of
a partial attendance of the members, and, without having given any previous
notice, that such a repeal would be moved, (as is usual, and ought to be always
the case, and always is the case when nothing unfair is meant) a member from
one of the outer wards made the motion for a repeal, and carried it by a majority
of those present. This we have received from report, and consequently we do
not vouch for the truth of it. But our information went further, and we were led
to believe that a certain gentleman, whose ability, activity and zeal have been
conspicuous, gave notice that at the next subsequent meeting, he should intro-
duce an ordinance relative to the subject, which should have for its object the
restraining of hogs from going at large, without the particular clause in the
former, which had rendered it obnoxious. In the belief that this information was
correct, we did not think it worth while to trouble the public with any observations on this unpleasant subject in the papers.

But we have this moment received a number of communications on this
subject, one of which informs us, that there exists no probability that the Board
will pass any ordinance having for its object the shutting up the swine. If so, if

the Board are determined on continuing a practice so disagreeable to a great part of the citizens; so offensive to the eye of decency; so dangerous to children; and even to grown persons, females especially; so destructive to our pavements; so filthy and so disgusting to the sight; and only continued for the sake of gratifying a very few of the inferior orders, such as chimney-sweeps & free blacks, then we propose to put the question to a fair trial, at the ensuing election, by designating the ticket for aldermen and assistants, that contains the names of such as are in favor of the hogs, as *The Hog Ticket*, and those who vote for it as *The Swinish Multitude*.

Evening Post, February 12, 1818

VALUES

In recent years there has been a great deal of discussion of the relationship between moral ideals, standards of conduct, and industrial development. In influential articles, labor historians Alan Dawley, Paul Faler, and Bruce Laurie argued that the growth of quantity production and industrial organization forced many artisans to adopt a stricter code of morality to respond effectively to the tactics of cost-conscious masters and merchants.[16] This was in contrast to the traditional pre-industrial artisan lifestyle that allowed considerable personal freedom at the workshop, that was seldom oriented to a clock or work schedule, and that was characterized by considerable hours spent in drinking and gambling, often accompanied by participation in blood sports such as cock fighting and bull baiting.[17]

There is ample evidence of pre-industrial customs in early national New York. The presence of large-scale alcoholic consumption is apparent from the statistics. In 1810, the Humane Society reported that one of every seven families (2,000) supported themselves by selling liquor. That year 1,300 groceries and 160 taverns had licenses to sell "strong drink," and by 1817 this figure exceeded 2,000. In the artisan wards, licenses were granted to small groceries to sell spirits by the drink, "a good glass for three cents," and also by the bottle, a quart of brandy bringing three shillings and a gallon $1.25 (a day's pay).[18] An article in the *Medical Repository* depicts this custom as it sarcastically describes a typical day's consumption by a worker (Document 23). Advertisements for bull and panther baiting in the sixth ward, at a special rink seating 2,000 spectators, illustrate the popularity of blood sports (Document 24).[19] Finally, a propensity to violence and slander was a further link of the artisan world to premodern culture. The Mayor's Court records are replete with cases of assault and battery between spouses or masters and apprentices.

While pre-industrial work culture could be "intellectually vacant" as well as indolent, brutal and debilitating, its strong sense of customary right allowed leverage and a chance for selective leisure.[20] A poem by bookbinder John Bradford describing the right of journeymen not to work by candlelight from March through October is a good example of the importance of custom in gaining leverage in working conditions (see Document 95). However, as a handbill distributed by the master carpenters reveals (see page 247), set hours were becoming more and more common, particularly in trades closely tied to the expanding American marketplace. These crafts demanded a stricter work discipline with greater attention to hours and performance. To be able to function within this marketplace and to be able to organize and establish any countervailing force, a different morality was necessary. More than that, however, the ideals of the American Revolution, particularly the republican pride of producers, dignity of craftsmanship and the desire to remain a significant political and economic force contributed toward the development of a different moral outlook.[21]

This attitude was well represented in the pages of the *Independent Mechanic*, a weekly published in 1811 and 1812 and intended to "please the fancy, improve the heart and strengthen the mind" of the "industrious mechanic." Edited by Joseph Harmer, a young printer just leaving the "contracted sphere of a journeyman," it was decidedly antipolitical, devoting its columns to bettering the working lives of artisans with practical advice and the domestic lives with articles on what constituted proper conduct.[22] The *Mechanic* was well aware of the presence of premodern habits, and many columns were devoted to the evils of drink (Document 25).[23] Also common were essays castigating members of other classes as the principal victims of these vices. One article, for example, described the habits of a wealthy glutton, a second the ruthlessness of a rapacious landlord, while a third depicted in detail the empty and useless lives of the well-born (Documents 26–28). The poor, too, were condemned for their unfortunate state and their lack of contribution to society (Document 29). The bonds and consolation of religion were the final ingredient for the proper household.

Central to this moral conception was the superiority of the artisans' moderate yet virtuous lifestyle typified by an epigraph in *Longworth's New York Directory* for 1806 (Document 30).[24] Indeed, this was a highly sensitive issue. Nothing angered and bothered artisans more than the contempt of the elite. A purported dialogue among young women over the possibility of marrying a son of a mechanic is but one example of many to be found in the *Mechanic* revealing this concern and indignation (Document 31).[25]

23. Drinking Habits of the Laboring Class

AN IDEA OF THE RATE AT WHICH DISTILLED SPIRITS ARE CONSUMED IN THE UNITED STATES

As a medical, commercial, and political subject of inquiry, the consumption of ardent spirits is very interesting. Economists, statesmen and moralists have long deplored the abuses of these products of the still. But it is probable the cause of their regret and lamentation will not be soon removed. As long as one class of people find a profit in distilling ardent spirits from the raw materials; a second in purchasing them by wholesale, or shipping them from country to country; and a third in dealing them by retail to those who consume them; there will be a distillers, merchants, and retail dealers in abundance, to satisfy the wants of him who wishes to regale himself with brandy, gin, whiskey, &c. When we consider the great amount of these articles brought to market, and reflect that they are all destined to pass into the human stomach, it becomes interesting to know minutely the rate and manner of their consumption. The following may serve as an example of what is frequently done by a labouring man in an American town, who passes for a sober citizen. As he walks out in the morning he takes what is called a *small* glass (half a gill) of bitters, gin, or something of the sort, at the first grog-shop he passes; and commonly takes a second whet (another half gill) before he gets to work. Generally he takes two more of these *small* glasses of raw and clear stuff (amounting to another gill) as he returns home to get his breakfast. Thus a half pint is disposed of before eight o'clock A.M.

On going out from breakfast he takes a *large* glass, or a whole gill, and in the middle of the forenoon another. To this is added a third as he comes home to eat his dinner. This amounts to three gills between eight and twelve o'clock.

He drinks another *large* glass as he goes about to work, at or before two P.M. another on the middle of the afternoon; and a third on returning from work at six or after, making three gills more by the time his day's work is ended.

The daily quantity of distilled spirits consumed by one of these persons is as follows:

Before Breakfast	2 gills.
Before dinner	3
By the time day's work is done	3
Total,	8 gills,

or one quart of distilled spirits, consumed by a single labouring man in a day, besides what he drinks in the evening; and the greater part of them can still keep about, and do their work, without being actually drunk. By degrees, however, it overcomes them, and they yield to the repeated and excessive stimulus of their strong draughts.

The retail cost of these doses of spirits is a heavy tax upon the individual, and amounts to as much as would by his family bread, butter and sweetening.

Morning drams, four half gills, at 3d.	1s.
Grog before noon, three gills, at 6d.	1 6d.
Grog after noon, three gills, at 6d.	1 6d.
	4 shillings

or half a dollar a day, spent out of his wages for rum, to be swallowed to his own ruin, and to the pinching and impoverishment of his family. There are hundreds of men who go on at this rate of drinking as long as health and money

Scott's Grocery on Pearl Street. At such stores which were located throughout the city, liquor was easily and commonly purchased. Many artisans found themselves in debt to the proprietors and occasionally were forced into debtors' prison.
FRANCESCA CANFIELD, WATERCOLOR, NYHS

hold out. In the city of New-York there are houses where strong liquors are thus retailed. Alcohol seems to be a greater curse to Christians than opium to Turks.

Medical Repository, 2d. series, 1 (1804), 333–334

24. Blood Sports

To all true lovers of Sport. You are hereby respectfully invited to attend at the New Circus in the Bowery, opposite Mr. [Francis] Spicer's Inn, where will be exhibited a Urus [26] and Bull bear, with dogs of the first blood, on Monday, Tuesday, and Wednesday next, precisely at 4 o'clock P.M. on each day. The Urus and Bull will be fought alternately with the same dogs, not only to gratify the spectators, but to convince the public, that the Urus, though far inferior to the Bull in size, and diminutive in appearance, is greatly superior in strength, activity, mettle and management.

The Proprietors have spared no expence to complete Circus in such a manner as that every spectator may be well accommodated, and have a fair view of this much admired sport.—N.B. Tickets to be had at the place of Performance only. First Box Seats, 4s. Second, 3s.—and Pit, 2s.

American Citizen, April 4, 1801

❧ ❧ ❧

Panther Baiting

To the Lovers of Sport. A Panther from the Wilderness of Niagara, will be Baited with Eight Dogs on Thursday the 23d July, on Bunker's Hill.

The vigour and activity of this animal is such as will astonish the spectators, a bait of this kind having never been exhibited before, either in Europe, Asia, Africa or America. The animal will be confined with a strong chain fourteen feet long, so that no danger whatever may be apprehended of its breaking loose. The sport to being at three o'clock. Admittance to the Boxes 6s. Pit 4s. The Panther may be seen, until the time of baiting, at the circus, Greenwich street. Admittance 1 shilling.

American Citizen, July 21, 1801

25. The Perils of Drink

FOR THE INDEPENDENT MECHANIC

ON DRUNKENNESS

Of all the vices to which the fallibility of our nature has subjected us, this is the most disgustful. It brings with it numberless disorders, accumulating both on the body and conscience, and renders us not only detested by society, but hateful even to ourselves. From the brightest prospects of earthly fame and happiness, it plunges us into the darkest depth of misery and despair, closing the bright scenes of happiness hereafter from view forever. How miserable must be the man addicted to this vice! How wounding to the feelings of an innocent man to be accused of it!—I have written this for the purpose of introducing a letter written from a man who was accused of habitual drunkenness, to his accuser. The former had indeed given some ground for suspicion, but was far from being guilty of the charge.

"Mr. W.

"Reports have circulated abroad which owe their origin to you, stamping upon the unblotted page of my character, in letters of the blackest dye, the name of drunkard! Christian forebearance teaches the expostulation, although the silver voice of friendship has by this report become discordant, and the hand of confidence is dubiously extended towards men. Sir, I am young, and an adventurer, my prospects all depending on my *character*. I have mother, brothers, sisters, and friends. The man who becomes a drunkard, sacrifices his youth and health, his prospects and his fame; he brings the grey hairs of his parents "with sorrow to the grave;" he brings disgrace upon his brothers and dishonour upon his sisters; and freezes the warm current of friendship, the nourisher of life and hope, the soother of sorrow, and the comforter in misfortune.

"A drunkard is a being who bears no connexion to this world; with whom the world has no connexion. Living in himself, he loaths mankind, and still is sickened with the food he lives on. A wretch, who stands a mark for "scorn to point her slowly moving finger at." Compassion exercises her functions with indifference, and charity, even charity, weeps, that the object is unworthy the exercise of her grace. Do I deserve this? . . . .

Independent Mechanic, August 10, 1811

26. The Empty Lives of the Idle Rich

. . . Mr. Editor, there is an evil which I should extemely well like to see some notice taken of. I allude to a certain class of men whom I often observe in my route to my daily labour (being a mechanic) walking with slow and solemn pace, perusing their letters on their way from the post office. I do not mean to complain, Mr. Editor, at their anxiety to see the contents of their letters, for that I know is natural to us all; but it is the affectation and self consequence displayed in the *manner*. I know, indeed, that men of business have not time to go home to read their letters, and therefore, *their* looking at them in the street, is often necessary. But as soon as they read them over, they put them into their pockets; this is as it should be. But, Mr. Editor, is it not ridiculous to see a young fellow, who wishes to attach a degree of consequence to himself, stand for an hour posing over half a dozen lines from a country friend, and not even content with that he takes up his line of march, with his letter up to his eyes, and his head bent in the attitude of deep study and meditation, and thus continues, probably, until he reads within a few doors of his master's shop. But perhaps, Mr. Editor, you will say that it *may be* a long letter, and wrote in a poor hand, and therefore that it would require some time to feret it out. This, indeed, might be the case, I readily grant; though that is not always so. I know from experience: for having accidentally got a peep at one of those consequential blade's letters, I discovered to my satisfaction, that his letter amounted to but *five lines*, written in quite large and legible hand; so coaxing my patience to watch his manoevres at the post office door for half an hour, and being not yet satisfied, I actually waited till he moved, and then took up my march after him. After having followed him for a mile and a half (during the whole of which time he was deeply concerned in perusing his five lines) I abandoned him, concluding, that instead of a quarter, I should lose half a day, if I kept on any longer.

It is to be hoped, Sir, that by thus noticing these pompous, vain and ridiculous practices of a certain class of young men . . . [we can] put a stop to a foolish pride in which they too far indulge themselves, and teach them a lesson, that the honest, blunt, and unaffected manners of a young mechanic, is far more praise-worthy, than the pedantic foppish airs of a would-be gentleman.

Ariel Mechanic

Independent Mechanic, May 25, 1811

27. Satire on a Ruthless Landlord

A FRAGMENT

He is a rascal!—why? Surely sir, he is a rascal! and thus plainly I'll make it appear; you must know in the first place, that he owes me ten dollars, and does not pay me. I called upon him last week; he appointed another day, which was yesterday, for me to call again, as he could not then settle with me. Agreeably to his appointment, I called yesterday morning, and he began to preach over a pithy mess of stuff, telling me that he had been disappointed; that the times were so extremely bad he was afraid he should be under the necessity of suing for farther indulgence, or go to gaol; and that his family was large and expensive— that his children had been and then were ill—that the doctor's bill was very extravagant—that he was very much embarrassed to get along—that sometimes he was almost tired of life—that he could die with pleasure, could he but pay all his debts—and a thousand other things, too numerous to be mentioned at present. I still say that he is a rascal! and as such he shall be dealt by: What if he has had a little trouble in his family, by George! is that a sufficient apology for putting me off from time to time; he talks about trouble!—go to his house; he pretends he has had sickness in his family: nonsense; his children are all barefooted, and look as hardy as so many young tygers—'tis false! He is a rascal; and I am determined to sue him for the debt, if he does not come to an immediate settlement; there is another quarter-day fast approaching, and he has not paid me in full yet for the last: I will sieze every rag in his house for security; I cannot endure such imposition. We landlords have a hard time of it; we are

The Independent Mechanic, *a weekly newspaper intended for artisans, was founded in 1811
by young printer Joseph Harmer. Fiercely apolitical (believing that craftsmen were invariably
manipulated and exploited by politicians and
parties) it offered practical and moral advice to
the mechanic community. Its contributors preached
a moderate course, free of drinking, gambling,
debt and dissipation. Condemning the idle rich
and the drunken beggar alike, it strongly advocated temperance and godliness.* INDEPENDENT
MECHANIC, APRIL 6, 1811

obliged to wait upon some of our tenants, day after day, and when they pay us,
it is with a sigh, and with a look that is expressive of the greatest reluctance. I
am determined, for the future, that no person shall occupy a house of mine, if
he does not pay me every cent. He tells me that the times are hard; I wonder if
he thought I was ignorant of that; sure I find the times hard enough, but then, I
do not make such a noise about it. He ought to be grateful to me for the lenity I
have already shown him, and not impertinently ask for further indulgence. I
will shew him what hard times are, if he is not more punctual in his payments,
for the future; he has never, yet, read the *preface* to hard times; his wife, too,
puts on a sorry face, and begins to whine when I come to see them, and deals
out to me a long account of their poverty, and inability to answer my demands,
with promptness and punctuality. He is a rascal! He told me, that he was
disposed to do any thing for my accommodation, if I would give him time; he
has had time, as much as any man; as much time as myself; as much time as the
richest man in the world; but what does he do with time? true, he works, and at
night, returns home with some provision for his family, and thus he lays out his
money. I tell him, frequently, to put out four, or five of his older ones to trades;
oh! sir, says he, they are not yet old enough; besides, if it be in my power, I am
resolved to give them some education, before I do it; and so goes his money;

and thus he robs me of my due; he is a rascal! I cannot, and will not bear it, much longer. He goes to church, every Sunday, and sits where I can see him; zounds! I wonder how a man, that is in debt, can have the brass to shew his face in church, where his creditors are! or at market; or indeed, any where, but at work. He is a rascal! and I a fool, for being so easy with him; the law must have its course: I will bring him up to the bull-ring: I will teach him how to deal with me: he asks for favors! how can he have the audacity to hope for favor; it is impudence for him, even to thank me, for the tender mercies I have already shown him; yes, I will go this day, and see that he is properly secured, Or no—I will wait until the next quarter's rent becomes due, and then, if he does not discharge the whole demand, I will stow him well, I warrant him; he is a rascal! that is as much as deserves to be said of him;—I will sweat him; I will fix him; ah! ah!—and that pretty cleverly too!!

GRIPUS

Independent Mechanic, September 12, 1811

28. On Vagrants

CENSOR

NO. X

INDUSTRY promotes *health*—seldom fails of producing *competence*, and not unfrequently, conduces to *wealth* and *independence*.

INDOLENCE engenders *disease*—seldom fails of producing *misery*, and not unfrequently conducts to a prison or the gallows.

When we reflect that, with a moderate exercise of industry, in this, our happy country, any person may be enabled to procure all the *necessaries*, and a proportionate *share* of the *luxuries* of life; when we contract the comforts, a neat, even though it should be a humble dwelling, affords with the wretchedness endured by the houseless, wandering vagrant; or, not to descend so low, when we compare the *real* pleasure which the industrious mechanic enjoys, as the evening sun sets on a well spent day, with the littleness and langour, in which the unoccupied idler drags on a weary life; when, in fine, we reflect, that in giving way to a lazy, slothful disposition, which rapidly increases with indulgence, we have no chance of gain, and, to a certainty, everthing to lose, our astonishment is excited, and our indignation roused, to see so many vagrants, (numbers of whom are apparently able to sustain the hardest labour, and who are not even *covered* "with *rags*,") infest our streets, by day, shocking the delicacy of our females, and disgusting the feelings of every one, who is not as debased as the wretches themselves; and by night, most probably, employed in appropriating to their own use the property of the honest and industrious.

That they must *eat* and *drink*, to support life, no one can deny; and also, that their beverage is not always drawn from the fountain's limpid rill, is sufficiently evident from their appearances, as they are to be seen, in almost every street in the city, stretched out upon the pavement, exposed to the scorching sun, nearly naked, and stupefied with liquor.

Here then, naturally arises a question: From what source do they draw their supplies, to procure this necessary food; and above all, money to purchase liquor sufficient to keep them in an almost continual state of intoxication? That they do not beg, (at least not generally,) I am pretty well assured; and that they will not work, admits of no contradiction. – One way, only is left: – they *steal*. They parade though the streets, watching an opportunity to purloin whatever portable thing they meet with in their way; this they find means to sell, or

While in the 1790s a number of artisans were influenced by the deism and free thought associated with Tom Paine. In the early nineteenth century, more were caught up in the enthusiasm of the Second Great Awakening. Quite a number attended small Methodist chapels like this one on John St. scattered within the outer wards. STOKES COLLECTION, NYPL

pawn, and with the money purchase liquor. Thus they proceed, until they become intoxicated, when they lay themselves down in the streets, no matter where, or how public, and sleep till they are sufficiently recruited to re-commence their depredations.

May we not, let me ask, among the many fires that occur in our city, a number of which are attributed to design, without risking much, lay a propor-tion to the charge of those miscreants, who with sufficient bodily strength for labour, have no visible means of support? It is not reasonable to suppose, that those, who *must live* by begging, or by *plunder*, would resort to this means of throwing the city into confusion, and the inhabitants off their guard; thereby multiplying opportunities for theft; and under the pretence of affording assistance, villainously rob the unhappy sufferers, at a time when they are too much distressed to detect the fraud, or punish the offender:—And does not the arrest of many, by our constables, and marshals, at almost every such deplorable time, in the very act of thieving, countenance the supposition?

Our proper officers, therefore, ought to be very assiduous in discharging their duty, by strictly enforcing the law against vagrants, and using all the authority in them vested, to rid the streets of their disagreeable and disgraceful, if not dangerous tenants. Our night watch, also, ought to be particularly instructed to take into their custody all persons of this suspicious appearance, numbers of whom may every night be found lying on the Battery, in the Park, and in all our markets, the Fly-market in particular . If this were done, we should at least be relieved from the disagreeable sensations, which must naturally arise, on seeing filthy wretches, half naked, and apparently covered with vermin, laying drunk in our path in the public streets; and the possibility of their committing depredations would be lessened; added to this, the miserable objects themselves would be benefited; and the public institution suffer no loss, as they should be compelled to earn a sufficiency to balance the expense of their own maintenance.

Independent Mechanic, August 3, 1811

29. Artisan Ideals

—I pay my debts;
  I steal from no man; would not cut a throat to gain
admission to a great man's purse,
   or a whore's bed; I'd not betray a friend

*Printers were very proud of their craft. They considered it to be the key to the furtherance of
knowledge and enlightenment. Anderson's depiction of a printing press within the republican eagle is
symbolic of artisan's sense of their value to American society. Printer Samuel Woodworth, a secretary of
the New York Typographical Society, wrote a poem that expressed the critical role of their profession:*

Hail! art of arts! all hail!
Thy praises mock the lyre;
To reach the boundless theme,
Its tones in vain aspire;
But grateful hearts which feel the bliss
Thy magic power bestows,

Respond to every strain like this,
How dull so'er it flows:
Chorus: Ours is the Heaven-descended art,
To give fair knowledge birth,
To mend the human heart,
And civilize the earth.

NYPL; GEORGE A. STEVENS, NEW YORK TYPOGRAPHICAL UNION NUMBER SIX

to get his fortune; I scorn to
    flatter a blown up fool above me or crush
the wretch below me.

Stonemason's listing from *Longworth's Directory of the City of New-York for 1805* (New York, 1805)

30. On Marrying a Cooper's Son

"Who is that?"
"La don't you know him! why not John W– –? oh fie!"
"What the cooper's son?"

"Yes and what is he now? he is still a son of a cooper; I mean he is not a lawyer, or a priest or some other professional gentleman. No, no, he is what I said he was, a cooper's son, the son of a cooper."

"But then I have heard it said, that he is a young gentleman of good abilities, and bids fair to prove a shining ornament in society. I am inclined to think also, that he is a worthy young man, from the little acquaintance I have with him."

"Nonsense! Still you think that he is a cooper's son, and nothing more than the son of a cooper."

"Why, my dear, what if he be the son of a cooper, may not the son of a cooper be a worthy man, and is not even a cooper, a character that is generally respected, and notwithstanding he is the son of a mechanic, he will no doubt be of as much consequence in society as the son of a nabob. Is it not reasonable to believe, that he will ever be considered by the wiser part of mankind no less deserving esteem on account of his origin?"

"I say that the young gentleman as you call him is the son of a cooper."

"What then? I know that a cooper is as honorable as a priest, or any character; and it is the most absurd thing in the world, for you to even suppose that John W——, is the less worthy for being the son of a respectable mechanic. If a person rise, by his own virtues, to eminence, he ought to be applauded, and commended. What if he can make no boast of the high standing of his father, or the illustrious name of a grandfather? He can speak for himself; and his exertions in laudable pursuits deserve the meed of praise, not the malicious and unmerited language of a traducer."

"Very well. Miss, go on if you will; speak of him, as you would speak of an hero, or a descendant of Alexander."

"I presume I speak of him as I ought; and should think myself unworthy to live, if I was habitually inclined to contaminate and blast the good name of people, who are worthy our imitation, and esteem."

"I suppose then, from the drift of your conversation, that you would with as little scruple consent to become his partner through life, as to be wedded to a man whose partners were of good blood and fortune."

"I must acknowledge that I would as soon comply to be his bride, as I would to any other person's, whose virtues and accomplishments were not adequate to his, though they might boast of their noble descent and lordling race of ancestors. Let it be asked, would you for the sake of titles and empty dignities, surrender every endearment of life? would you sacrifice your peace, liberty and repose, and take a malicious viper in your bosom, in preference to a kind, beneficent, and humane man: merely because he was of more noble descent? Would you sooner become the vassal, to a debauchee, a spend thrift, and a blasphemer, than a companion and associate to a man of feeling, and sensibility? Would you, in short, be seen weeping for that happiness, which you thought to obtain in the high stations of life, and regretting when too late, the time you left the mansions of cheerfulness? Would you be seen imploring a haughty villian, with tears of unfeigned sorrow, to abandon his mad career, in the rounds of

Benjamin Franklin long remained a hero to the artisan community. Many societies were named after him and his writings, particularly those of "Poor Richard," remained popular. The emphasis on the importance of manual labor and the condemnation of the lazy rich and the indolent poor were common. A scene from POOR RICHARD ILLUSTRATED: LESSONS FOR YOUNG AND OLD. YALE UNIVERSITY LIBRARY

dissipation and vice? Could you then suffer the haughty indifference with which he would treat you? Look well to these things, my young woman, and you will no longer despise, or affect to despise, a character so worthy and irreproachable, as that of the good cooper's son. I shall see you again shortly, and shall then be happy to know your mind. So I bid you good bye."

Independent Mechanic, January 4, 1812

A WOMAN'S WORLD

While much has been written about the importance of women in their role of transmitting republican ideals to the next generation, it is less clear that these writers had the artisan classes in mind. For while "republican mothers" were not expected to enter the workplace, the daughters of craftsmen often had to find employment. Generally the only jobs available were in the tailoring trade, as seamstresses and mantua makers (silk work), or in the homes of the elite, as personal servants. Occasionally, on an artisan's death, his widow took over the business. Women could also be found as grocers and boarding house keepers. There was also at least one factory established in New York which hired large numbers of women to do needlework.

Many wives of artisans stayed home raising children, maintaining the house, marketing and cleaning. There is all too little extant evidence about family relations between artisans and their wives and the values of women in artisan households. The *Independent Mechanic* does, however, provide a few

Six women at work in a millinery shop. Dress making and mantua making (silk work) were two trades dominated by female labor. ANDERSON COLLECTION, NYPL

Most women did not work for salaries. Some helped out at home in their spouse's trade. The above scene depicts a woman, accompanied by her child, working in a decorative profession either sewing or embroidering. ANDERSON COLLECTION, NYPL

A woman's dress, 1815–1820. Considerable craftsmanship was involved in the fabrication of these garments, and was often performed by women. MCNY

important glimpses. A number of articles appeared concerning the proper manner of female upbringing and deportment, with the stress on meek and domestic behavior and on cleanliness and modesty. Too, *Mechanic* correspondents exhibited fear of women falling into the snares of 'female vice' such as slander and gossip, excessive vanity, and an inclination to spend beyond their means. The latter fault is well illustrated in a letter written by a most unhappy tradesman (Document 32).

Women occasionally used the *Mechanic* to discuss their interests. In one instance, in rebutting a male complainant, "Friend to Females," "Sarah Touchstone" defended her right to take children to church. In another "Miss Mackaboy," responding to the same "Friend's" complaints about women's use of tobacco, argued for the privilege of taking snuff (Documents 33–34). These documents, if they do not reveal women as active in politics and public affairs, do reveal feminine courage—perhaps a Revolutionary legacy—to defend the prerogatives of their sphere. It is likely that the republican ideology so prominent within the mechanic community had some impact on the women within that society.[27]

31. A Profligate Wife

FOR THE INDEPENDENT MECHANIC

CENSOR

NO. VIII

Marriage is Life's *lottery*, which hath many blanks;
And he whom Fortune with a *prize* doth favor,
The gift her choicest blessing should esteem.

The following letter, from a discontented husband, I received a few days since, and which I have no doubt will be acceptable to some of my readers. Mr. Censor,

I am unfortunately a married man that can not live comfortably with my wife; and our uneasiness is altogether owing to her conduct.

Now, as your paper comes regularly to our house, and is pretty generally read by her, I hope you will be so good as to publish a little wholesome advice in one of your numbers, that may tend to convince *her*, as well as any other woman, who may give their husbands like cause of complaint. That you may be the better able to feel for me, I will give you a fair statement of my case, from the beginning to the present time.

I am a mechanic, and am called a good workman, on which account I am able to keep in constant employ, and earn a good deal of money. While a single man, I was not fond of frolicking, and in about a year and half after I was free, I had saved a pretty good sum. I then began to look about me for a wife, and pitched upon one that seemed to be every way calculated to make a fine companion for a steady mechanic. She appeared good tempered, sufficiently accomplished for a wife for me, *extremely neat* in her person, but without being extravagant in her dress; and to make all complete, she did not seem to be over fond of company-keeping. I accordingly made my addresses to her, and in a short time finally determined to ask her for my wife. I made her fully acquainted with my *then* present circumstances and my future prospects; and entreated her to maturely consider whether she would be content to live in the manner she might expect, if·she accepted me for a husband; at the same time assuring her, that nothing should be wanting to make her life happy, that my industry could supply. She accepted the terms, and in a short time we were married.

All went well for about three months, when she began to form a new set of female acquaintances, some in the same circumstances with herself, but who were enabled, by foolishly squandering their husband's substance, to dress in all the extravagance of every new fashion, give tea parties once or twice a week, resort to the theatre, and, in short, to launch out into every kind of extravagance, unfitting for a mechanic's wife. She no sooner got well acquainted with the *ladies* in question, than she began to be very discontented. Our furniture was become too common. The *rag carpet* was a disgrace to the floor. Mrs. _____ had a fine Turkey carpet, and her husband did not make as much money as I did. Our chairs were not fit a decent person to sit on, because Mrs. _____ had a set of white and gold, with painted *rush bottoms*. Our *calico* curtains ought to be burnt; she was ashamed to look at them, after she had seen Mrs. _____'s white muslin ones, with net fringe and *gilt* cornices. She was quite ashamed to ask a few ladies to tea, after having spent an afternoon at Mrs. _____'s, whose set of china cost *forty dollars*. In short our tables and irons, lookingglass, and every article in the house ought to be sent to vendue, they were a disgrace to a decent family. I endeavoured to reason with her, but in vain; a remonstrance always produced a fit of the *pouts*, which generally lasted until I was forced to give her something which I was truly ashamed to do; further, she would refuse to be seen twice in the same gown or hat; she should be *known* by her clothes, always in the same dress. In short an article was scarcely soiled till it became so horribly old-fashioned that she could not possibly wear it unless it was at least *altered* and *new trimmed*, to give it a change of appearance.

Scarce a week passed, in which the husbands of some of her extravagant friends did not appear in the list of *insolvents*. Mrs. _____'s carpet, Mrs. _____'s china, and Mrs. _____'s curtains, were all sold by the hammer of the auctioneer. These instances I brought as warnings but in vain; and to save myself from a similar fate, I was obliged to lock up my money, and forbid her to run me in debt.

From this time she dashed into another extreme, she discharged our servant girl, declaring that if she could not appear like a Christian (as she termed it) she would not be seen out of the house, and would be completely the mope I wanted her. She now appeared continually in a state always out of humor, and from being ashamed to be seen unless decked out in a manner unbecoming a trademan's wife, she was now so careless of herself, that I was, in truth, ashamed that any one *should* see her. And thus has she continued to the present day. You must think, then, Mr. Censor, that my life is not very agreeably spent. We have a growing family, to make a decent provision for which, I work hard, and it is truly distressing to me, after my day's labour is over, to come home to a house, in which I had been accustomed to meet the smiling face of a sweet tempered wife, and could sit down to my comfortable supper, happy myself, by seeing all contented about me; but which is now so sadly reversed, that I find nothing but frowning ill-humor, and slovenly neglect. Instead of that neatness, which formerly proved my wife was anxious to make herself agreeable to me, I now find a shameful inattention even to common and necessary cleanliness; which fully evinces a total disregard, as well of my good opinion, or happiness, as of the opinion of the world at large.

Your, &c.
A TRADESMAN

Scarce anything tends more to breed discontent between married people, than an avowed indifference, on the part of the females, to cleanliness, and neatness in their persons. Can it be supposed that a man in his senses, could ever give the preference before marriage, to a girl who paid no attention to her appearance, but was always to be seen as if she employed in the kitchen? Everyone will answer—No. And where can there be a greater insult offered to a man, one only excepted, than for his wife to so far deviate from that neatness of habit, which first fixed his attention, as to bring the blush of shame into his face when a friend calls at his house. Is it not a tacit declaration that she values not his love, or his good opinion, that she is joined for life to a man she dislikes, and that in his approbation there is no inducement of sufficient weight to balance the trouble she should have, in rendering herself agreeable. To this, everyone must answer—Yes.

I would recommend to all married ladies to think seriously on this subject, and some, perhaps, may find their own lives rendered more happy, from profiting by the example in the foregoing letter.

Independent Mechanic, July 21, 1811

32. On Taking Infants to Church

Mr. Editor,

    I know of no subject which deserves more to be noticed, than that of women taking their infants to church. It is an evil of such magnitude, that no woman of consideration or decency, will be guilty of it. It is indecent, because no woman who has that nice and scrupulous regard for herself, which, as a female, ought to be her first and greatest consideration will expose her bare bosom to a gaping multitude of men; and this she is necessitated to do frequently, in order to pacify her babe. Indeed, often it is the case, that when the minister in the sacred desk, is in the most solemn, affecting, and interesting part of his discourse; and when too his audience are loath to hear the sound of a footstep, fearful that they may lose the train of his reasoning, and when the whole congregation are in the most respectful silence, that the ears of all are stunned, the imagination confused, and the soul tortured by cries and screeches of an infant. What, I ask, is more vexatious? What can be more painful? The poor child is not to blame, but the mother who introduces it. Some may say that because a woman has been blest with the birth of a child, she ought not to be deprived of an opportunity of hearing divine worship. But to those, I answer, this is no argument; for a woman cannot attend to the minister and to the child at the same time; and even if she could, it can in no possible shape be justified, that the rest of the congregation should be disturbed, for "better that one die, than the whole should perish." I say again, it is a grievous nuisance, wholly unjustifiable; and no woman ought to be suffered to enter the threshold of a church, with an infant in her arms, unless for the purpose of having it christened. A moral woman can be as good at home as at church, and better, when they have infants in their arms. Besides, other evil consequences flow from it: many an infant receives a death-cold, from their being wrapped up warm in church, and after service are exposed to the damp dews of night and chilling blasts. That mother who possesses a tender feeling for her babe will not sport with its health. May this short notice be received as friendly advice from one who is a

FRIEND TO FEMALES

Independent Mechanic, December 21, 1811

* * * * *

Mr. Editor:

I would beg leave through the medium of your papers, to address a few lines to answer to a morose old jockey who came out in your last in the character of

"A FRIEND TO FEMALES"

I cannot say that I thank the gentleman for his pretended friendly advice; and as no person can like their church better than I do, I must attend as often as my family affairs will permit. After having paid this tribute of my God, I feel as happy through the week as possible. I feel as if I had something very heavy taken from my breast. I go through my weekly toils with much more cheerfulness and pleasure, than when I play the truant. To stay at home because I have been happily blessed with a child is ridiculous. I am sure that my son (God bless his little dimpled cheeks!) never disturbed any one of the congregation, although he is my companion at the house of God. Even while I am writing, it is smiling in my face as if it knew its injured mother busied in vindicating her wrongs; and would seem to say—must my mother be abused, because her circumstances will not allow her a nurse to leave at home?—Shame on him who is so thoughtless.

This boasted friend to females says, "that no woman of any consideration or decency would be guilty of it," meaning the practice of taking infants to church. A most admirable assertion! But give me leave to tell him, that *consideration* is the sole cause of their attention to church—the consideration of their immortal souls. God never blest a woman with a birth to give her an excuse for neglecting her church; but on the contrary, that she should be more attentive as she has a family to bring up, and she should be more pious in order that she may bring up her children in the way they should go. It is indeed an afflicting sight, to see, on the Lord's day, so many idle profligate children strolling about the streets; and what is the cause? it is not, as he says, the fault of the child, but the mother, in not conducting them to church.

"Expose her bosom to a gaping multitude of men." A gaping multitude of men, did he say? Yes; and I am sorry to be under the disagreeable necessity of joining with him in the assertion; for how many deluded wretches are there, who only enter the house of the Lord to gape, and put females modesty to the blush, by their rude behaviour. If they came there to hear the word of God, they would not be gaping at the mother's naked bosom. He says—"when the minister is in the most interesting part of his discourse, the ears of the congregation are stunned by the cries and screeches of an infant" a most wonderful *infant*, that can stun the ears of a whole congregation with its weak and unfinished organs, and prevent him from hearing the preacher! Upon my word, I never heard such absurdity in my life. I am confident, if a person goes to church from devotion, they will not be disturbed by a mother's naked breast, or the cries of her child.

While urban life allowed for some convenience, in the early nineteenth century women's traditional chores, as depicted by New Yorker Anderson, remained laborious and time consuming. ANDERSON COLLECTION, NYPL

Again—he asserts "that the mother cannot attend to the minister and her child at the same time." I am not have [sic] of his opinion for I contend that her mind is better fitted to receive what the minister put forth, than when without her child. When she looks on the infant, it reminds her of what she once was, of what she now is, and with the pleasing sensations of what she probably may be, when this earth has no more claim to her earthly form. But it is impossible for a man to attend to the minister's discourse while gaping for a woman's naked bosom. That "a moral woman can be better at home than at church, particularly if she has an infant," is impossible, if she intends to teach her children the worship of God; for if she has several, while attending to one, in the house, the rest steals out and joins the wicked boys in the street; if she sends them to church alone, it is ten to one they will be decoyed away by the enticing proposal of some fascinating play: but the mother attending church herself prevents all these evils, and 'tis an old saying and a true one that "*as the old* cock crows the young one learns." If I may be pardoned for using a proverb.

SARAH TOUCHSTONE

Independent Mechanic, December 28, 1811

33. On Women's Right To Snuff

FOR THE INDEPENDENT MECHANIC

THE SNUFF-TAKER'S REPLY

What! if we take a little snuff,
    To pass an idle hour away;
'Tis harmless as the smoker's puff,
    Our female friends and mothers say.
Sometimes we think you like to go
    To porter-houses for good beer:
And where's the harm?—no harm, Oh! no:
    No harm at all, indeed, my dear;
Then for segars of pipe you call,
    And smoke and puff, and puff and smoke,
(Till clouds on clouds ascend the wall,)
    Like Vulcan's forge, when Aetna broke!
Why set your head on fire, dear sir?
    Why with your mouth volcano make?
And why your maw a reservoir—
    A ton of double ale to take?
You like your smoke, I like my snuff,
    In either sir, where is the crime?
To leave off yours is hard enough,
    As hard for me to leave off mine.

We women say that you are bad,
    For drinking ale, and guzzling gin.
Since you have said that females had
    By taking snuff committed sin.
As women preach, so men must hear,
    Sound doctrines to their creed apply:
But when men teach, we often fear,
    They'll tell us things we may deny.
Tobacco is delicious, ah!
    And snuff must be no doubt, the same;
What's then the odds, my dear, I say?
    The only difference is the name.
You tell us that you'd rather live
    A batchelor a thousand years,
Than your consent to Hymen give,
    Than with a SNUFFER *soothe* your cares.
It may be so; but should we care
    Were you indulged in such a choice;
The ladies never will despair
    While *snuff is comfort—not a vice.*

MISS MACKABOY[28]

Independent Mechanic, October 19, 1811

PART TWO

Politics

*F*or craftsmen, the line of first defense for artisan republicanism was electoral politics. It was in this vibrant arena that the gains of 1776 would either become a permanent part of American society or else be lost in favor of a return to an aristocratic, monarchical government and community. Artisans were a self-conscious and potent constituency. No party could hold office without a major share of their votes.[1] Yet, the position of artisans in the early republic was not that of the revolutionary era. In 1776 craftsmen were at the center of power; no major decision was taken without consulting the Mechanics Committee.[2] In New York politics from the 1790s on, however, they worked within a framework of large national parties. While they were a critical element of these organizations, they did not control them or the issues of partisanship. Politics, consequently, was often frustrating. Still, it remained the central forum in which craftsmen could assert their various concerns and attempt to see that they became public policy. Equally important, electoral politics was the most visible and significant forum in which mechanics could declare that they were as important to the body politic as were the merchants or the lawyers.

THE 1790S

The 1790's was a decade of momentous political contention as Jeffersonians and Hamiltonians fought for their particular conception of American republicanism. The stakes were high: the future of the American government commencing operation under the authority of the articles and by-laws drafted in Philadelphia in 1787.[3] In New York, as in other states, parties and politicians waged bitter fights within a new political setting in which local leaders found it necessary to seek national as well as state and local ties.

The dominant party in New York City at the beginning of this era, and the one that commanded the broad support of the mechanic community, was the Federalist Party. Under Alexander Hamilton and John Jay, authors of the famed *Federalist*, they had led the state campaign for ratification of the Constitution. Headed by the city's most prominent merchants and attorneys, their espousal of a strong new nation that commanded national and international respect, was able to protect commerce, to implement tariffs, to pay its debts, and to create favorable business conditions, attracted artisans into a powerful electoral coalition. While expecting the deferential support of mechanics as a matter of course, the Federalists were not unaware of the Revolution's heritage of enhanced political consciousness among all sectors of the population, and wisely included craftsmen on their Assembly slate. In 1789, this ticket, established at a joint meeting of the Merchants and Mechanics Committees, carried by a tally of 2,342 to 373.[4]

As strong as the Federalist hold on the mechanic constituency was in 1789, within six years they were unable to hold even a majority of the city's artisans. A series of deeply felt local and national events galvanized many of New York's mechanics, turning them away from the Federalists and into the fold of the Democratic-Republicans, an incipient political party aligned with the Jeffersonian movement and marked by egalitarian and civil libertarian ideals. An open, middling organization whose leaders were to be found mingling willingly with prominent mechanics, the Jeffersonians supported artisans' particular concern for craft protection through tariffs or bounties, opposed restrictive municipal regulation, and gave assistance to immigrants. Most importantly, they understood the artisan's conception of republican government, both for expanding economic horizons and for prominent recognition as the producing class.[5]

The Federalist outlook was most compatible with that of the British Whigs who governed England. Their foreign policy was pro-British, much to the dismay of most craftsmen who still remained hostile to their former oppressor. Too, Federalists became increasingly hostile to the French Revolution. They were suspicious of revolutionary ideologies which they saw as hostile to the property-owning segment of society. They backed President Washington's condemnation of the Democratic Societies and supported the Alien and Sedition laws curtailing freedom of speech and freedom of the press. Moreover, they firmly opposed any alteration of municipal voting laws which restricted suffrage in the important election of aldermen (as well as assessors, collectors and constables) to property-holders. This disenfranchised three-fourths of the city's mechanics (Documents 34–35), causing much friction and more distance between artisans and their erstwhile political allies.[6]

Local issues proved costly as well to the Federalists. This was particularly true in the Keteltas affair, stemming from the arrest of two ferrymen, Burk and Crady, for insolence to an alderman. The men were whipped without due process. When William Keteltas, a Republican lawyer, protested to the Federalist-controlled State Assembly seeking impeachment of the officers, he found no sympathy; when he condemned that body, he was arrested for contempt. Keteltas became a celebrated hero for standing up to aristocratic arrogance (Document 36).[7] Federalists also lost support with individual trades over municipal regulation. This is exemplified by an attempt of the Federalist Common Council to force tallow chandlers to remove from city limits on grounds of health, a move opposed by Republicans (Document 37). Expecting artisans to defer to their leadership, Federalists found it almost intolerable that this class would turn against its leadership and values. Yet for a young, ambitious patriotic sailmaker like Stephen Allen, this was part and parcel of his decision not to support the Federalists when he chose a party in the 1790s (Document 38).

34. Federalist Defense of Suffrage Restrictions

TO THE FREEHOLDERS AND FREEMEN OF THE CITY OF NEW-YORK

To-morrow being the day appointed by law for the ELECTION OF CHARTER OFFICERS, the citizens are invited to pay due attention to this important object.

They will recollect, that by the Charter of the city, the corporation is invested with extensive powers and a large estate. If these powers are exercised with discretion, they may be rendered subservient to public happiness in many particulars; but on the other hand, if unfortunately they should be entrusted to the tools of ambitious and designing men, they may become instruments of faction and oppression for the worst of purposes. It is truly a nice and arduous task to regulate the police of a great commercial city, inhabited by persons of almost every description; where the jarring interests of contending individuals are to be consulted and reconciled as far as may be possible. To execute such a task with any propriety would require some talents, much experience, and great probity. The last is essentially requisite, and give me leave to add, that every Magistrate should not only possess an unsullied character, but also have a considerable stake in the community. I do not mean to insinuate that vice is the constant concomitant of poverty, or virtue inseparable from riches. I know that in several instances the reverse will be found true; but considering the frailty of human nature, and the present state of society and manners, independence of circumstance and respect for property, afford no bad security for general good behavior. It is obvious that a certain share of property is a safe qualification in many cases, both for the electors and those whom they are to elect.—It is obvious, also, that any man, whose system of politics tends to deprive property of all its influence and consideration, and to excite irreconcilable enmity between the rich and poor of the same society, must be dangerous.—Such men flatter the populace for the acquisition of power, and abuse the rich that they may be enabled to plunder them. The public property of the city is such, as may in the care of safe and prudent persons, be a lasting fund for many purposes of public ornament and utility. In other hands, it may be speedily dissipated, even under popular pretexts, for the gratification of rapacity and inordinate ambition. Should we elect such persons to the Office of Aldermen, we may probably see freemen enough made to secure all future Elections for Charter officers, and if in this state of things it should be our misfortune at any future period to have a Chief Magistrate of the city stained by the imputation, and hardened by the use of fraudulent practices; prodigal in his disposition; destitute of principle, and greedy of wealth—my fellow citizens may imagine, and would be forced to deplore the consequences.

I sincerely hope that their zeal and exertions at the present and future elections, may avert the evil.

A CITIZEN

Evening Post, November 16, 1801

35. The Consequences of Suffrage Reform

But now, fellow citizens, what do you imagine is proposed by these *friends of order?* Nothing less than that the legislature should break down the charter of your city for the purpose of extending the right of suffrage to every good democrat, both native and imported within five years? But what is a

> **AMERICAN TICKET,**
>
> *Patriotic Americans,*
>
> A N D
>
> **HONEST FOREIGNERS.**
>
> NO GENET—NO EMMET—NO CLINTON.
>
> *NO DICTATORS—NO JACOBINS.*
>
> **NO GOVERNED GOVERNOR,**
>
> B U T
>
> *An Independent Executive.*
>
> **REPUBLICANISM AND OUR COUNTRY, FOR EVER.**
>
> DOWN WITH THE FIRST CONSUL.
>
> DOWN WITH HIS LEGION OF HONOUR.

A 1794 Federalist broadside linking Democratic-Republican Governor George Clinton with the controversial French ambassador Edmund Genet. Genet had compromised his position by partisan involvement in American politics against Federalist pro-British policies. The Federalists were attempting to link Clinton and Genet and at the same time attacking the French Revolution and its "jacobin" American supporters. NYHS

charter in the eyes of such people as your Cheethams and Duanes, who if the proper time shall ever arrive will with equal readiness bawl out for the erection of a guillotine in the park and endeavour practically to shew the possibility of perpetual motion in the action of its bloody knife. The event of yesterday may convince them that such a period is farther distant than they have hoped.[8]

Evening Post, November 17, 1802

36. The Keteltas Affair: On Federalist Arrogance

For the *New-York Journal* &c.
    Citizen Greenleaf
By inserting the following, you will oblige one of your correspondents.

I FIND from the perusal of your paper of last Friday, that the conduct of our *worthy Magistrates*, in punishing some of the Swinish Multitude, for not treating them with that degree of respect which their high office entitled them to, has given cause of offence to one of that *groveling throng*. In order, therefore, that their dignity and importance may not hereafter be exposed to any insult from an ignorant public, I would most humbly beg that the following, or some similar plan should be adopted, viz.—that all men in high offices should at the public expence be provided with some distinguishing badge, such as a gold chain, to be worne round their necks, as is the custom in some kingdoms in Europe; or if that should have a slavish appearance, let a gold metal be struck off with the following inscription—"sum praestontior omnibus, inclinalinated mihi;" or if that would not suit, let it be in these words, "I am born to govern, therefore approach me with reverence." If either of these modes were to be adopted, no one then would dare to act in such a manner as to infringe upon their majesty; or if they did, let some exemplary punishment be inflicted, even worse if possible than twenty-five, or thirty lashes on the bare back, in order that *rascals* might be taught to fear and adore their rulers. I would further propose that a large ship, almost worne out in the service of our well beloved ally George,[9] should be brought and stationed in either of the rivers which bound this city, for the purpose of confining such unruly master ferrymen or others, who would wilfully trample upon the dignity of their stations; and further, that the management of the said ship should be given to any one of our magistrates, who may be thought most fit for that office, by having from experience, learned the best method of chastising rascals on board such vessels heretofore. Hoping that these incoherent ideas may be taken in good part, I subscribe myself with the most profound respect,

A Friend to the MIGHTY

New York Journal, December 30, 1795

37. Federalist Persecution of the Tallow Chandlers

Citizen Greenleaf,

A late ACT *of the Legislature*[10] seems to render it necessary, that every citizen who is a friend to himself, but cannot vie with the great, should be upon the watch, and be attentive to his own interest. Self defence either of property or person is esteemed the first law of nature. Every member of society, not even excepting the good peaceable Quakers, has therefore the right of saying, touch me not. Mankind unite and make a common cause with each other, to frustrate the designs of those who would burn, rob or destroy the property of an individual; but why is it not as good for a man to have one half of his property burnt or destroyed, and he injoy the other half peaceably and quietly, as to be paid for what he may esteem perhaps one half of the value of his property, and himself totally driven from it, or if not driven from it, in effect disqualified by law from making any use of it. It is a common observation, that "every man is best judge of his own affairs;"—If so, it is utterly impossible that any number of indifferent men should be adequate to the task of estimating the damage and injury it would be to a person, settled down in business, to be ousted and *driven out of town*! But even suppose the *Talllow Chandlers* once situated upon the pinnacle of Bunker's Hill, what security have they that they shall long remain there undisturbed? as soon as that will be known or heard, rolling along, with the accompanyments of wealth, will come from *nabob*, some wise and pompous Treaty maker, or may be some son of Esculapius[11] with his wife, and we will not suppose with how many concubines, who perhaps finding his delicate smellers a little offended, and casting his eyes, will exclaim, "you dirty stinking dogs, you shall continue there no longer. March for Kingsbridge."[12] Thus, driven from pillar to post, even "from Dan to Bathsheba," the chandlers will have no rest for the sole of their feet, and like the rolling stone will be able to gather no moss.

IMPARTIALITY

New York Journal, February 13, 1797

38. Stephen Allen: on Choosing a Political Party

. . . I was not long deciding which of these parties to join, for on the one hand I beheld all the old Royalists and Tories whom I had known while yet a boy attaching themselves to the Federalists, while on the other many of the old Whigs who had ever been friends of the Revolution were joining the Republicans, and from this view and my early predilections in favor of the freedom and independence of my country, altho I was but a novice in politics, I was induced to join the Republican party, and have ever since adhered to it, through good and bad report, believing it to be founded on fundamental and immutable principles. But although I was warmly attached to the principles, and by my vote and counsel endeavored to promote the success of the party I had espoused, I did not permit my politics to interfere with my business or to draw me off from giving it the most strict and regular attention. My political opinions I always considered as an immutable and sacred right which I determined to enjoy at all events, and I always noted to others, in this respect, what I claimed for myself, never attempting to control or improperly influence any man in my employ, and never inquired of him his opinion either in politics or religion; but the same indulgence was not extended to me by others, for some of the Federal merchants who employed me were eternally harping on my politics in order that they might find some excuse for a withdrawal of their patronage. I never denied however the party to which I was attached, but always contended, whenever the subject was forced upon me, that politics had nothing to do with trade, and that I always considered due and strict attention to business and the interest of my employers as paramount to every other consideration, except the peaceable and independent enjoyment of my opinions, or which no man had a right, nor would I permit him on any occasion, to call his right in question. I lost some customers whose aristocratic feelings would not permit others to enjoy the same feelings which they claimed for themselves, but such illiberal persecution only tended to confirm me the stronger in the sentiments I had espoused, and this system of coercing the minds of men, which appeared to have been adopted as a party measure by the Federalists, together with other high-handed proceedings all having the same end in view, was eventually the cause of destroying their ascendency in the government of the country and of bringing into power the friends of equal rights and Republican rule.

"The Memoirs of Stephen Allen," ed. John C. Travis, typescript, NYHS, p. 50

REPUBLICAN
ASCENDANCY

I n the hard-fought election of 1800 in which both sides used careful organization and spirited appeals, the Democratic-Republicans decisively carried the artisan vote. With it, they elected the entire slate of Jeffersonian assemblymen. This proved essential in carrying New York's electoral votes for Jefferson—without which he could not have been elected. From this pivotal contest until the severe economic hardships caused by the Embargo, the Democratic-Republicans consistently carried 60 to 70 percent of the outer mechanic wards and, in so doing, maintained political dominance.

The success of this young party was due in large part to its ability to offer artisans prosperity, a greater political role, and respect. In addition, the Jeffersonians considerably enhanced their appeal by recalling and identifying with the meaning that the American Revolution held within the mechanic community: that the artisan was an essential element of the body politic and that hardworking tradesmen contributed more to the worth of the young republic than those of higher social standing. In response to the Federalists' restrictive attitude towards artisan suffrage, for example, the Democratic-Republicans responded that mechanics paid their taxes and were respectable and valuable citizens entitled by the Revolution and Constitution to full participation in the political process (Document 39). In presenting their message to artisans, Republicans constantly referred to Federalist ideology while building on the democratization of politics that brought them to power in the 1790s. In the various ward meetings prior to state and local elections, nominating committees would present candidates for approval of local party members, a procedure also used by the opposition. During the campaign, Republicans effectively pilloried the Federalists as opposed to the aspiration of artisans for political participation and representation, insensitive to their concerns, and willing to employ economic coercion to prevent mechanics from the full exercise of their rights. Too, charges that Federalist leaders and candidates had been loyalist or loyalist sympathizers remained potent among the fiercely patriotic and Anglophobic craftsmen population (Documents 40–44).[13]

The Federalists were markedly unsuccessful in winning back their once solid mechanic constituency. Perhaps a poem, borrowed from an anti-Jacobin English publication, which they published in the *Washington Republican*, a short-lived Federalist newspaper established to communicate with artisans, best explains their difficulty (Document 45). The static and condescending attitude to craftsmen's political and economic ambitions could only alienate the voters it was attempting to reach, but the Federalists were unable to understand this. They did make a number of responses to Republican charges, such as accusing Democratic-Republicans of having loyalist backgrounds or defending carpenter Stephen Rudd, an active artisan politico, from the accusations of a Republican newspaper editor that he willingly served in the British Navy during the Revolution (Document 46). While demonstrating that Republicans were not free of deferential expectations, these charges were largely unsuccessful. The Federalists were more arrogant, possessed more loyalist backgrounds and did expect the unthinking obedience of those beneath them on the social ladder. Finally, they were prone to use coercive economic tactics, ploys that often brought them greater frustration.

39. Democratic-Republicans on Suffrage Reform

COMMUNICATION

Fellow Citizens

The federal free holder objects to the increase of freemen,[14] because it may communicate to men of small property the same right which he possesses and as it is real estate which is most liable to be affected by municipal regulation and taxation, the choice of the Corporation is peculiarly interesting to the proprietors of such property. But does not every house holder pay a certain proportion of the city taxes? And as it is a principle of our Constitution, that no man ought to be taxed without his consent, should not the freeholders, if they alone are to have the exclusive privilege of electing the corporation, pay all the necessary taxes, and not impose any upon those who have no controul over their municipal representations. This should be the commutation, if their fellow citizens are to be excluded from the enjoyment of the franchise of this city.

We will admit that the freedom of the city ought not to be indiscriminately conferred, because we are of opinion that freemen may become destitute of principle, prosperity, and property and as the character is most indelible, the right accompanying it must be exercised to the injury of the public; but those citizens who pay rent and taxes—who have an interest in our general, as well as local prosperity, ought to participate in common with the freeholders in the choice of corporate magistrates.—The constitution of this state wisely admits such men to be electors of the House of Assembly. Is the Corporation of New York a body of so much more importance than that house, or the immediate representatives of the people in congress, that men qualified to elect the latter should be ineligible to choose the former?

Happily we live in an age when the rights of men in society are better understood and more respected than when our character was formed. We have lopped off many of the monarchical relics, which had their origin in the views and customs of colonial dependence, and the exclusion of the citizens from all participation in the election of the magistrates to whom they must be subject, is a deprivation of national and constitutional right, intolerable under our republican form of government, hostile to its spirit, and injurious to its welfare . . . .

American Citizen, March 31, 1801

40. On Artisans and the Gentry

"THE COMPLIMENTS OF THE SEASON."

To the Mechanics—We mechanics and plain men are never noticed by federalists except at and about the election. One would suppose that the oculist had at these times performed an operation on their eyes, for on all other occasions, they pass us if they were blind and could not see far off.

But now, why so complaisant? They can see, and bow the head, and sometimes go so far as to shake us by the hand. Since these gentry have eleven months out of twelve to cut capers, we should pay them in kind. We should not see them nor bow to them, and in fact not know them at all. This shall be my conduct.

A MECHANIC

American Citizen, April 11, 1807

*Political broadsides, with bold type and arresting
headlines, were a common means of communica-
ting with artisan voters. This 1804 example,
supporting Jefferson and vice-presidential candidate George Clinton, equated the Federalists with
the still hated British. Mayor Varick and prominent Federalist Rufus King were the particular
targets in this case.* NYHS, 1804

REPUBLICANS

Turn out, turn out and save your Country from ruin !

From an *Emperor*—from a *King*—from the iron grasp of a *British Tory Faction*—an unprincipled ban-
ditti of British speculators.   The hireling tools and emissaries of his majesty king George the 3d have
thronged our city and diffused the poison of principles among us.

DOWN WITH THE TORIES, DOWN WITH THE BRITISH FACTION,

Before they have it in their power to enslave you, and reduce your families to distress by heavy taxation.
Republicans want no Tribute-liars—they want no ship Ocean-liars—they want no Rufus King's for Lords
—they want no Varick to lord it over them—they want no Jones for senator, who fought with the British
against the Americans in time of the war.—But they want in their places such men as

Jefferson & Clinton,

who fought their Country's Battles in the year '76

🙠   🙠   🙠

Mechanics—What is the reason that on the federal assembly ticket there
is not a single Mechanic? It must be either that no Mechanic would serve the
managers of the party, or that they hold a mechanic in too much contempt to
abominate even one of that numerous and respectable class of citizens.[15]

American Citizen, April 12, 1806

41. Federalist Aldermen and the Concerns of Artisans

ADDRESSED TO CITIZENS NOT WORTH QUITE 2000 PER YEAR!

What is the true reason for passing those laws prohibiting and imposing heavy fines on wooden buildings within certain limits in the city?–Laws which drive us who are Mechanics and Cartmen and Laborers, further and further into the suburbs, and will hardly let us remain in peace even there?–Laws which were unheard of in times when George Clinton was Governor, with a Republican legislature, strongly recommended by the Mayor and this Corporation. But let me ask these lawmakers for the reasons for this law–If I own a lot of ground in the middle or lower parts of the town and cannot afford to build of brick or stone, why may not I build such a house as suits me best, and my family are content to live in? The answer, Why? Why, because your house may get on fire, and the Mayor, or perhaps Robert Lenox, or James Watson, or John B. Church, or General Hamilton, or Robert Bowne,[16] or some other great man, or rich man, may live next to you–and they ought not to be disturbed or endangered by your misfortune. Aye, but his house is equally liable to take fire first– and, in either case, who is in the most danger, my house of wood, containing all I am worth in the world, or his brick walls; with his money safe at the Bank?–True, that varies the case a little,–but the sooner the wooden houses are burned out of the way the better; they spoil the beauty of the city, and are an eye-sore to the rich people, and people from England who like to live in the neighborhood of each other, and have the streets better paved; and their horses and coaches to stand in brick stables–It was also certainly high time you should be removed beyond the city???–Mr. Mayor or Robert Benson having taken it into their hands to build there abouts–Besides, you people of the outwards are too busy enquiring the reasons of laws, and in what the governments have done on other matters.–Well, then it seems we and our wooden houses are to be huddled together in the skirts of the town, far enough from the place of business, and far enough from the places where the Mayor has taken care to station the Fire Engines, safely to protect the brick buildings–and all for fear certain purse proud merchants and men in office might possibly be disturbed in the night by the cries of our wives and children perishing in the flames!–Mr. Mayor, we remember these and many other good things you have done for us.

A CARPENTER *of the Seventh Ward*

American Citizen, April 28, 1801

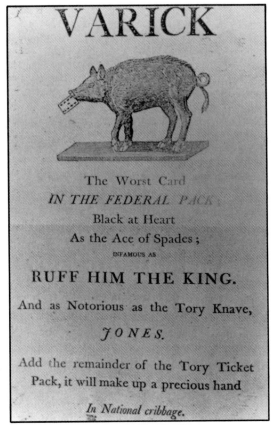

The Worst Card
IN THE FEDERAL PACK,
Black at Heart
As the Ace of Spades ;
INFAMOUS AS

RUFF HIM THE KING.

And as Notorious as the Tory Knave,

JONES.

Add the remainder of the Tory Ticket
Pack, it will make up a precious hand

In National cribbage.

In the critical election of 1800, the bearing of Mayor Varick, and particularly his use of power to intimidate the cartmen, proved a powerful issue. The Democratic-Republicans carried the artisan wards by large majorities. NYHS

42. On Federalist Coercion of Cartmen

How was one of our body treated by the son of an *old tory* no later than last Saturday because he told him like an honest man *that his counting house full of dollars should not tempt him to vote against his conscience.* That tyrant kicked the man out of the house. On hearing of that daring assault, my old veins swelled with indignation. I recalled the cause which was ever my pride and boast, and I felt more attached to it than ever.

My friends! Are we depending upon the charity of the merchants? Will their puny clerks carry the burthens that we do? No, no! For what we receive we give our attention and labor, therefore we have as good a right to be independent, as the lawyer is of his clients, the doctor of his patients or the merchant of his customers.

Are we so base and vicious that it should be necessary to reduce us to a state worse than that of negro slaves; to be deprived not only of a free choice, but to be forced to vote against our will.

The conspiracy which terrified you last year, can never be revived in so formidable a shape. I now see men the most respectable for character and consequence, willing to support your rights. Be firm—be unanimous and you may defy your enemies and secure your freedom.

AN INDEPENDENT CARTMAN

American Citizen, April 28, 1800

43. Federalist Intimidation Tactics in a Mechanic Ward

Seventh Ward–For several years past the *federal party* have resorted in vast numbers to the upper wards, but particularly to the *Seventh* to interrupt the electors in voting. Last spring, General Stevens collected a number of sailors and others, prepared drums, arms and colors, and was on the point of marching his collection to the poll of the seventh ward when the Mayor approached to prevent disturbance. At the same time, *federal committees of interruption* were assembled around the poll to defeat the very purposes of the election law, and in effect to render null and void the most essential rights of the people. These disorderly practices have been witnessed by the republicans with a patience which has evinced that they are really more "disposed to suffer than to right themselves by resistance." The federal party at this moment rely principally for success on intended interruption to voting in the upper wards—particularly in the *seventh*. They have gone so far, as I am informed and believe, as to appoint, at the present election, a *committee of interruption* consisting of ninety persons for each day of the election. Are we thus to be overawed by combination—to be deprived of our rights by turbulence? How far will federalists go in endeavors to excite commotion? No one has a right *to vote or to challenge out of the ward in which he resides*. Why then the very numerous assemblage of federalists at the seventh ward, which we have so frequently witnessed, and which it seems we must again witness, if not to interrupt the voters in the exercise of their rights—if not to occasion commotion?

American Citizen, April 27, 1807

EXPOSURE
OF FEDERAL MEANNESS
AND DESPOTISM.

Fellow Citizens—LET us support our Independence ? If we are Mechanics Labourers and Artizans—Why should we surrender our opinions and our rights to the arbitrary mandate of a Tory Employer, and that employer, perhaps a foreign emissary ! A few years ago the worthy Mr. Coddington was insulted and *whipped* by a son of the same Neilson, who *invited the British Fleet* to protect our Commerce, and became instrumental to the death of PIERCE. Remember this ! Mark them!

Now, Bribery, and denunciation are threatened ! No man who dares to oppose Federal Men is to be employed by them !! *Look at the following Affidavit ?* Read ! Consider ! Then determine for yourselves. Is it possible there can exist one republican in this city who will sell his principles *for all the federal party could offer ?* Is there *ONE?*

AFFIDAVIT.

City of New York, *ss.* Garret Van Horne, Junior, of the city of New York, Carpenter, being duly sworn, doth depose and say, that this day, the 27th April, at the Fifth Ward Poll, William Bridges of the same place, Architect and Surveyor, did tell him this Deponent, "That after May, work would be *dull* and that he the said William " Bridges had Two or Three Houses to build, and that if he, this Deponent would vote " for the Federal Ticket, he Mr. William Bridges would give him this deponent a JOB ;" or words to that effect, and further this Deponent saith not.

Garret Vanborne, Jun.

Sworn before me this 27th april, 1808.
DAVID M. ROSS, *Notary Public* for the State of *New York*

Many Federalist employers expected political deference—even obedience—from their employees. When this was refused, as it was more and more frequently with the rise of the Jeffersonians, they often resorted to economic coercion. NYHS

ᘍ

44. Democratic-Republicans on Federalist Carpenter Stephen Rudd

Stephen Rudd, House Carpenter—This man is unworthy of notice except as the creature of the TORIES.

. . . .

I must now tell the reader who Rudd the House Carpenter is, whose fame has been thus trumpeted by the friends of the "American Ticket."[17]

I am sorry to state that he is by birth *Irishman*, for the reader will say with me in sequel that he is a blot on the Irish character. This Rudd, thus employed as a tool by the friends of the *"American Ticket,"* was in our Revolution a BRITISH SOLDIER! Rudd was in the pay of the King of England, whose "conduct was marked by every act that may define the tyrant." Rudd, in that service, fought against and with the rest of the British force sought to subdue and enslave the WHIGS OF AMERICA! Rudd was one of those wretches who was paid by the King of England to destroy every American whig! This merchant, whom the Tories have now the impudence to term *"Disciple of Washington,"* was armed as a British soldier against that illustrious chief, and as a British soldier, would have stabbed him to the heart. And yet this fellow—this wretch—this TORY—harangues his brother *Federalists* in their war meetings, and addresses them in the *Evening Post,* in support of the "American Ticket!" Since the Revolution at the close of which he was discharged from the British service, Rudd has resided here. Trying to repent of his great sins, he joined the respectable Society of Methodists. But he had been so hardened in revolutionary wickedness, that in the Methodist Society it again broke out. From this society he was, I am informed, EXPELLED for his immorality! . . .

American Citizen, April 27, 1807

45. Federalist Satire on Artisans and Republican Ideology

The following is so just a satire on the ridiculous affectation of humanity among a certain class of people, that I never read it but with fresh pleasure. An idea that the laboring part of society are the most miserable is as prevalent as it is unjust. The Knife-grinder, snoring under the friendly shelter of a butcher's stall, is more free from the heart-corroding cares of life than the merchant extended on a bed of down. The former hears the winds whistle about him, whilst the latter slumbers on the rock of anxiety, fearing that his speculations may be thwarted, his ships buried on the ocean, or his riches swallowed by the flames.

The Friend of Humanity and the Knife-Grinder

"Needy knife grinder! Whither are you going?
Rough is the road, your wheel is out of order,
Bleak blows the blast—your hat has got a hole in it,
                              So have your breeches!

Weary knife grinder!—little think the proud ones
Who in their coaches roll along the turnpike road,
What hard work 'tis crying all day "Knifes and
                              Scissors to grind O!"

Tell me, Knife-grinder, how came you to grind knives?
Did some rich man tyrannically use you?
Was it the Squire? or Parson of the Parish?
                                        Or the Attorney?

Was it the Squire for killing of his game? or
Covetous Parson for his tythes destraining?
Or roguish attorney, made you lose your little
                                        All in a law suit.

Have not you read the Rights of Man, by Tom Paine?
Drops of compassion tremble on my eyelids,
Ready to fall as soon as you have told your
                                        Pitiful Story."

Knife Grinder

"Stay! God bless you, I have more to tell, Sir,
Only this night a drinking at the Checquers,
This poor old hat and breeches, as you see, were
                                        Torn in a Scuffle.

Constables came up for to take me into
Custody; They took me before the Justice;
Justice Oldmixon put me in the Parish Stocks, for
                                        a Vagrant.

I should be glad to drink to your honor's health in
A Pot of beer, if you will give me sixpence,
But for my part I never love to meddle
                                        With politics, Sir."

Friend of Humanity

I give thee sixpence! I will see thee *d—'d* first—
Wretch! Whom no sence of wrongs can rouse to vengeance—
Sordid, unfeeling, reprobate, degraded,
                                        Spiritless outcast!"

(kicks the knife grinder, overturns his wheel, and exits in a transport of
republican enthusiasm and universal philanthropy)

Washington Republican, August 5, 1809

Thomas Jefferson residing over a supposed meeting of the Democratic-Republican Society. The figure with the pen resembles Tom Paine. FREE PUBLIC LIBRARY OF PHILADELPHIA

🌑

46. Defense of Stephen Rudd, Federalist Carpenter

For The Evening Post

Mr. Coleman, [18]

In conformity with my promise, I now take up my pen to refute the charges made against me in the Citizen. I would have contented my self, and treated them with silent contempt, had not the cause which I espouse demanded of me a refutation.

Mr. Cheat'em[19] is much hurt, that the title of gentleman should be applied to a House Carpenter, a mechanic who, in his estimation, can stand no comparison with a hatter.

Mr. Cheat'em thinks me a blot on the Irish character. — That is, I am not the *sort* of Irishman which suits the views of his faction.

He says I was a British soldier in the day of Great Britain, and in that service fought against and sought to subdue and enslave every American whig.

How far this is true will be seen from a brief historical account of my first departure from Ireland till my return back.

In the city of Dublin, the place of my nativity, I was impressed into the *navy* service about the age of between 16 and 17 years, bro't to England, and from thence to America. Halifax, Nova Scotia, was the first place I put my foot on shore for the space of eight months. – I worked in the navy yard, till the ship, which was called the Robust, was ready for sea. We then joined admiral Arbuthnot, at Sandy Hook, from thence we sailed to the southward, and during a period of eighteen months I never put my foot on shore; when, after an engagement with the French fleet, we came up to New York to refit. Here I worked on board the ship till she was ready for sea, when she was ordered for England. Some days before she sailed, another carpenter and myself agreed to make our escape to the Americans, and accordingly eloped, and got to Long Island. We were not many days there, before we were taken by a party of 16th light dragoons. To save ourselves from being brought to New York, we joined them, & in the space of four months I was raised to a sergeant, and acting quarter master, when my comrade deserted and came to New York, and informed against me. I was ordered to be brought to New York, and was examined by Admiral Digby and Prince William Henry, who both said they would have me hanged. – I was accordingly put in the main guard house, and kept there a considerable time; when ordered for trial, my officers would have been tried by the general Court Martial, the Admiral said I should be tried on board a ship. I was at length tried by the general Court Martial, where I saw, for the first time, since his desertion, my old comrade's evidence against me. In my defence, I was obliged to have recourse to this argument, that I never left his majesty, and if I was compelled to serve him, the least I could have was a choice in what department to serve him; however, the court took compassion on my youth, and sparing my life, consigned me over to the navy. The Admiral treated me very hard, confined me in Irons some months; when, after an Address I made to Captain Clayton, he procured my enlargement from the Admiral, and appointed me Carpenters mate; but I was never to have my feet on shore while the ship was in America. I went to England, and was paid wages for the time I was on board of her, which was about 18 months, and that was all the wages I ever got for between four and five years service – a musket or great gun I never fired in my life.

. . . .

The public is well acquainted with the character of *Mr. Cheat them*. It would be superfluous for me to mention one word about him. His character is already so black that the plumage of the raven cannot make one additional tenth to it, and I greatly fear he will be enveloped in blackness and darkness forever.

STEPHEN RUDD H.C.

Evening Post, April 28, 1807

THE EMBARGO AND
THE WAR OF 1812

Despite the seemingly insurmountable Democratic-Republican advantage in the early years of the nineteenth century, the Federalists did mount a strong political comeback that included considerable gains in the artisan wards. As a means short of war of protecting American ships from seizure and sailors from impressment by the British navy, President Jefferson, with the approval of Congress in 1807, implemented an Embargo on all foreign shipping. For an international port city such as New York, whose economy was dependent upon commerce, this was a devastating blow that saw widespread unemployment, underemployment and bankruptcy as grass began to grow upon the wharves. Unpopular and unsuccessful, the Embargo was allowed to expire in 1809 but the Madison administration in attempting to cope with the same problem also invoked restrictive acts and in 1812 led Congress to declare war on Great Britain.[20] The war years, while occasionally prosperous for well-placed individuals, were fraught with uncertainty and risk as trade slowed and inflation became rampant. In addition, in order to pay for the war, Madison and Congress instituted taxes that were particularly onerous to craftsmen, especially those producing luxury goods such as goldsmiths and coachmakers. Equally imposing were the provisions in the tax bill allowing unannounced searches of workshops.[21]

Republicans argued that American honor was at stake, that British depredations could not be tolerated and that the pro-British Federalists verged on being Tories in disguise. The sacrifice necessitated by the Embargo and War were necessary to ensure American independence (Documents 47–50). The Federalists, in turn, persuasively responded that they could restore prosperity, that the city was needlessly making sacrifices for no gain and that impending financial doom loomed shortly ahead (Documents 51–53). It was a time of tense political partisanship as mechanics were asked to place their national pride and the defense of republicanism ahead of their pocketbook. The Federalists regained enough artisan support—though short of a majority—to make the elections for these years very close.[22]

47. Democratic-Republicans on Patriotism and the Embargo

Mechanics, Trad*emen* and Labourers . . .

An election is approaching when you will be called upon to discriminate between those who will deprive you of your liberties and those who strive to perpetuate them. The federal party, composed of old tories, refugees, and apostate citizens, have again endured to take the field. The fair temple erected by your hands and dedicated to liberty is sacreligiously assailed—Sons of departed heroes I fly to its defence—let not rude hand mar the sacred fabric—repeat the oath taken by your fathers on the alter of '76—that you would sooner perish than live slaves. These same tories strove in that eventful period to rivet them to the Royal Color of George the 3d. But their arms, nerved for battle by a gracious providence, enabled them to crush the chariot wheels and scatter them into air. Independence followed these glorious efforts—swear then to preserve it—transmit the boon to your children as a sacred legacy, unsullied and untainted by impure hands—rest assured, mechanics, that the man who in this trying hour, suffers his hair to be shorn by the harlot federalism, is either a fool or a TRAITOR. If they talk to you about the Embargo, tell, and you may tell them truly, that their villanous falsehoods produced it—tell them too of their alien law, their sedition law, their standing army, their stamp act, &c., &c. and thus stop their mouths. Their folly can only be equalled by their impudence, when they thus unblushingly come forward to oppose you in the pursuit of your political rights. Rally round your government determined to defend it to the last extremity, defend it against foreign foes and domestic traitors. Look at the heading of their ticket—"No Embargo," "American Ticket." Consummate impudence.—"No Embargo," I say so too, with all my heart, if all the old and young tories would take shipping and be off. It would be a happy riddance for America. "American Ticket," petty Americans, who would sell us to old England tomorrow. American ticket truly.—Mechanics, look to these wolves in sheeps clothing—look to these snakes in the grass, or you may be stung to the heart.

A MECHANIC

American Citizen, April 21, 1808

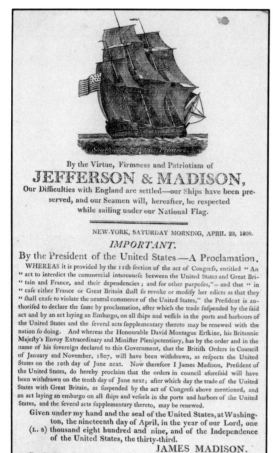

By the Virtue, Firmness and Patriotism of
JEFFERSON & MADISON,
Our Difficulties with England are settled—our Ships have been preserved, and our Seamen will, hereafter, be respected
while sailing under our National Flag.

NEW-YORK, SATURDAY MORNING, APRIL 22, 1809.

IMPORTANT.

By the President of the United States.—A Proclamation.

WHEREAS it is provided by the 11th fection of the act of Congrefs, entitled "An
"act to interdict the commercial intercourfe between the United States and Great Bri-
"tain and France, and their dependencies; and for other purpofes,"—and that " in
"cafe either France or Great Britain fhall fo revoke or modify her edicts as that they
"fhall ceafe to violate the neutral commerce of the United States," the Prefident is au-
thorifed to declare the fame by proclamation, after which the trade fufpended by the faid
act and by an act laying an Embargo, on all fhips and veffels in the ports and harbours of
the United States and the feveral acts fupplementary thereto may be renewed with the
nation fo doing. And whereas the Honourable David Montague Erfkine, his Britannic
Majefty's Envoy Extraordinary and Minifter Plenipotentiary, has by the order and in the
name of his fovereign declared to this Government, that the Britifh Orders in Council
of January and November, 1807, will have been withdrawn, as refpects the United
States on the 10th day of June next. Now therefore I James Madison, Prefident of
the United States, do hereby proclaim that the orders in council aforefaid will have
been withdrawn on the tenth day of June next; after which day the trade of the United
States with Great Britain, as fufpended by the act of Congrefs above mentioned, and
an act laying an embargo on all fhips and veffels in the ports and harbors of the United
States, and the feveral acts fupplementary thereto, may be renewed.

Given under my hand and the feal of the United States, at Wafhing-
ton, the nineteenth day of April, in the year of our Lord, one
(L. S) thoufand eight hundred and nine, and of the Independence
of the United States, the thirty-third.

JAMES MADISON.

By the President,
RT. SMITH, *Secretary of State.*

Democratic-Republican pronouncements and advertisements emphasized the importance of national honor. This broadside, praising Jefferson and Madison's attempts to peacefully influence Great Britain, declares that England had acceded to the Non-Intercourse Act and revoked the Orders in Council. Alas, Madison was mistaken and soon had to reverse himself. NYHS

48. Stephen Allen on the War of 1812

On the 18th June, 1812, the United States declared war against Great Britain. The people and government of the country had for a long time borne the most aggravated insults from the British who, by capturing our property on the high seas and condemning it while we were at peace with them, impressing our seamen and forcing them into their service against their inclination or will, insulting our flag on all occasions with impunity, and heaping upon us abuses of the most opprobrious character, had brought down upon them the execration

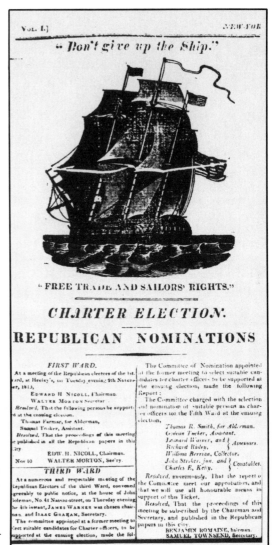

So intense was partisan and patriotic spirit during the War that even local elections for aldermen and constables stirred fierce debate over policy. This is the Republican announcement of charter nominations, November, 1814. NATIONAL ADVO-CATE, NOVEMBER 13, 1813

and hatred of a large majority of the American people. The policy of our government however was peace, at least so long as it could be maintained with honor, but the time had now arrived when it became a duty to resist, and the nation accordingly prepared for war. Now it was that every citizen was called upon to exert his energies in defence of his country, and when he who refused the assistance within his power must bear the odium of disaffection to the cause of liberty and independence.

These considerations, however, had little weight with the Federal party in this country, and this opposition to the war and the administration of Mr. Madison was carried to a most fearful extent. They endeavored to induce the people, and succeeded with many, to withhold any aid to Government by the way of loan, under the idea that the Union would be dissolved, and the eastern states cut off from the western; and in order that the idea might have greater weight, they called a convention at Hartford, Connecticut,[23] which was attended by delegates from all the Federal states to deliberate on the subject of a dissolution!! Indeed no means were left untried to weaken the hands of government and force them into a dishonorable peace with the enemy. The effect however was very different from what the leaders of the Federal party had anticipated, for instead of dividing it tended to unite and strengthen the friends of government; and the elections which took place during that period pretty generally resulted in the choice of those friendly to the Republican administration of the country, both for representatives in Congress and our state legislature.

Individually I felt much interested, both because I was sensible from experience that the privileges enjoyed were here of the highest order and therefore worth contending for, and because I felt a strong conviction of the justice of the cause we were engaged in. I accordingly exerted all the influence and means that I possessed to bring the war to an honorable conclusion. At the commencement of the contest, I enrolled myself in one of the voluntary companies, composed of persons exempted from the performance of military duty, and regularly met with them for improvement in discipline and tactics. I worked on the works for the defense of the city, which it was deemed necessary to raise on Long Island and other places, and I loaned the government all the money I was in any way enabled to spare from my business.

Memoirs of Stephen Allen, pp. 55–56

49. Democratic-Republicans on Taxes, Sacrifice, and Patriotism

Taxes! Taxes! Taxes! Taxes are sad things and terrible hardships, to be sure. But who shall justly complain of them? Shall those who by their support of British claims and encouragement of British arrogance, produced the war, which has created these taxes? Shall those who, have necessity claimed against the government for not prosecuting the war with vigor, while they were destitute of the means, now refuse to furnish those means, already from necessity appropriated in advance? Shall the war-worn soldier and weather-beaten sailor suffer and starve for their pay, sooner than obtain it from the collection of taxes? Shall every defender or creditor of our country lose 6¼ per

The democratization of politics that took place during the American Revolution continued at the local level. In each ward, active and interested citizens of each party gathered at a common meeting place to nominate candidates for assembly and for municipal offices. The results of the meetings were then published in the respective Republican or Federalist newspapers. This advertisement, from the mechanic sixth ward (Clarkson Crolius, the chairman, was a well known republican potter) also contains a resolution declaring the importance of defending national honor "in a just and necessary war." NATIONAL ADVOCATE, NOVEMBER 13, 1813

cent. (a year's interest) in his treasury notes, because taxes are burdensome to them? What system, justice, honor and gratitude?

In 1798 taxes, excise and stamp duties were imposed, more grievous than any of the present day, because so unnecessary.[24] Yet they were defended by those who now affect with such extraordinary sympathy for the pockets of the electors. Ten dollars for a just and necessary cause, should be paid more cheerfully than ten shillings for wanton profligacy and useless waste. And it is truly preposterous in the friends of the British government, to complain of the expense of taxation on this country, while they approve of the English system, which takes one-fourth of a man's earnings for the public use. If republican taxes are whips, those of the federalists would be scorpions.

Columbian, April 25, 1814

50. *The Independent Mechanic* on the War of 1812

The following message[25] and manifesto is published, even at this late date, for certain weighty and substantial reasons: among the foremost of them is, the desire of many to have, on file documents so nearly touching the vital interests of the union. Next to the Declaration of Independence these papers

THE TORY EDITOR *and his* APES *Giveing their pitiful advice to the* AMERICAN SAILORS

A common charge against the Federalists was that they had little in concern for the common man, whether it be the artisan or, in this case, the American sailor (tar). In this engraving, the well known English artist William Charles (then in residence in New York) depicts the Federalist (Tory) editor warning sailors of the dangers of capture and imprisonment if they fight against Britain.
WILLIAM CHARLES, ENGRAVING, 1812. NYPL

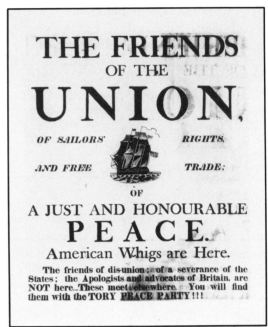

Republicans commonly attacked the Federalists as "Tories" for their opposition to the war. Those who advocated peace at any price rather than a "Just and Honourable PEACE" were enemies of the union. NYPL

will be treasured up as preeminently important to the present generation, and the step taken by our government in consequence of them, may effect such a change, and give such a cast to our political character, that posterity will feel a gratification in the opportunity thus afforded of perusing them—Many of our readers, perhaps, have not had, or neglected the opportunity of reading these documents at the time of their first publication, who would now, when the War has assumed a body and form, feel a peculiar interest in the subject of them. After this recapitulation of wrongs and indignities, none but a cowardly sycophant, or an enemy to the country would be the advocates of further forbearance. The wretch who, for mean sordid interest, would sacrifice the honor of his country, deserves to be held up to the public view, and cannot fail to excite the contempt and scorn of every man of principle in the community.— Warlike operations had scarcely commenced, when flags of truce from the enemy made their appearance. Whether this was a piece of finesse to trifle with our government as heretofore, and gain time to better prepare for the unexpected event, or whether, having pushed their purpose to the extremest point, and tried the extent of our forbearance, they had a desire of meeting with amicable terms a little this side the boundary line of abject servility, is still questionable. All eyes were then fixed on government. The patriotic citizens of the country were anxiously waiting an answer to the enquiry "Will the President accede to an armistice? Shall hostilities cease just as the arm of vengeance is raised? Is the long catalogue of injuries, so recently before our eyes, so easily, forgotten?"—

To the eternal honor of the executive, the sentiments of the Committee on Foreign Relations were reiterated.—*"The period has now arrived, when the United States must support their character and station among the nations of the earth, or submit to the most shameful degradation.* FOREBEARANCE HAS CEASED TO BE A VIRTUE."

Ed.

Independent Mechanic, September 19, 1812

51. Federalist Appeal to Artisans: Commerce Binds All

Federal Republicans!—Turn out and do your duty! Let the Mechanics recollect that with COMMERCE, this city will flourish—without COMMERCE, it must moulder into ruin.

Ship Carpenters! Blacksmiths! Rope Makers! and Mariners! remember that it is on *Commerce* you look for your subsistence. If that be palsied, it must prove your ruin—Be active, be vigilant—'Tis a noble cause in which you are engaged, and to prove it effectual, requires your noble exertions. If you turn out and do your duty, the clouds of democracy must vanish, and again the sun of Federalism illumine our hemisphere.

Evening Post, April 24, 1810

52. Federalists on Artisans and Democratic-Republican Taxes

The rights of freemen—Let this be the watchword at the polls; let it be the sentiment that fills every elector's mind. It is not for this or that party we are called upon to assert our rights.—The rights and existence of freemen are at stake. We have been long enough imposed upon and duped with the hypocritical cry, of *free trade* and *sailor's rights* while the interests of the one have been abandoned to destruction and the others have been driven from our shores. This has been the false and hollow pretension for a series of extravagant expences and thoughtless prodigality, till we find ourselves, at last, overwhelmed with a national debt, whose amount renders its discharge totally hopeless in our day. In their desperation, the men in power have laid upon the community a load of taxes, under which it staggers, without being able to shake it off or to relieve itself. Nay, the payment of one tax is only taking the first step in the circle; the more we pay, the more remains to be paid. Sixteen millions is the annual interest of the national debt, and the current expenses of government is fourteen millions, making an aggregate of THIRTY MILLIONS, entailed upon us and our posterity, and at the end of a century to come, we have still the principal before us. – Here's *"a sight that might appall the devil."*

In the attempt to collect these taxes, they have promulgated laws that break in upon the rights of every freeman. The mechanic is exposed to the impertinent curiosity of every saucy collector, who chuses to enter his shop and examine into the mysteries of his trade, or who takes a fancy to pry into his private accounts. The manufacturer, who was promised all the fostering care of government to aid and protect him against foreign competition, and to secure him a preference in his own market, now finds an oppressive load of taxes laid upon his infant attempts, that press him to the earth; and though he *may rise early, set up late, and eat the bread of carefulness,* yet it profiteth him not; the fruit of his labour must go into the hands of the collectors and other minions of government, and after enriching these vermin, the remainder may find its way into the treasury. But by the *Furniture Tax,* every man in the land, be he high or be he low, rich or poor, is liable to have his house entered by men in the shape of collectors, if they suspect the account rendered, to examine his furniture; its quality; take an account of his spoons and his glasses, and set it all down in his list for taxation. And tho' he will for the present, admit that a collector is of course an honest man, yet what is to prevent a thief or pickpocket from imposing himself upon the unsuspicious as a collector or deputy collector, and as such entering our parlors, where he may riot at leisure upon spoons, tankards, watches and other valuables to which he may take a fancy, and decamp unmolested, leaving as to charge it to the account of government. The consequences that may follow from this odious infamous and unheard of tax law are not even imagined. And what renders it the more inexcusable in this country, is its very little productiveness. Indeed, it is very certain, that in a great proportion of the country it will not defray its own expenses. In the western states, and in all that part of the country that does not abound in superfluities, few indeed will there be, in the course of a thousand miles, that will return a cent's worth of household furniture above 200 dollars, after deducting the necessaries the law excepts. So that the law is as strongly marked by egregious folly as by odious oppression.

Let those, therefore, who hold in just abhorrence such laws and their authors, give evidence of their sentiments by their ballots at the approaching election.

I speak in round numbers and from a slight calculation.

MEMENTO
FOR THE ELECTORS.

TAXES.

LAND TAX,
HOUSE TAX—WATCH TAX
CARRIAGE TAX—WAGGON
TAX—HARNESS TAX—LICENCE
TAX—AUCTION TAX—STILL TAX,
LEATHER TAX—BOOT TAX—HAT TAX
CAP TAX—LADIES HAT TAX—SU-
GAR TAX—TOBACCO TAX—
SNUFF TAX—SEGAR TAX
BAR IRON TAX—SLIT
IRON TAX—BRAD
TAX—ROLL'D
IRON TAX
PIG
IRON
TAX—CUT
NAIL TAX—UM-
BRELLA TAX—FUR-
NITURE TAX—STAMP
TAX—SPRIG TAX—PAPER
TAX—DOUBLE POSTAGE TAX,
CANDLE TAX—PLAYING CARD
TAX,—SADDLE TAX—BRIDLE TAX—
BEER TAX—ALE TAX—POR-
TER TAX—WHISKEY TAX
DOUBLE DUTIES, &c.
LOANS—TREASURY
NOTES—STAND-
ING ARMY.
&c. &c.

" *A wise and frugal government shall not take*
from the mouth of labour the bread it has earned."

[Jefferson's Inaugural Speech.]

Federalist appeals emphasized the burdens of war, including the various taxes imposed by the Democratic-Republicans to pay for military costs.
EVENING POST, 1814

&a. &a. &a.

Shoemakers, ahoy! Have you been at Mr. Thompson's, the Collector, and given bonds with two sufficient sureties, to pay the duty upon your work? If you make a single shoe or boot above 3 dollars in value, without having given bond to secure the duty to the government, you do it at your peril, and are subject to a penalty of no less than five hundred dollars. What is your situation better than that of Virginia negroes? You must account for every pair of boots you make to

Mr. Thompson, the Collector; you must tell him how much you ask for them, who you make them for, and how many pair you make, and to crown the whole, all this must be done under oath. No, that does not crown the whole, one thing more; whenever a customer breaks or runs away or cheats you, in addition to the loss of the article itself and the labor, you must pay the duty upon it to government. This is the crowner, the cap-sheaf.

Silver-Smiths, Carpenters, Joiners, Hatters, Tailors, Tobacconists, Boat-Builders, Chair-Makers, Sail-Makers, Tallow-Chandlers, Distillers, Coach-Makers, Watch-Makers, Tinmen, Blacksmiths, and ye mechanics and manufacturers of all articles and commodities, of whatever name or nature, *be ye also ready*. A fine of five hundred dollars awaits you, unless you comply with the provisions of these arbitrary, iniquitous laws, passed by Congress the 16th of February.

Evening Post, April 24, 1815

53. *The Examiner* on the Folly of Democratic-Republican Loyalty

The poor, who at the best, are always uncomfortable, must rejoice, although they are reduced to beggary, because, forsooth, such a man, a good republican, manages the loan; or because, such a one is enriching himself as a contractor, and he is no less of a republican, than all those who make a *trade*, and a profitable one they all make, of their republicanism. Indeed the republican party prospers, and prospers much, if while the mass of them are becoming every day poorer, the leaders are becoming every day richer from the very same cause. "The republican party is triumphant! Huzza for the republican party!" Shouts the poor infatuated maniac, who returns reeling home from the democratic orgies at *Martlings*.[26] "John have you got money to buy us bread tomorrow morning," cries his sorrowful wife. "How shall we get our winters wood, John? And quarter day will be round again soon, and how is our rent to be paid, John?" "O daddy see my shoes," cries poor Nancy, "my toes are sticking out, and in these cold mornings, they are most frozen going about for things." And my coat (says Stephen) is almost worn out, it can't be patched any more; I wish you would get me a new coat. And daddy, the madam says she must be paid for Nancy's schooling and mine, or she can't have us come any more." But John is a republican; to him the republican party is all in all; John can let his children starve and freeze, but he would not forego the pleasure

Federalists as well as Jeffersonians claimed that their policies favored American independence and prosperity. They argued that free commerce would relieve the economic distress of the cities. This Anderson engraving linking commerce and American freedom with the symbol of American liberty, could well have been used by the Federalists. If "Commerce" and "Free Trade" are equated, then it might also have been employed by the Democratic-Republicans. Both parties claimed that they were the only organization able to restore America to its Revolutionary origins. ANDERSON COLLECTION, NYPL

of spending his only shilling at Tammany Hall, and huzzaing for the republican party, from any compassion to his own offspring. The return of old Washingtonian times, when peace and plenty rendered every honest man's fireside a little paradise to him, are hateful to John, because the tories want such times, and are trying to bring them about again, and John hates the tories.

Examiner,[27] October 22, 1814

FACTIONALISM AND INDEPENDENT POLITICAL ACTION

T he Democratic-Republicans were plagued with factionalism throughout the early nineteenth century, particularly from 1802 to 1807 when the Federalists offered little opposition, and after 1816 when the Federalists all but left the political scene. These groups usually centered around dissident or outcast Republicans such as Aaron Burr, Dewitt Clinton, and Morgan Lewis.[28] As these groups battled in state and municipal elections, they too appealed to the mechanic constituency using the same themes employed against the Federalist enemy: loyalism, contempt for artisans, economic coercion (Document 54).

Such infighting among Republicans, along with the disregard for artisan interests and sensibilities that—as Federalists charged repeatedly—the Republicans did at times display, could not but alienate a number of craftsmen from participation in the political process. This is evident in the high percentage of eligible tradesmen (44 percent) who did not vote.[29] It is also apparent in articles printed in the staunchly antipolitical *Independent Mechanic*, one of which is reprinted here (Document 55), that argued that it was in the best interest of mechanics to abstain from partisan politics. An alternative to abstention would have been independent political activity, an action artisans engaged in with success in the Revolutionary and post-Revolutionary eras. There were significant though limited appeals for such a movement during the economic dislocation caused by the Embargo and War of 1812 (Document 56). However, no serious steps were taken in this direction. Internal divisions (ethnicity, journeymen versus masters, tariff positions), the lack of a politically oriented artisan newspaper, the presence of few clear-cut mechanic issues and the co-optation of potential artisan leaders by the major parties were the most significant factors inhibiting such movement.

This political satire depicts the enormous power of the Mayor (in this case Marinus Willett). The Mayor's authority to license cartmen and of revoking licensing and disciplining drivers was immense. This illustration was used by the Clintonians against the Lewisites in a battle of Republican factions. Attempting to win cartmen's votes, it reminds drivers that after his appointment in 1807, Willett, a Lewisite, recalled all cartmen's licenses and ordered the haulers to reapply. This was seen as an act of political intimidation. "Family Electioneering," WILLIAM CHARLES, ENGRAVING, 1807, WINTERTHUR MUSEUM

54. Factional Appeals to Artisans

On Governor Lewis's Contempt for Artisans

Mechanics—I state the following fact on the authority of a gentleman whose name is left with me.

A Mechanic who had done work for Governor Lewis[30] called upon him with his bill to which Governor Lewis objected as containing some charges which he thought exorbitant. In consequence of the objections, the mechanic proposed to refer the charges to the decision of three mechanics, who were judges of the work: to this proposition Governor Lewis replied that "HE WOULD BE DAMNED IF HE WOULD TRUST A MECHANIC"!

If this fact be denied it shall be substantiated *on oath*.

Mechanics! what think you of the insulting declaration?

American Citizen, April 28, 1807

🐦 🐦 🐦

Clintonian Appeal to Artisans

MECHANICS, remember that lawyers who would solicit your votes on election days, and asking you to drink grog with them to coax you to give them fat offices, would scorn to look upon you after the election is over. The mechanic ticket for assembly is headed by NOAH BROWN.[31]

Columbian, April 26, 1821

55. For the Withdrawal of Artisans from Politics

Mr. Editor,

Being an inhabitant of this city, and one that has devoted a great part of my time to political squabbles, but from which, hereafter, I am determined to keep myself aloof, having learnt from experience, that my ambition to support men, in order that measures might be adopted that would prove beneficial to my country, was no more than a political phrenzy, or mad infatuation, a disorder with which too many of our modern politicians seem to be affected; I have, therefore, in a cool hour of reflection, and after a candid investigation, determined to pursue a quite different course, which, I feel confident, will prove infinitely more to my advantage.

I have a family, which I tenderly love, but that I have shamefully neglected them, I cannot deny. Many have been the evenings when my little one was sporting around me, seeming anxious to get instruction, to learn the first movements of life, and receive those parental caresses, which it is natural for a parent to give a child; and when, too, my wife has implored me to spend the evening at home, that I have abruptly left her and my little one, even amid their anxiety for my stay, to haunt the ale-house, or to attend some political meeting. And these kind of attendances were more beneficial to the tavern-keeper, and more destructive to my purse, than all the bawling influence that I possessed, was of advantage to my country.

It is true, that when engaged ardently for the benefit of others, I have often received the flattering compliment from those in whose interest I was so warm, of being an active fellow for the cause, and highly deserving of having all the drudgery to do. But this flattery, while it answered the ends of others, was poisoning my frame rapidly; and evidently, as I had the sagacity to discover, would bring my family to destruction. But, as my hopes of comfort and happiness of life had taken a deep root in the love of my wife and child, my heart began to grow sick at the picture before me. "Time," I exclaimed "is money, and time gives me bread and meat for my table: why, then, am I struggling for the benefit of others, at the loss of my own individual happiness, and the destruction of my family?"

What, I would ask, has it ever benefited a mechanic to lose a week in electioneering purposes, spending his money in riotous and debauched company, and joining the dregs and filth of society, in midnight caucuses, orgies and revels, making enemies of friends, and wasting his substance and reputation? None under heaven. Yet it is a solemn fact, that many a man whose circumstances in life were respectable has been totally ruined by it.

"Curse politics," said I as I retired from the political mob, "I am determined no more to have any thing to do with them. Let those who fatten from such employment do the dirty work." But scarcely had I got clear of the multitudes, before I was accosted with "Sir, I hope you are not going to leave the political field!" and "My dear sir, pray be vigilant, or all is lost!" by those who at those times, are ever ready to take you by the hand, and make the most *sincere* professions of friendship and fellowship; but who, probably before the sun of the last day of the election hath retired behind the western hills, will view you as nothing better than the abject slave of party and of factions ready for purposes of any kind, however base and dishonourable. And too often it happens that those kind of men, from their respectable standing in society, are too apt to lead and sway the unsuspecting men. But things like these, base as they are, are now become so fashionable, that the leaders of a party, just before an election, will take upon themselves to count the number of individuals over whom their power extends, and bet upon the result, from the assurance of their own poisonous and baneful influence.

. . . .

The present existing tyrants of the old world have been enabled to build castles and palaces, and to wear imperial and royal diadems, by means of those detestable artifices, which they practised upon the unsuspecting and credulous. But, alas! beware of demogogues, who by artful and insidious means, and by

> ### REPUBLICAN ELECTORS, ATTEND!
>
> The polls have been open two days for the election of a suitable person to represent the city of New-York in Congress. Out of six thousand votes there has not been four hundred taken. What is the meaning of this supineness on the part of the Republicans? This is worthy of enquiry. Will any man of common sense say, that the people of this city are indifferent who shall represent them; no, fellow citizens. The fact is, that the committee of nomination did actually determine on Mr. George I Warner, as the most suitable candidate, but certain of the leading men who direct the affairs of this city, could not submit to the idea of being represented by a Mechanic, however uniform his Republicanism, or however well qualified for the station. It is a fact which will not be denied, that Mr. Warner possesses talents very superior to the Merchant candidate. But Mr. Mumford is a Merchant, and as the junto could not procure a lawyer for their candidate, they immediately convened the Merchants, and the combined interest of the lawyers and Merchants, overpowered the Mechanics.
>
> Republicans, can the best interests of our free country be supported by any particular classes? no, it must be the union of all. We must be represented by talents and long tried Republicanism, whether it be found in the Lawyer, the Merchant, or the Mechanic.—Therefore, rouse and prove yourselves worthy of your professions, and give your support to the true Republican, the tried Friend of the party, GEORGE I. WARNER, and you will be supported by thousands of your fellow
>
> G.DeC.C. **ELECTORS**.

While Democratic-Republicans commonly attacked the Federalists for ignoring the concerns and interests of craftsmen, within the Republican establishment anti-artisan sentiment could also be found. This was particularly prominent in years such as 1804 when the Federalists failed to mount a serious challenge. In this case the Republicans are accused of failing to nominate a mechanic for Congress. NYPL

false pretensions to liberty and happiness, are endeavouring to enslave mankind. Beware of those who wish to rule and who talk of dealing out justice to all, with even handed impartiality. Their professions are as sweet honey, but their actions are as bitter as gall.

TIMOLEON[32]

Independent Mechanic, June 29, 1811

❧

56. For the Formation of a Mechanic Slate

To all real Lovers of Liberty

My friends and fellow citizens. The time is fast approaching when we shall be called upon to give our votes at the ensuing election, by the different contesting parties in this city; but my friends, reason and liberty, and the welfare of our country call aloud to us to consider to what an abject state of slavery we are brought. When we attend the polls to vote the tickets that we hand for the boxes are cut and dried for us before hand: by the two great rival societies of this city, the Tammany, &c., and the leading characters are men seeking offices only; not our welfare. With these men all patriotism is buried in the tomb of avarice. Think of this ye industrious Mechanics and Labourers who work hard from day to day, and can hardly provide bread for your families; think I say how many wretches the money that is lavished away on gormandising placemen would make happy, and consider that a great part of the money is drawn from the pockets of we that work & toil from year to year without advancing one step forward to prosperity: thus gloomy indeed is the prospect before us; great political engines are at work, and we the Mechanics and Labourers are to be the dupes, and to set and keep them in motion.–Do look my friends at the distracted state of our country owing to the different factions that are continually starting up. If a remedy is not speedily applied, we shall like Rome fall a sacrifice to some aspiring demagogue, and our government will be a Monarchy or military tyranny and we shall be compelled to submit to a double despotism, of church and state. We find that our general government is destitute of energy sufficient to enforce the laws. If the laws that are made cannot be put in force, they ought of course to be repealed. A Government or body politic, without energy, may be compared to a human body without legs.

Fellow Citizens, it is high time that the tocsin of alarm be sounded, and that some remedy be applied to cure those evils. Let us not be dragged to the polls by demagogues. The immortal Washington was opposed to all political cabals, and the writer belongs to none of them nor ever will. Let us, the Mechanics and Labourers, come out from among them and be separate, for it is not the virtue or the talents of the candidates that are to serve in the Legislature, that the leaders consult, but how much property do they possess, how far and to what lengths will they go to serve the leaders, and how many places will they provide for them. Look back my friends to the close of your revolution, and you will find your Legislature was composed of the honest Farmer and the virtuous Mechanic. But now you must vote for very different men, if you vote agreeable to the wishes of the leaders. Let us my friends, make our OWN TICKETS and vote for those virtuous citizens that never held an office; and that never expect any. By doing this we shall break up that PARTY SPIRIT, that will otherwise one day prove the bane and ruin of our beloved country.

We find that the two factions in this city are constantly calumniating each other. Let us as friends convince them at the next elections, that we are no partisans, but that we are partial only to our Republican Government and country.–And in order to accomplish so desirable an object, let those who have independent minds call public ward meetings, and choose their own candidates, and form their own tickets. This my friends is in our power, we being the majority, and by doing this the OFFICE HUNTERS will bewail their fate in sackcloth and ashes; and thus we shall save ourselves, our posterity, and our country from ruin.

A REAL AMERICAN

American Citizen, March 22, 1810

PART THREE

The Marketplace

*T*ogether with the creation of genuine republican government, a central meaning of the *American Revolution for artisans was the opportunity to realize entrepreneurial ambitions. Craftsmen, already in the Colonial Era a community of singular ambition, expected to further expand their economic horizons now that the fetters of British mercantilism were lifted and a stong American government in place. Much of their opposition to British measures focused on the suppression of their right to participate in the marketplace. As noted, for many craftsmen one of the central meanings of artisan republicanism was capitalism for the common man; that is, an open, accessible marketplace that would permit the meritorious—however humble their origins—to rise in the social order. American raw materials, combined with individual initiative and enterprise, offered the chance to all hard-working farmers and artisans to attain entrepreneurial independence and a better standard of living.*[1]

This Jeffersonian creed became more deeply embedded in the consciousness of craftsmen through the prosperity brought to the city of New York in the early republic. Thomas C. Cochran describes a "business revolution" in the economy of the new nation. Buoyed by expanding trade created by the exigencies of the Napoleonic Wars and by increased consumer demand, merchants expanded operations and reinvested capital. Active daily newspapers and improved postal communication produced greater security of information, while stable and systematic business procedures such as incorporation also contributed to a positive business atmosphere. New York, with its excellent harbor and hinterlands and the most entrepreneurial daring in the nation, became the focus of the country's commerce, the hub of inter-urban commodity flow. As enterprises—new and old—flourished, the city's population quintupled between 1790 and 1830, and its total capital value increased by 850 percent.[2]

For successful master craftsmen, the marketplace provided considerable financial gain. An occupational wealth analysis of the fourth ward in 1815 conducted by Edmund P. Willis, a ward he considered most typical of the city's entire population, found that the majority of master craftsmen possessed between $2000 and $5000 in assets, a very comfortable sum and not far below that of merchants and attorneys. Some of the more successful *tradesmen amassed even greater fortunes, such as baker Thomas Mercein ($2600 in 1808; $11,000 in 1815), potter Clarkson Crolius ($8300 in 1808; $22,400 in 1815), and glazier Jacob Sherred ($120,000 in 1815).*[3]

A number of masters sought their fortunes in enterprises oriented to quantity production, trades that often involved large numbers of employees and extensive marketing. This was particularly true in shoemaking, building (masonry and carpentry), tailoring, printing, and cabinetmaking. These crafts, which experienced considerable labor unrest, will be considered in Part IV. However, they, like the traditional crafts discussed in this part, used similar types of promotion, investment, organization, and invention, and both could involve considerable expenditure.

THE WORKPLACE

Running a craft enterprise was not a simple task. Even the smaller operations entailed concerns with procuring supplies, handling workmen, quality control, credit, rent, etc. The daily expenses of three bakers (Document 57) give a sense of the many details involved in an artisan's business day from obtaining raw material and labor to maintaining horses and equipment. The day book of turner James Ruthven, typical of countless ledgers of artisan proprietors, describes the production and repair work of a small-scale independent craftsman. The description of a saddler's workshop/store reveals the complex nature of traditional crafts in the early 1800s (Documents 57–59). The saddlery was a relatively large-scale operation with eighteen employees. Stores and workshops were interspersed throughout the house and warehouse entailing different aspects of the leather crafts, including trunk making, harness making

As busy as the port of New York was in 1788, forty years later, when this engraving was made, it was at an even higher state of activity. The construction of the Erie Canal made New York the hub of American commerce. South Street and Maiden Lane, STOKES COLLECTION, NYPL

and saddle making. John Smart, the owner, displays a proud sense of the producer ethic in commenting on the "nearly eight years unwearied application and by the particular attention to the quality of the work done at it . . ."

Artisans were keen inventors, eager to devise and sell practical applications and to take advantage of other's ideas. During the Revolution, homemade technology had helped the Americans live without British goods and to wage war. Moreover, new invention could keep the United States free of dependence on Britain for its manufactures, and would furthermore be geared toward practical items befitting a republic rather than the luxury goods common to the aristocracy across the Atlantic. In this manner, for new technology to remain true to artisan republicanism it had to remain tied to the decentralized production of skilled craftsmen, rather than to the large manufactories or factories that were emerging in Britain.[4] No American city was more open to change and innovation than New York. Newspaper advertisements fully portray the various new devices offered to artisans to fill the various needs of the metropolis's inhabitants and businesses (Document 60).

57. Typical Baker's Expenses

Expenses:

2 barrels of flour at $9.53	$19.06
Wood for oven	.50
Yeast (average)	.50
One workman (including board)	1.00
House rent (based on $212.50 yearly rent)	.58
Salt	.06
Candles	.12
Carting (for 2 barrels of flour)	.09
Wear and tear of wagon, baskets and peals	.12
Personal labor and attendance	1.25
Horse feed	.50
Total	$23.78

Income:

192 loaves (according to November 1 assize)	$22.19
Sale of 2 barrels at .31 (many broken)	.62
Total	$22.81

Daily loss	$.98[5]

Mercantile Advertiser, November 19, 1801

58. Day Book of James Ruthven, Turner and Carver

1793		£	s	d	
Feb. 3	Beading a Teapot	5			Barley
	Beading a Sugar dish	5			
	9 boxes	4			Skinner
	13 forks	1	6		Caldwell
	Beading a Milkpot	3			Van Voorhees
	2 handles		10		Stevenson
	2 Pillars	1			Dodge
7	A Cover pattern	16			Stevenson Foundry
	4 Chafing Handles	1			Mount
	4 Bucket Pins	1			Shapless
	4 Flask Screws	8			Brinkeroff
Amount of Account of Stevensons Foundry		3	3	6	
	Altering a Pattern	1	6		Jesop
	4 Brass Pullies	1			T. Smith
	Beading a Bowl	4	6		Debous
	A Golden Bowl	1			
	2 Urns	3			Bailey

1803					
Jan. 22	A Teapot Bezel Milled	2			
	A Coffee pot bezel	3			Faben
	2 pint mugs	6			
	30 Backgammon men	6	3		Robert Calder
	3 oval patterns @ 5£.	15			Forniquet
	24 A handle	6			Stevenson
	16 Skimmer handles	5	4		Houstoium
	2½ lbs. stones @	3	9		Sayres
	1/6				Forbes
	4 Cup hips	10			A Wright
	48 small balusters	12			
n.b. 27	Jansen's Acct.				
	rendered	6	10	0 pd.	
	Brinkeroff's Acct.				
	rendered	1	3	0 pd.	
	Repairing a public	1			Caldwell
	A Ring	1		6	Forbes

1793 & 1803

NYHS

A Turner's shop. EDWARD HAZEN, THE PANORAMA OF PROFESSIONS AND TRADES OR EVERY MAN'S BOOK (PHILADELPHIA, 1836), NYHS

59. Sadler's House and Workshop: A Description

A Bargain of a Valuable Establishment—John Smart, Sadler, &c. No. 159 Water-street, intending to decline the business, offers for sale his Stock in Trade, consisting of a large and general assortment of Sadlery. Also, the House and Store occupied by him as a Sadler's Shop and Warehouse.

The Establishment is the growth of nearly eight years' unwearied application, and by the particular attention paid to the quality of work done at it, its character in that particular stands unrivalled by any similar establishment in the United States, and is far superior to any thing of the kind in N. York. The House, corner of Water and Fletcher streets, is a frame building, 20 feet front and rear and 30 feet deep, two-stories high and has a large garret and cellar; the cellar is occupied as a work-shop for the Trunk and Harness Making, and is calculated to accommodate six workmen; the first floor is also occupied as a work and sale shop, it has convenient work-benches for six men, and well arranged glass cases sufficient to contain five or six dozen saddles and as many bridles, part of said cases are calculated to shew plated bridles and whips to much advantage, a small mahogany case for bits and stirrups, and a large case for plated harness; under the whip and bridle cases are nineteen small drawers, convenient for plated goods, whips, &c. under the saddle cases are large drawers for leather, &c. and on the said floor there are several other drawers, shelves, &c. in the most convenient style for the business. On the second floor there is a harness case sufficiently large to contain two or three dozen sets of chair harness, a work-bench for three men, and sundry other convenient fixtures. The garret is used to contain the hair, wool, hides, trunk boxes, &c. necessary to the business.

The store, No. 16 Fletcher-street, adjoining the house, is 21 feet front and rear, and 20 feet deep. It is a three-story Fire-Proof Building, the cellar of which is used as a work-shop, it is nine feet high, and fixed for six men, and has three large windows in front, and an area, wall and iron railing. The first floor is

New York contained a number of tanneries, particularly in the Fourth Ward. These helped supply shoemakers, saddlers and other leather workers with the large number of processed hides that they required. ANDERSON COLLECTION, NYPL

a 12 foot ceiling, fixed for a ware room, handsomely shelved, a counter, desk, book cases, &c. in the most complete order, the next story is calculated for a leather store, with drawers that will contain 12 dozen hogskins, this story is ten feet in the clear. The third story is 8 feet in the clear; the break-work of the garret is two and a half feet high, and contains a wheel with its band, tackle, fall and slings, in the most complete order for hoisting goods. – The manufactory has progressed so far as to enable the proprietor to employ on an average twelve men and six apprentices through the last year, not withstanding the obstruction occasioned by the fall epidemic; and upon a fair calculation, six men more may be employed in the ensuing season.

A number of excellent customers from the Southern States are much attached to the manner of executing work at this place, who buy largely, and pay in good acceptances in New York. The retail business is in a very prosperous train; so much so, that it has afforded higher prices for best work than any shop in this city could obtain, with the decided preference and unqualified approbation of its numerous and generous supporters.

The stock at present consists of almost every article used in the Sadlery Business and Harness Making; also all kinds of Trunk materials. Any person inclining to purchase the business as it stands, will find the price very low and terms easy – Possession may be had on the first of May next. –

New-York Gazette and General Advertiser, February 21, 1804

60. Baker's Oven for Shipbread

TO BAKERS. The proprietors of the Patent, for manufacturing ship and other bread, will dispose of Rights for using the Machinery of that invention, in one or more States of the Union, or in any foreign country.

The great benefit of this Invention must be obvious. – The mixing, breaking or kneading and moulding of the breads, is done in an easy and expeditious manner, so as to save nearly all the manual labour practised in the common way; besides making the bread more complete in every respect, and the principal part of the work may be done by Boys from 10 to 14 years of age. It is already in actual operation in the State of Connecticut, therefore, those facts have been fully proved, and the bread is known to keep good in warm climates and on long voyages. – The Proprietors are willing to join a Person or company to erect works to be used in this State or City, should that mode be preferred to purchasing a Right.

Further Particulars may be known by applying at No. 164 Front-street.
N.B. The Machinery may be constructed to go either by a small stream or
Water or Horses.–

The New-York Gazette and General Advertiser, February 25, 1801

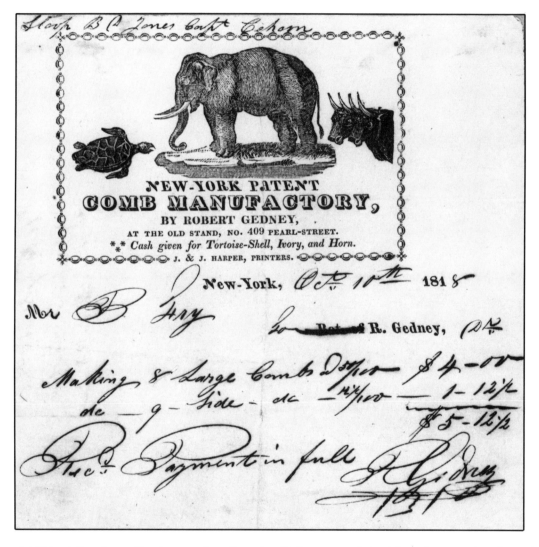

*A bill in dollars for making large and small combs. Half cents are derived from the conversion of
shillings into dollars (eight shillings to the dollar). The elephant is part of the traditional emblem of
comb makers.* NYHS

MEANS OF ENTERPRISE

I n their search for profit and expansion, artisans often ventured into partnerships that provided more capital and security than an individual could raise. While often helpful, they did have liabilities, and notices of dissolution were common. The testimony of Stephen Allen is illustrative. A precocious apprentice and then journeyman during the American Revolution, he was eager to strike out on his own. Having no capital, he found a partnership the best means. His first such relationship netted him $4000 in seven years (1788–1791). After that, personal difficulties developed, causing him to go it alone. A later partnership (1807–1809) brought in $32,000; thereafter, he prospered on his own. In addition to financial success, he became an alderman and ultimately the first artisan to become Mayor of the City of New York. His memoir, a critical document in artisan history, describes his unrelenting efforts and sacrifice to achieve financial independence (Document 61).

Occasionally, mechanics would pool resources into a mutual joint stock venture such as the New York Slate Company, organized by building craftsmen to quarry slate and sell it to local builders or use it themselves (Document 62). In addition, master craftsmen formed mutual associations to further their individual businesses. The Blacksmith Society, for example, an organization of masters, made large-scale purchases of coal for its members and for sale to the public (Document 63). Also common was the fixing of prices citywide. This was true of shoeing smiths (Document 64), printers (Illustration) and bookbinders among others. Clearly an attempt to control competition, these efforts perhaps were throwbacks to the tradition of the "just price" common in the eighteenth century in England and America. However, they depended upon the cooperation of all involved craftsmen, and in a generally unregulated free market economy, this was increasingly difficult to attain. A common but also increasingly unsuccessful tactic in countering violators was social ostracism. The "Curse," by bookbinder poet John Bradford, is a dramatic illustration of the extent of the wrath of fellow craftsmen and their employees towards violators (Document 65).

As ambitious entrepreneurs, master craftsmen were eager to reach the buying public. The City's numerous daily and weekly newspapers offered the major forum, and artisans filled their pages with ingenious appeals to purchasers. Moccasin maker William Jackson, who ran a large-scale footwear manufactory while selling patent medicine on the side, appealed to patriotism, humor and, most importantly, the economic self-interest of merchants faced by the cut-off of trade during the Napoleonic Wars (Document 66).

61. Stephen Allen: His Business Career

. . . The next year (1789) business was much better, and I obtained a situation in a sail-loft belonging to Thomas Hillson.–There were then a number of the Friends who owned shipping, and Hillson being the only one in the city at that period connected with the society, and who carried on the business of sail-making, he obtained the whole of their work, and consequently was enabled to keep two or three hands constantly employed. He therefore engaged Augustus Wright and myself by the year, at low wages, and boarded us at his house, but we were compelled to lodge in the sail-loft. This Hillson was one of these eccentric characters who are occasionally met with in the world. His dress was of the most slovenly kind, with elbows through his coat. His other garments filthy and with slouched hat, he appeared more like a beggar, than a man in the decent walks of life.–When in the company of the Friends, he was all meekness and suavity, and could use the plain language of that sect with fluency, but at other times he was the height of vulgarity and would swear like a pirate. He was times careless and prodigal of his money, and at others penurious to a fault. In his temper he was whimsical and passionate, and was often tyranical to those under his control wherever he had an opportunity of showing off with impunity, but to those who possessed independence enough to resist him, he was docile and meek.–

With all this impropriety of conduct and oddity of character, Hillson possessed one good trait, for at the time I am speaking of he provided well for his family and laid by sufficient money to build him a very decent house in this city. We continued to work as journeymen in this loft until the year 1787, when Hillson concluded to take a partner in his business and finally proposed the matter to and offered me the situation–On the 1st of May, 1788, we commenced our partnership under the firm of Hillson and Allen. About the same period Augustus Wright who for so many years had been my shop-mate, received a similar offer of partnership from a sail-maker of the name of Cone, which he accepted also, and they commenced business on the same date that we did.

I now attended to the business of my sail-loft with redoubled assiduity and industry while my partner Hillson spent a large portion of his time in walking the docks, as he said in pursuit of business. My acquaintance with the customers of our establishment was very limited, particularly at the commencement of our partnership and during the first and second year of its continuance, inasmuch as they were principally such as had employed Hillson previous to our connection, and the collecting of the money with other outdoor business, being mostly performed by him, it was seldom that an opportunity offered for me to become acquainted with them, and I had therefore no choice but to be contented with matters as they were conducted, which threw upon me all the labor of the establishment, together with the keeping of books and accounts. Remonstrances had no other effect than to irritate and promote altercation, and I found that instead of amendment, matters grew worse.—Finding that no change in his conduct was likely to be effected, I told him that I would dissolve our partnership, be the consequences what they might. To this threat he paid no attention whatever and I therefore stated to the person of whom we rented the sail-loft, the situation of our concern, and my reasons for the determination I had formed of dissolving my connection with Hillson, and then left it at his option, either to continue me as his tenant or to rent the place to Hillson. He preferred that I should continue in the loft, which was of some importance, as we generally did as much work for the landlord as would pay the rent. I accordingly informed Hillson of the arrangement, and at the same time tendered him a part of the loft for any work he might have, until he could provide himself with another. This partnership therefore, which had existed for nearly four years was finally dissolved on the first day of December, 1791, and I commenced business on my own account.

My prospects were not very flattering, for a large portion of our customers in the shipping business were the particular friends of Hillson, drawn to him by his Quaker connections and those among the boatmen and coasters who were also attached to him on account of his constant association with them on all occasions. He had acquired also a great name with the Long Island people for cutting a handsome sail, many of whom were our employers. With a full view of all these advantages on his side and disadvantages on my own, I did not suffer myself to despair of being enabled by industry and strict attention to business to make a living, for I had long before this come to the determination of using the utmost economy in all my concerns, in order to keep myself from obligations of every sort, and to lay by something in case of misfortune, or accident to myself or family. With a view of accumulating some property therefore, I purchased a small house in Chestnut Street, while still in company with Hillson, although my purchase money was then far beyond my means, being twelve hundred and fifty dollars, when I possessed only fifty dollars, and a part of this sum I had to borrow of Mrs. Marschalk in order to make the first payment. My motive in making the purchase was to avoid the May day removals (three of which, as Poor Richard has told us, are as bad as a fire) and I concluded also that the owing of this debt would prove a stimulus to our economy until it was discharged.[6] My agreement with the person of whom I had purchased was that he should receive any sum that I might wish to pay, not less than fifty dollars, and accordingly no sooner was I in possession of that or a larger amount which could be spared with convenience, than I proceeded to have it endorsed on the bond, thus lessening the debt and preventing the accumulation of interest.[7]

The first year I was in business after the dissolution of co-partnership with Hillson, my profits were quite small and did not pay expenses. I made the most of the work, however, which came to me by working early and late, so long as there was anything to be done, and hiring as few journeymen as possible; and I prided myself upon being able to say that no person who employed me was ever disappointed, for the work was always done at the time promised.–

It has been the uniform custom of those following the business of sail making to obtain the materials such as sail duck, bolt rope, twine, thimbles, marlin and lines, from the ship chandlers, giving them the retail profit on those articles, which it had always appeared to me belonged to the manufacturers of the sails; and I had determined whenever my means would permit to furnish these articles myself. I commenced therefore, about this time to purchase a portion of the articles alluded to from the importer, in such quantities as my means would admit, and prudence appeared to warrant, and charged them in my bills at the prices fixed upon them by the ship chandlers.–

In order that I might ascertain whether I was gaining anything by my business, and how much, I had adopted the practice, (and which ought to be followed by all who wish and expect to gain a fortune) of annually examining my affairs by taking an inventory of stock on hand and debts due, as also the debts I owed, by which means I was able to see how I had thrived for the year. Thus I found that on the 1st of January, 1796, after having been in business about eight years, I was worth at least four thousand dollars more than when I commenced. I now determined to commence the purchase of small lots of sail duck, for which purpose I attended sales at auction where I frequently made advantagous cost purchases that netted me a large profit. I also purchased small lots at private sale when opportunity offered but only from those who had sufficient confidence in my integrity and punctuality in payment, and who were willing to sell without receiving a note at hand for the amount, for so fearful was I that a demand might be made for the payment on a day when through some unforseen disappointment I might not be able to meet it, that I preferred the loss of profit on a purchase to the loss of my credit.–

The Revolution in France which commenced in 1793 [sic] and the beligerent state of all Europe had called into action the whole commercial resources of our country, and every kind of business flourished, but particularly the business I was following. And, as I had started with the determination of gaining by honorable means a competent support for myself and family, whenever business was given me to do I exerted every nerve to perform it by the

Scenes in a sail-loft as sails are sewn, woven and stitched by sailmakers. From the certificate of membership of the Society of Master Sailmakers, 1793. NYHS

time required, in order that no disappointments might be experienced by my employers, and that at the same time, by quick despatch my profits might be augmented. Year after year, during the fall and winter months, which was always the most busy season, have I labored at least fourteen hours out of the twenty-four. My practice was, in order to save time, to take breakfast before daylight and with a lantern containing a light, proceed to the sail-loft with the apprentices, there kindle our fire, and commence our work, perhaps an hour before the journeymen would arrive (as they worked only by the day) which in winter was 7 o'clock. – And at night we worked by candle light till 9 o'clock, and sometimes later, according as we were pressed for time, to complete the business engaged to be done; but I never worked on a Sunday, preferring the most unremitted and hardest labor through the week to the violation of the Sabbath.

Memoirs of Stephen Allen, pp. 45–50

62. New York Slate Company

WHEN an association is felt to be a public benefit, what encouragement ought it to receive from the community at large? Such we presume is the NEW YORK SLATE COMPANY.

In the year 1802 they formed themselves into an association, principally composed of mechanics in the building line, for the express purpose of preparing slate within this state. After nearly four years assiduous attention in prosecuting and carrying on the business they have expended about one hundred thousand dollars, and the Company have as yet derived little or no benefit therefrom besides the heavy expense attending and undertaking of this nature. They have constantly in their employ about one hundred men, viz. it is–Quarrymen, Dressers, Packers, Cartmen, Boatmen, &c. etc. demanding the expenditure of about fifteen thousand dollars per annum which is regularly paid in Cash. The Company view with regret the long established prejudice in favor of Slate im-

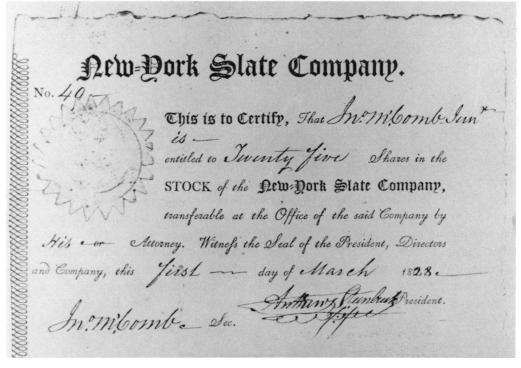

A Certificate of stock ownership in a company organized by a group of artisans. The holder, John McComb, was a prominent builder who supervised the construction of the new City Hall. NYHS

ported from Great Britain and Ireland, which operates to impede the sale of theirs, notwithstanding the extravagant price formerly paid of from fifteen to twenty-two dollars per square, while this Company's Slate, equal if not superior in quality is now sold at the moderate price of from six to nine dollars per square and it is a well known fact that the common sort of Foreign Slate that is generally imported does not stand the violence of this climate—competition in trade is certainly a public benefit. The Company neither wishes nor expects a monopoly—all they ask is, that their fellow citizens would reserve their own judgment after examining the quality and other advantages herein mentioned which they can do by calling at the Company's Yard, New Albany Basin; or on

Joseph Newton
109 Greenwich-Street

Prices Are as Follows

11	per square $6
12	
13	per square $7
14–30	per square $9

All slate taken from the Company's yard is to be paid for sixty days after delivery.

All Slate C. Wise Company yard.

For exportation ten percent drawback, payable on note ninety days after delivery. The Company stows them in the vessel.

American Citizen, September 30, 1805

63. Cooperative Venture: Blacksmiths' Purchase of Coal

FOR SALE

By the Blacksmith Society,

VIRGINIA COAL, of the best quality fit for the Grate or Forge. As the Smiths are constantly consuming this article, it is presumed they are the best judges of it; the public, therefore, may rely on having them genuine from the vessel, without being intermixed with all kinds of rubbish, which has been the case of many years in this city. They will be sold without any further profit than to defray yardage and carting.

    N.B. Apply to Mr. Randolph, at the old distillery, corner of Murray and Greenwich-streets, where the coals are to be seen.

Evening Post, February 20, 1806

64. Trade-Wide Price Structure: The Shoe Smiths

NOTICE

We the Master Shoeing Smiths of the city of New-York, find ourselves under the necessity of advancing the prices for Shoeing of Horses, on account of the enormous price of iron, coals and labour: we therefore take this method to inform the owners of horses, and our employers that we the subscribers have adopted the following prices, by which we presume that ample justice will be rendered to ourselves and the public in general.

All shoes steeled at the toes	15 shillings per set
[ditto] plain	14 shillings per set
Four removes and steeled at the toes,	8 shillings
Bar shoes,	8 shillings a shoe

Joseaph Henville,
Honh. Robarts,
Wm. Carvear,
John Bell,
Christopher Riddel,
Saml McGinniss,
Patrick Fitzpatrick & Nowlan.
Wm. Retallack,
Richd. D. Graves,
Wm. Batchelor,
Abraham Hipwell,
James Gridley,
James McGinniss

Evening Post, November 13, 1814

The following is the printed handbill shown:

> New-York, May 18, 1795.
>
> The following are the Established Prices of
>
> # PRINTING,
>
> Done at the respective OFFICES of the Subscribers:---
>
> | | L. | s. | d. |
> | --- | --- | --- | --- |
> | FOR Every sheet of common-work, of demi paper, printed on brevier, of which 1000 copies are printed, | 6 | 10 | 0 |
> | For every sheet of ditto, on burgeois, of which 1000 copies are printed, | 6 | 0 | 0 |
> | For every sheet of long primer, or small pica, on demi paper, of which 1000 copies are printed, | 5 | 0 | 0 |
> | For every sheet of pica or english, of which 1000 copies are printed, | 4 | 10 | 0 |
> | For every additional thousand, | 1 | 10 | 0 |
>
> If the work should be French, Latin, Rules, Figures, &c. an advanced price to be paid, (of one fifth at least.)
>
> N. B. In the above cases, the person employing the printer to furnish paper.
>
> | | | | |
> | --- | --- | --- | --- |
> | For printing and furnishing a single pack of large cards, | 0 | 10 | 0 |
> | For every additional pack of large do. | 0 | 6 | 0 |
> | For a single pack of small cards, | 0 | 8 | 0 |
> | For every additional small do. | 0 | 5 | 0 |
> | For 50 or 100 quarto handbills, | 0 | 10 | 0 |
>
> For every additional hundred, five shillings, unless more than 1000 are printed, in which case a deduction of one fourth may be made.
>
> For 100 folio handbills, 20 shillings, the printer furnishing paper.
>
> For every additional hundred, one dollar, unless more than 500 are printed, and then, as above, a deduction of one fourth may be made.
>
> ## BLANKS OF ALL KINDS.
>
> For any number, under five quires, 7 shillings per quire.
>
> For every additional quire, not exceeding ten quires, 6 shillings per quire.
>
> For every additional quire, after ten, 4 shillings per quire.
>
> N. B. The person employing the printer, to furnish paper.
>
> WE do further agree, That if either of us shall do work at a less rate than is here established, we will forfeit the sum of twenty pounds, to be appropriated as a majority of us shall think proper.
>
> Tiebout and Obrien,   Arch. McLean,
> Wayland and Davis,   Thomas Greenleaf.
> Roberson and Gowan,   John Buel,
> George Forman,   T. & J. Swords,
> Hurtin and Commardinger, George Bunce & Co.
> John Harrison,

Master Printers were willing to establish common prices for their services. They also established penalties against enterprises undercutting these rates. CHARLOTTE T. MORGAN, THE ORIGINS AND HISTORY OF THE NEW YORK EMPLOYING PRINTERS ORGANIZATION (NEW YORK, 1930)

65. Violation of Trade-Wide Price Structure: Bookbinders

CURSE ON BOOKBINDER UNDERSELLING PRICES

A Most solemn Curse, pronounced by Ben Burnisher, upon a Master Bookbinder, who endeavoured to injure the business, by working under price.[8]

> May rats and mice devour your paste,
> Your paper and your leather;
> May your hand-letters be defac'd,
> Your types all mix'd together;

May all your pallets, stamps and rolls,
Be on their faces batter'd;
Your beating-stone pick'd full of holes,
Your hamm'r in pieces shatter'd.

And may your standing-press fall down,
Your press-boards all be cracked;
May your law leather all turn brown,
Each law-book edge get blacked.

May you be bother'd—all your life,
With workmen—brandy lovers;
With sandy boards, a dull plough knife,
Thin paste and horny covers.

And may your gilding all rub off,
Your rolls burn through the leather;
And you henceforward be obliged
To finish—in dry weather.

And may your colours be too strong,
So as to rot the leather;
May all your books be titled wrong,
Each fly-sheet past'd together.

May your lying presses all get broke,
Your books be wrong collated;
And may you with foul charcoal smoke
Be almost suffocated.

May your apprent'ces run away,
Your business be diminish'd;
And may booksellers never pay
You, when your work is finish'd.

God grant that you distress'd may be,
From constable to the beadle;
And live till you can't feel or see
Your press pin from your needle.

Independent Mechanic, June 29, 1811

66. Advertisement: Mockasin Maker and Medicine

WILLIAM JACKSON

MOCKASIN MAKER TO THE INHABITANTS OF THIS RENOWNED
CITY OF GOTHAM

And many other Citizens under the Republican Government of the United States

TAKES this method of returning his sincere thanks to his numerous and respectable customers for their very liberal countence and support. Those gentlemen who have heretofore exchanged Cash for Mockasins of Jackson, and who fear that they will not be supplied next season in consequence of the Non-Importation Act, are respectfully requested to calm their fears, and make themselves perfectly easy on that score—Jackson, through the polite attention of the Emperor Huggins,[9] King of *Grease*, &c. who has a confidential Correspondent in the Cabinet, was enabled to anticipate this last Non-Importation Act; and, therefore, not only imported a sufficient quantity of the most elegant Carpeting, sufficient to make Mockasins for all the Ladies and Gentlemen in the United States, (not forgetting the *French* state of New-Orleans,) for three or four years to come, but he has likewise imported sixty-seven of the best workmen in Europe, to assist him in this *infant* establishment. Wholesale merchants who wish to make a rapid fortune by *selling* these incomparable Mockasins, must be supplied on moderate terms *for cash* (none of your *trust* customers for a large amount) and retailers who wish to make themselves *snug* and *comfortable*, by vending these articles, are requested to send their orders in time. This request is made, not from any interested motives on the part of the manufacturer, but merely to prevent his Mockasins lying on the shelf, and himself being eat out of house and home by his sixty-seven imported *gormandizers*. Mr. Jackson deems it unnecessary to state that he has prevented more coughs, colds, asthmas and consumptions, by his LIFE PRESERVERS, than all the quacks in New-York have by their drugs; he therefore presumes that between him and the ladies and gentlemen of these United States the same *understanding* will continue heretofore.

William Jackson

🐦 🐦 🐦

Season of Shud, Weeks of Catching 8.

Apropos. – W.J. is confidently informed that the Physicians of New-York had a meeting this spring to find out the cause of their monstrous decrease of practice last winter. After mature investigation it was sufficiently ascertained that JACKSON was the only cause. – Convinced of their utility, they resolved, that instead of bleeding, purging, &c. that they would hereafter recommend the use of JACKSON'S MOCKASINS.

Morning Post, May 13, 1811

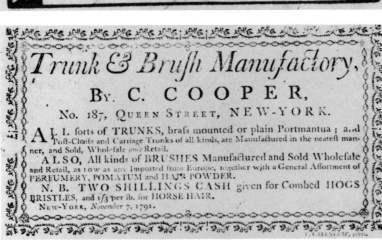

Artisans were adept at using advertisement in the form of newspaper ads, handbills and business cards. Business cards were an important means of attracting notice and of stressing the importance of the profession. Handbills allowed for even greater detail. NYHS; INDEPENDENT MECHANIC; EVENING POST

NEW DRESSING ROOM.

A. TRUMENTO, No. 1 Wall-street, just returned from Italy, has the honour to inform the gentlemen, that he cuts and dresses hair in the latest style, and in a manner so as to adopt it to the phisiognomy. He has for sale a quantity of RAZORS of the first quality, if they do not please on trial, the purchasers are at liberty to return them, and receive the money. He has likewise procured a very fine hone, and engages to restore razors to a very keen edge—and should they not cut he will receive no recompence.—Those gentlemen who may please to honor him with their patronage, may depend on the most particular and respectful attendance.

N. B. Gentlemen who subscribe by the quarter will have their razors, &c. kept exclus. of

BRUSH WARE-HOUSE.

JAMES COOK, Brush Manufacturer, from Philadelphia, respectfully informs the public that he has opened a Brush warehouse No. 174 Broadway, two doors above Maiden-lane, where he offers for sale, wholesale and retail, from his manufactory No. 238 Market street, Philadelphia, a general assortment of fancy brushes of the latest and most approved patterns, consisting of fancy clothes, hat, penetrating hair, hearth, flesh, table, silver wired tooth Brushes, &c. Also, the much approved Saggina clothes Brushes, made from the root of a tree growing on the mountains of Italy; and the new invented electric hair Brushes, superior to any other kind now in use. All sorts of common Brushes, fancy and common Bellows, all of which will be disposed of at the Philadelphia prices. Painters can be supplied with ground paint, sash and graining Brushes, of the first quality. Russia Bristles of the first quality, for shoemakers use. All sorts of New York Brushes manufactured.

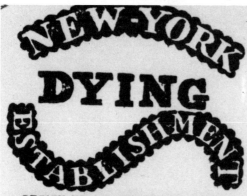

OFFICE NO. 101 WILLIAM-STREET.

THE proprietors of the above establishment continue to receive orders for dying at their extensive buildings on Staten Island, and are amply provided with experienced workmen, machinery and materials for conducting the business in all its branches. They beg leave to assure the public that they have spared no expence nor efforts to obviate the objections which have been generally made to American dying and to render it equal in all respects to that of Europe or any other part of the world.

Silk, Woollen and Cotton articles of all descriptions dyed of any color, and at the most reasonable rates.

They also dye and cleanse ladies and gentlemen's garments of all descriptions; and, in particular, their

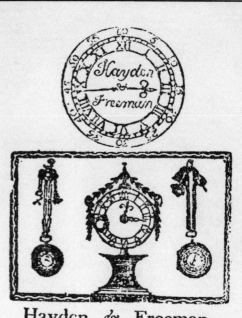

Hayden & Freeman,

WATCH and CLOCK MAKERS

SADDLERY.

THE subscriber offers for sale his Stock, which consists of a large assortment of Saddles, Bridles, Trunks, of all descriptions, Harness, Hobby Horses, Sleigh Backs, Leopard and Bear skins. This is a good opening for any person in the business, who can advance a few thousand dollars; or those that stand in need of any of the above articles, either by wholesale or retail. They can supply themselves on better terms than hitherto known in this city, by applying at his store No. 141, Water-street, corner of Depeyster-street.

Aug. 3 tf   JOHN HASKETT.

PLATT & FAULKNER,
MERCHANT TAILORS,
NO. 129 WILLIAM STREET.

HAVE the honor to inform their friends, and the inhabitants of New-York in general, that they still continue business in all the various lines of their profession. From a long course of practice in most of the principal cities in the United States, they are induced to hope with confidence that whatever article is entrusted to their execution in the line of their business will be finished with a dispatch and neatness, which will not abuse the favor of their patrons. They have established correspondence with the principal houses of their profession in the United States, and receive regularly from London, the newest and most correct fashions.

They have constantly on hand an excellent assortment of CLOTHS and FANCY GOODS, forming a variety which cannot fail to gratify their customers.

Any Gentleman providing his own goods, will be punctually attended to, and his favors thankfully acknowledged.

Work done at the shortest notice, at a moderate price, for Cash, or approved credit.

☞ FIVE or SIX Journeymen Tailors wanted immediately. None need apply but those who can produce unquestionable recommendations as to ability.   tf   Sept 14

MANHATTAN INN,
SIGN OF THE STAGE AND PACKETS

WILLIAM MORGAN respectfully informs the public, that he has removed from 35 Greenwich-street, to No. 5 Ann-street; where he will be happy to entertain company, and assure those who may favor him with a call, that the excellence of his liquors, beer, and other refreshments, cannot be exceeded. Suppers of oysters, chickens, and relishes of every description, will be served up with taste and dispatch. As his situation is very central, being only a few doors from the intersection of Broadway and Chatham row, and the rooms airy, parties will meet with every convenience.

N. B. Six or eight boarders can be accommodated with board, with rooms to themselves if required, at a very moderate rate.
                                     August 24

MARTINOT & ROE,

UMBRELLA and PARASOL MANUFACTURER. No. 70 Maiden-Lane, two doors from William-street, New York, respectfully inform their friends and the public, that they have constantly on hand large and fashionable assortment of silk, cotton, and gingham UMBRELLAS and PARASOLS of the first quality, which they will dispose of on moderate terms, wholesale and retail.

❡ B. Umbrellas and Parasols repaired and covered in the neatest manner.

May 18 6m

JOSIAH DUNN

E. MILLON,
FRENCH MERCHANT TAILOR
AND LADIES, HABIT MAKER,
(Lately from Paris.)
No. 54 MAIDEN LANE,

RETURNS his most grateful thanks to his customers and friends, for that support which they have so liberally granted him, and assures them that his utmost endeavours to please, shall still remain steadfast, both by the goodness of his work and his punctuality at stated periods.

E. MILLON still makes Ladies, Riding Dresses and Coats in the first stile. He has on hand Cloths and Cassimers of all qualities and prices.

All orders gratefully received and punctually attended to   Sept. 28.—1m.

RICHARD MARSH,
No. 66 John-Street.

RESPECTFULLY informs his friends and the public that he continues to carry on the business of FANCY and WINDSOR CHAIR MAKING, of the newest fashions, and on the most reasonable and accommodating terms. Those of his friends who please to honor him with their commands may rest assured that the utmost punctuality and correctness will be observed.

N. B. He also informs his friends, that he has opened a livery stable at the above place, where gentlemen can be accommodated with horses & carriages at the shortest notice.

JACOB KATEN,
Boot and Shoe Maker,
No. 240,
GREENWICH STREET,

A few doors from Murray-street,

RESPECTFULLY informs his friends and the public in general, that he continues to carry on the above business, in all its various branches, and humbly solicits a continuance of the encouragement he has already received, which he will endeavour to merit, by an immediate attention to all orders he may be favoured with.

May 11.

WILLIAM MERRILL,
House-Carpenter, Ship & Shop Joiner,
Corner of Pine and Front-streets,

BEGS permission to acquaint the Public and his Friends, that he still carries on the above branches of business; and while he feels grateful for past favours, will be happy to be honored with a continuance of their patronage. Those who encourage him may rest assured of having their work executed with promptitude & fidelity. CISTERNS made, and warranted water tight.
April 20.

PROPOSAL,
BY JOHN TIEBOUT,
NO. 238 WATER-STREET, NEW-YORK,
For Publishing by Subscription the
PILGRIM'S PROGRESS
From this world to that which is to come.

DELIVERED under the Similitude of a Dream, in two parts. By JOHN BUNYAN. I have used Similitudes—Hosea xii. 10. A new edition, divided into chapters. With the life of the Author. To which are added, Explanatory and Practical Notes, by Messrs. Mason, Scott, and Burder. Embellished with elegant cuts, by Anderson.

ADDRESS.

THE high estimation to which the *Pilgrim's Progress* has been held for above a century, sufficiently evinces its inviolable worth.

FANCY CHAIR STORE.

JOHN K. COWPERTHWAITE,
NO. 4 CHATHAM-SQUARE,
Two doors below the new Watch house, New York

Has on hand an elegant assortment of FANCY AND WINDSOR CHAIRS, settees and Children's Chairs of the newest fashions and well finished, which he offers for sale on the most reasonable terms.

All orders will be thankfully received and punctually attended to.

N. B. Old Chairs repaired, painted, and re-gilt.

July 27   tf

New-York Music School,

FOR teaching the art of performing on various sorts of Musical wind and String instruments, in a short, true and comprehensive manner. Also, Military Bands taught correctly and likewise engaged on the shortest notice, by JAMES H. HOFFMAN,
41, Anthony street.

New-York Sacred Musical Society.

THE New-York Sacred Musical Society, under the direction of Messrs. HILL & ALLEN, will be opened on the second Monday in October, two evenings in each week, for the reception of learners in the art of Singing; if a sufficient number shall subscribe previous to that time.

A collection of excellent music will be ready for delivery on the first evening, printed with NEW PATENT NOTES much more accurate and easy to learn than any heretofore used.

Those who subscribe will pay for their tuition one dollar on the first evening, and one on the last evening in each quarter.

N. B. The society will meet at the School room in Rose-street.   Sept. 28.

Wanted Immediatly,

AN Apprentice to the Boot and Shoe-making business. Apply to No. 91 Pearl-st.— Sep 28.

GREEN TREE
PORTER HOUSE,
NO. 37 FAIR STREET,

J. FRANK acquaints the public in general, that with a view to his own emolument and their comfort, he has commenced duty as a PUBLICAN, in the above well-known and long established Inn, where will constantly be provided the best Liquors, Porter, Ale &c. Also Beef steaks, Oysters, Chickens, Small Relishes, &c. &c. at the shortest notice.

Parties and Companies accommodated with convenient rooms, and provided with Dinners, Suppers, &c. with dispatch.

❧ Choice DUBLIN PORTER will be on draught in a few days   Oct 5—tf

DANCING ACADEMY.
MR. KENEDY

RESPECTFULLY informs the ladies and gentlemen of this city that he intends opening his Academy for the winter season at Mr. WILLIAMS's Long Room, No. 51 Bowery. His first public will be on Thursday the 10th inst. His days of tuition will be Fridays and Saturdays, from 3 o'clock P. M. until 6 for ladies, and from

A page of advertisements from the Independent Mechanic.

NEW-YORK AIR FURNACE.

PETER T. CURTENIUS, and Co.

HAVE repaired the New-York Air-Furnace, *and have procured the best Workmen, together with the necessary Apparatus to carry on the Manufacture of* Cast-Iron, *in the completest and best Manner, so that the Ware they make will be equal to any imported from Europe, and the Price less.*

The WARE manufactured at this Furnace, consists of the following Articles, viz.

Pots and Kettles of various sizes from one to fifteen gallons, Tea Kettles, Pye Pans, Skillets, Griddles, Pot-Ash Kettles and Coolers, Whaling Kettles, Boilers for Tallow-Chandlers and Sugar-Works, Stoves for Sugar-Bakers, Mill-Cases, Cast Bars for Sugar-Works and Distilleries, Rollers and Shears for Slitting-Mills, Hearth and Jamb Plates, cast agreeable to any pattern, Close Stoves for Work-shops, Franklin Stoves neatly decorated with carved work, Bath Stove-Grates elegantly ornamented with carvings, Chimney Backs, Ships Cabouses of the new construction, with bake ovens, in which the same fire that roasts and boils the meat bakes the bread, Mill Rounds and Gudgeons, Saw-Mill Cranks, Calcining Plates for making Pearl Ashes, Cast Iron Screws for Falling and Paper Mills, Fullers Plates cast to any size, Sash Weights, Forge Hammers and Anvils, Plow Plates, Half Hundreds, Quarters, Fourteen and Seven Pound Weights; Cart, Waggon, Coach, Phaeton, Chair and Sulky Boxes, &c. &c. &c. ——— *Also,* Bells for *Churches, made of the best Bell Metal, from fifty to one thousand weight.*

N. B. Persons who want any Backs or other Ware, cast agreeable to particular Patterns, will please to send their Patterns to the Furnace, *near Mr. Atlee's Brewery, North-River, or leave them at the House of* Peter T. Curtenius, *No.* 48. *Great Dock-Street, near the Exchange.*

New-York: Printed by J. M'Lean, No. 41, *Hanover-Square.*

Ironmaking was a hazardous and risky business in New York. Many firms were short lived. NYHS

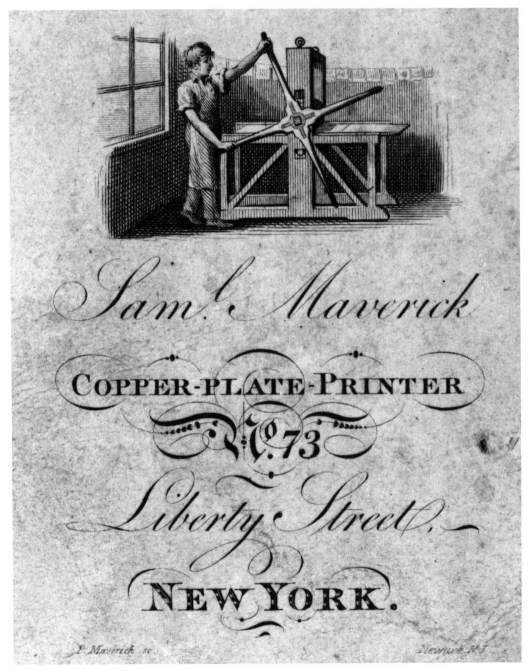

Broadside of Copper-Plate printer Samuel Maverick. NYHS

BANKING AND CREDIT

In order to expand their enterprises and take advantage of the burgeoning American and international markets, mechanics sought investment capital. While bankers were a major source of credit in the early republic, artisans were often turned away in favor of more prominent and more financially secure merchants. Too, banks commonly disdained doing business with mechanics because of the small amounts handled and the questionable nature of some notes. This proved no little source of frustration, and artisans sought to establish a bank that would service craftsmen as its primary function. Some mechanics were among the sponsors of the Manhattan Bank in 1799.[10] The first institution dedicated to tradesmen was the Mechanics Bank, chartered after a successful campaign in 1810 for $1.5 million, the largest capitalization of any city bank to that date (Documents 67–68).

The Charter of the Mechanics Bank provided that mechanics be given preference in the purchase of stock, that seven members of the Board of Directors be members of the sponsoring agency, the General Society of Mechanics and Tradesmen (an association of the city's most prominent masters) and that $600,000 be set aside for use by city tradesmen. Unfortunately, the Society loosened its membership standards and allowed nonartisans of high financial standing to join the Society and assume control of the bank. These directors oriented the bank's transactions more toward personal profit than toward the interests of mechanics. This caused much internal discord within the Society. According to fellow director Stephen Allen, it also caused the bankruptcy of seven members of the Board of Directors.[11] Although the bank survived, it separated from the Mechanics Society and proved a major disappointment to the artisan community. Also disappointing was a private bank venture organized by ironmonger Jacob Barker to service tradesmen's needs. Artisans attempted to rescue it from an attempt by the state legislature to outlaw all private banks (Document 69), but were unable to save it from succumbing to the Panic of 1819. Its failure caused considerable distress within the mechanic community.

Craftsmen, as part of their business practices, commonly extended credit. At any particular moment they would have a number of accounts outstanding, or else would hold the notes of out-of-city banks. This led to considerable problems either in the lack of or delay in payment, or else in the unreliability of bank notes. Mechanics often complained bitterly about the first problem, focussing their anger on the prominent who selfishly and condescendingly threatened the livelihood of the producer class (Document 70). Artisans also occasionally refused to accept credit, but in so doing seriously risked the loss of trade.

67. In Support of the Mechanics Bank

THE NEW BANK

A highly respectable Petition has gone to the Legislature from the Mechanics, and others in the City of New-York, praying for the incorporation of another Bank, to be called "The Mechanics Bank," and the best grounded hopes are entertained for its ultimate success.

Independent of the wealth, respectability and intelligence of this valuable body of the community—claims of themselves irresistible, I cannot but advocate the measure for other reasons equally weighty and important.

First—the amount of Banking Capital in this city is not commensurate with its opulence and commerce, and not proportionally so large as the capital in any other Atlantic city in the continent of America.—consequently there frequently remains in the market at the mercy of usurers a large amount of undoubted paper.

Secondly—the capricious, irregular, and arbitrary manner in which the affairs of *more than one* of our Banks are administered. Instead of loaning their funds with impartiality—a system of gross monopoly and favouritism notoriously exist, and for purposes which the private practices of several of their directors can best explain. At one period the honest unsuspecting merchant, lured by their liberality, is induced to share their favour unsparingly—when of a sudden without any visible cause he is taught to repent his credulity by a capricious rejection of his paper, when his wants are most urgent. If he remonstrates, instead of candidly avowing the truth, that their favourites who are deeply in debt, must not be abandoned—the question is evaded by some shallow pretext.

A Merchant

American Citizen, March 2, 1810

68. On Artisans' Need for the Mechanics Bank

MECHANICS BANK

. . . The solid funds of the city authorize and its fair and legitimate calls require an augmented Banking capital. The million and a half applied for by the Mechanic Society would not be disproportionate either to our property or our wants. The Bank too, contemplating as the petitioners do that a majority of its direction shall always be Mechanics, would extend relief to a valuable class of our citizens who generally stand in need of it. Fifty and $100 Notes which Mechanics issue are too trifling for notice at the present Banks. The middling class of the community therefore, which in all nations is the most valuable as well in peace as in war, are now excluded from Bank advantages. The intended Bank, if granted would embrace them, and by doing so add spirit to enterprise, vigour to industries, and wealth to the state.

American Citizen, March 8, 1810

A check made upon the Mechanics' Bank in 1853. Despite the bad faith and mismanagement of a number of the first directors, the bank survived and became a major institution in New York City, eventually becoming part of Chase Manhattan. While it never fulfilled the hopes of the artisan community for easy credit, much of its business was among well-to-do craftsmen. NYHS

69. Artisans' Support of Private (Exchange) Bank

At a very numerous and respectable meeting convened at Tammany Hall, agreeably to public notice, on Saturday evening, the 4th day of April 1818, JACOB HALSEY was appointed Chairman, and CHARLES N. BALDWIN, Secretary.

The following preamble and resolutions being read were unanimously adopted.

Whereas, a bill has passed the Senate, and is now pending before the House of Assembly of this state, prohibiting private banking and exempting the Exchange Bank of this city from its provisions for only three years: And whereas, should said bill become a law, it would operate very injuriously to a large proportion of the citizens of this district, inasmuch as it would destroy all competition with the incorporated banks, benefit the rich, oppress and benefit the poor, extend the power of existing aristocracies already too great, and ultimately terminate the banking transactions of an individual, whose loans have been highly advantageous to many laborious and industrious mechanics and neighboring farmers; and who commenced in this business with lawful authority embarking his fortune in its pursuit, and three years of his life having been devoted to his labors, in relation to which, this meeting cannot better express their sentiments than in the language of the honorable committee of the Senate—"that if any bill restraining private banking should pass, the proprietor of this institution should be exempt therefrom, without limitation or restriction, as an act of justice to which he is entitled upon every principle of private right, and public decency."

Therefore resolved, that every act of incorporation is a species of monopoly, and ought not to be granted, except in those cases where competent individuals cannot be found to carry on the business upon their own responsibility equal to the wants of the community.

Resolved, That in the opinion of this meeting, judging as well from our own experience, as from the report to the honorable Assembly, of their committee on currency, the conduct of the incorporated Banks has not been such as to entitle them to any particular benificence or reward from the Legislature.
. . .

Resolved, As the opinion of this meeting, that banking can be conducted by individuals, as much more beneficially for themselves and advantageously for the public, as any other business may be managed by an individual better than by an incorporated company.

Resolved, That previous to the establishment of the Exchange Bank, a great proportion of the Mechanics and small traders of this city did not participate in bank favors, although necessitated to receive the notes of their employers, and although they were necessarily compelled to suffer a due proportion of the evils inseparable from a paper system.

Resolved, That at all times since the establishment of this institution they have received a liberal support, the funds of the Bank, and the time of the proprietor being almost exclusively devoted to that class of the community, while the capital of the incorporated Banks has been generally employed in accomodating directors or the friends of directors, and other large dealers whose extensive speculations would attract the funds of every institution where they could obtain an ascendancy or even an influence.

Evening Post, April 16, 1818

70. The Difficulties of Collecting Debts: A Dialogue

Excuses, Or A New Way of Paying Debts.

Nearly a similar case with the following actually occurred with a poor but respectable mechanic, who had an account against a gentleman for less than five dollars. SAMUEL PRESTO.

Jan. 1st, called. 'O! this is Mr. L.'s bill – call any day next week.'

9th, called. 'Not at home.' When will he be home? 'Any time to-morrow.'

10th, called. 'Has a gentleman with him.' Wait an hour. 'Oh! this is the bill; look in on Tuesday.'

Tuesday, called. 'Leave the bill, I will look it over.'

Thursday, called. 'Not at home; gone to the hall.'

20th, called. 'There seems to be a mistake in the bill – I know nothing of this item – take it back and examine your books.'

24th, called. 'Just gone out.'

29th, called. 'I am busy now, I will call down and settle it.'

Feb. 16th, called. 'Bless me, I quite forgot to call – this bill not yet discharged! Bring me a receipt any time to-morrow or next day.'

17th, called. 'Gone out riding, and will not be back till the last of next week.'

March 1st, called. 'What! did I not settle that bill? surely that bill is paid; don't you remember calling here about ten days ago?' Yes, sir, I called, but you were then busy. 'Well, I'll examine – call next week.' Will you be good enough to fix a day? 'What insolence! If you make use of any more such language, I shall complain to your employer; at any rate, I am determined to procure a less troublesome mechanic; so, impudence, here's the amount of your bill; write a receipt in full in this book, and tell your employer I mean to have no further dealings with him.'

Independent Mechanic, August 10, 1811

TARIFF PROTECTION

A major factor in the overwhelming artisan support given the United States Constitution was the belief that a strong national government would institute tariffs and provide other encouragement for America's fledgling manufactures. And, on July 4, 1789, Congress did implement a general import duty with a "protective intent." It allowed certain needed raw materials in duty-free (wools, hides, copper, etc.) and imposed a general 5 percent *ad valorem* duty and other taxes on selected imports such as coaches, hats, and paper. A 10 percent discount was also extended to goods carried in American vessels, and a special duty of fifty cents per ton was charged on goods carried in foreign-built and foreign-owned ships.[12]

This measure, however, produced more revenue than protection, and artisans continued to encounter the difficult competition of the more sophisticated European and, particularly, British manufactures. Consequently, craftsmen forwarded numerous appeals to Washington requesting greater assistance. In a republican vein, the journeymen hatters insisted on the high quality of American goods as opposed to British imports. Moreover, they pointed out that American merchants, a non-productive class, were colluding with British merchants to undersell American-produced goods. Were not the Constitution and the republic established to support hard-working, productive journeymen (Document 71)? In a similar vein, the brewers argued that the support of beer production would much increase the public health (Document 72). Congress did grant a number of individual requests but refused to institute a truly protectionist policy, arguing that higher tariffs might restrict foreign markets for agricultural goods, thereby also injuring domestic craft enterprise (Document 73). After the War of 1812, however, in the wake of growing nationalism and severe taxes imposed on domestic manufactures, a real measure of protection passed Congress (1816).[13]

71. New York Journeymen Hatters: For Protection

COMMUNICATED TO THE HOUSE OF REPRESENTATIVES, DECEMBER 7, 1807.

To the Honorable the Senate and House of Representatives of the United States of America in Congress assembled, the petition of the subscribers, citizens of the United States and inhabitants of the city of New York, members of "the Journeymen Hatters Society" of that city, respectfully showeth:

That your petitioners have served regularly as apprentices to the hatting business, and are now working as journeymen to the said trade, and did expect, by their industry and attention to that art, to gain an honest livelihood for themselves and families; and that your petitioners, having full confidence in your honorable body, that you will give every encouragement and protection to the manufacturers of the United States, and lend every lawful assistance to those citizens thereof, who are immediately dependent on the encouragement which your honorable body in humble petition, praying that an additional impost

New York City was a center in the manufacture of American hats. European imports posed a serious threat to this craft. ANDERSON COLLECTION, NYPL

duty may be laid on hats. And as reasons therefor, your petitioners beg leave to state that, by the constant importations of that article, our home manufactures in that particular have diminished, and probably will continue to suffer, and perhaps finally go to ruin. Your petitioners further represent, that the present duty laid on hats is so inconsiderable, that mercantile men, particularly in this city, are enabled to import, and actually do import, from Europe, and sell, hats, at a less price than those of American manufacture; which obliges many, who have served a long time as apprentices and journeymen to the said trade, to abandon it, and resort to other means for supporting themselves and families. And your petitioners beg leave further to state to your honorable body, that the materials in this country, used for making hats, are equal, if not superior, to foreign produce of the same; and they are confident that the hats of the United States are superior to the European manufacture of the same article.

Wherefore, and inasmuch as your petitioners are attached to the liberties of this country, and are willing to hazard every thing for the maintenance of its rights and independence, they pray that your honorable body will, after having taken into consideration these circumstances, grant the prayer of your petitioners, and lay an additional impost upon the importing of hats from foreign countries, whereby your petitioners, and many others, similarly circumstanced, would be relieved from their present embarrassment, and the daily expectation of being deprived of employment in that art, which it has been their study for years to acquire.

Signed in behalf of the Society.

JAMES McCABE, *President*
AARON COATES, *Secretary.*

American State Papers, Finance, Vol. 2, p. 257

72. New York Brewers: For the Promotion of American Beer

PROTECTION TO MANUFACTURES.
COMMUNICATED TO THE HOUSE OF REPRESENTATIVES, FEBRUARY 3, 1812.

To the Senate and Representatives in Congress assembled:
The subscribers, brewers of malt liquor, in the city of New York, having long had to encounter with Many impediments to the extension of their business, so as to render it profitable either to themselves, or as an useful branch of manufactory to the community at large, take the liberty to suggest to

Congress, that while the consumption of ardent spirits continues to form so common a drink, for the generality of people, particularly among the laboring part of society, it will operate against the use of malt liquors, which circumstance, together with the quality of foreign beer heretofore imported, has lessened the consumption of the article manufactured at home, and which, in the event of the intercourse being opened, may again be the case.

With this view of the subject, we are induced to solicit the attention of Congress, in order that some legislative aid and encouragement may be afforded in the premises.

It is not for us to expatiate on the benefits which may result to the community, as to the preference, in point of health, which malt liquor may have to that of ardent spirits, or of the policy of encouraging the one, and of discouraging the other, even in a moral point of view; these are considerations, so connected with individual and general good, and so according with the system adopted by Congress, for promoting the manufactories of our country, and so congenial with the spirit of the nation, that we shall forbear expressing much on the subject.

We, therefore, submit to your consideration the propriety of adopting such measures as may be promotive of encouraging the manufactory, and use, of malt liquors, in the United States.

MURRAY & MILBANK, *and others.*
New York, 1st month, 19, (*January*) 1812.

American State Papers, Finance, Vol. 2, p. 528

73. Report of the House of Representatives Committee on Commerce and Manufactures on Memorials and Petitions

. . . much has been done already to encourage the domestic industry of our citizens.[14]

That industry, under such aids as the government by these means has given at a time when population is so rapidly increasing, has caused useful arts and manufactures to rise up and thrive in almost every part of the country, our works in wood, copper, hemp, leather and iron are already excellent and extensive. And if we do not excel in the manufacture of the finer articles of cotton, silk, wool and the metals, we may felicitate ourselves that by reason of the ease of gaining subsistence and the high price of wages, our fellow citizens born to happier destinies are not chained to the wretchedness of a strict discipline in such manufactories.

Our citizens are distinguished for their ingenuity and skill, they have invented many expedients by machinery to shorten and cheapen labor. The machine for making wool and cotton cards, the machines for ginning cotton, the machine for cutting and headless nails, the machinery for elevating wheat and for raising and stirring meal in mills, and the improvements in manufactures of musquets, class with the most useful inventions with which the age has been adorned.

. . .

In the meantime it ought to be considered, that there is great scope for agriculture, tillage, and rural employment in the United States. Agriculture is the great occupation which set in motion all kinds of manufacturers. It furnishes both the raw materials, and the articles of subsistence, to those who are engaged in manufacturing employments. The cultivation of the earth is therefore absolutely necessary to provide the ingredients for artizans to work upon, and the food for enabling them to live, while they are engaged in labor. This being the fact, the great question arises, whether we shall furnish raw materials and food to manufacturers in our own country, or in foreign lands? . . .

In a country devoted to agriculture, the cluster of arts and trades which minister to its wants spring up, of course, and almost from necessity. The plainer, coarser, and more useful fabrics in wood, wool, leather, iron, flax are manufactured with tolerable skill; while the more fine, costly, and high wrought articles of those several kinds can be procured more conveniently from foreign parts. And while the country consumer pays for the former with one part of his spare produce, he barters away the other part to procure a proportion of the latter.

There may be some danger in refusing to admit the manufactures of foreign countries; for by the adoption of such a measure we should have no market abroad for our produce, and industry would lose one of its chief incentives at home.[15]

. . .

American Citizen, February 9, 1804

MONOPOLY AND THE FEAR OF FACTORIES

T he presence and growth of factories in Great Britain was both well-known and feared by the entire artisan community: apprentice, journeyman, and master. Masters feared that the entry of such enterprises in America would cause them to lose control of their business to affluent industrialists and, eventually, to lose their personal independence and wealth. Journeymen and apprentices feared that factories would spell an end to whatever hope they had of becoming masters themselves and would also allow proprietors to lower their wages to subsistence or less. Mechanics believed that large-scale joint stock enterprises backed by mercantile capital would be able to monopolize a trade, driving out smaller and more vulnerable artisan operations through economic warfare. More than this, large-scale factories would overturn the proper republican political economy, based on agriculture and small-scale household manufacture, leading to extremes of wealth and poverty and to the political corruption of the new republic.[16]

This issue came to the fore most clearly and most dramatically in a dispute between the city and its bakers over the regulation of the price of bread. Angry that their profits were limited by the assize, a longstanding customary law that tied the price of loaf bread to the cost of flour,[17] bakers in the 1790s vigorously argued for the right to free enterprise: to sell bread at the price they pleased, letting the market regulate the price. This quest was granted by the Common Council in 1800 (Document 74). When the cost of flour declined a year later and bakers failed to lower their prices accordingly, the public—which relied on bread as the major staple in their diet (particularly among the poor and middling classes)—became indignant. The bakers angrily defended their actions and position (Document 75), but the pressure was too great. The Council reinstituted the assize, and the bakers in turn retaliated with a one-day work stoppage. This bold strike then triggered further angry public outcries (Document 76) highlighted by a meeting of a number of the city's most prominent merchants at the Tontine Coffee House. There they determined to form a factory-like operation for the manufacture and sale of bread: The New York Bread Company. Shares were quickly sold and, much to the consternation of the city's bakers, the enterprise prepared to go into production.[18] Quickly the debate shifted into an inquiry of whether "monopolistic" companies would be permitted to endanger artisan trades—a debate that raged throughout the city's newspapers and led to large meetings of concerned mechanics (Documents 77–79). The Bread Company did go into operation and with some success, but its life was cut short by a major fire a few years later.[19]

The baker's strike and the inception of The New York Bread Company are highly significant events, contrasting the bakers' dislike of regulation and desire to enter the marketplace unrestrained with their fear of the kind of corporation to which an open marketplace could give birth. Their detestation of regulation and supervision continued after the demise of the Bread Company, as their entrepreneurial spirit appeared stronger than their fear of the factory.[20]

A second important incident which deeply aroused mechanics' fears of monopoly took place in 1803 when Mayor Livingston proposed to the Mechanics Society that public workshops be established to provide the poor and disadvantaged—namely widows, orphans, handicapped, unskilled and ex-convicts—with artisan skills. The city's artisan community reacted with dismay and alarm to this proposal, fearing that it would create a public monopoly that would undersell mechanics as well as jeopardize their standing by placing them on the same level as criminals and outcasts (Document 80). This plan was hotly debated and eventually became a political issue. Artisans deemed it sufficiently grave to organize citywide to defeat the measure when it was presented to the State Legislature.[21]

Artisans' fear of factory enterprise was well-founded. While it would take years, large-scale manufactories that began to operate in the United States at this era would eventually overtake most artisan crafts. Most new American factories were located in New England, but a few began to operate in New York in the Jeffersonian age. The Federal Manufacturing Census of 1820 reveals the extent of a number of such operations. Among the businesses included in this survey were a marble and monument manufactory backed by $70,000 in capital, that employed one hundred men and fifty boys, paid annual wages of $90,000, and produced wares worth $120,000 per year; and an iron foundry, backed by $200,000, that employed seventy men and twelve boys, paid out $50,000 per year in wages, and used two steam engines and a boring mill to produce steam engine castings, screws, boilers and housewares.[22] The highly successful Lorillard tobacco manufactory processed from 250,000 to 300,000 pounds of tobacco a year, and a new textile concern produced satin and broad clothes using steam-powered spindles and looms. This latter manufactory, not unlike the ones in New England, was still struggling at this time to maintain a profit margin and to compete with similarly produced goods shipped in from Europe.

74. Committee of the Common Council on the Regulation of Bakers

That having met a Committee from the Bakers in this City and having heard all their reasonings on the subject they are of the Opinion that perhaps the only Mode this Board can adopt to afford Relief to the Petitioners and the Citizens at large would be to regulate in future the weight of Bread only and not the Price, leaving that to the Bakers. This would create an emulation among the Bakers and would of course produce good Bread and in the opinion of the Committee at a reasonable Price. The Committee are further of Opinion that all Loaf Bread baked for sale should be of the weight of one pound and an half and of three pounds and that any Loaf Bread offered for sale on a less weight should be liable to seizure and the Baker fined.

Jacob De la Montaigne
Selah Strong

Minutes of the Common Council, July 14, 1800

75. In Defense of the Bakers

For the American Citizen

Messrs. Printers,
Observing a paragraph in Friday's *Citizen* referring to the condition of the bakers of this city, I take upon myself to relate a few facts, which, I trust, will place the matter in a different light; the writer of the paragraph says the price of a one shilling loaf of bread is now the same as when flour sold for twelve dollars per barrel, though the barrel now costs only nine dollars. This I deny. Flour is now selling at 9½ dollars for southern flour, and indeed some flour merchants have this day asked for 10 dollars, and it should also be remembered that though the price of flour may be low today, yet the whole stock that a baker has

to buy is generally laid in for eight and twelve weeks. Now it is said to the meanest capacity, that if in baker's stock it cost him 12 dollars or 13 (which a great part has) he surely can no way afford to work up that flour at the rate of 8 dollars. I do not remember ever to have seen any lamentable paragraph bemoan the poor bakers' fate when he received an assize for selling his flour at $10 when he bought it at 12. Yet this has frequently been the case, and the hardships the greater, because the evil rested upon a few individuals. But in the other case if any evil at all, it is borne by so many that no one can feel it. The law respecting the assize of bread at present, says, that every loaf shall weigh one, two, three and four pounds, but the price is left to the workman. Can any thing be more reasonable or just?

What right, or if right is assumed, what justice is there in any law, which limits the profit of one class of citizen's labor, and leaves every other free as the air? Would the merchant be satisfied, if a law should say, your wine and your rum, your sugar and your tea has cost you so much, yet you shall not take more than so much profit when you sell it again? There is as much reason and justice in the corporation saying to his shoemaker, your side of leather costs you 20 shillings, you shall not get more than 8 shillings for a pair of shoes, as for them to limit the profit of any other business. The bakers are associated for the purpose of apportioning the price of bread to that of flour, under the present regulations of the Corporation. But the greater part of the public are averse to have any odd pence attached to a pound [loaf] or even deducted from it. This has already been tried. Not only the grocers of the city, but many others of the in-

Emblem of the Society of Bakers as displayed at the celebration in honor of the completion of the Erie Canal. The design was taken directly from that of the London Bakers Society. NYHS

habitants formed an association and compelled the bakers to sell their bread at even money, or take it home again. The typographist further states, that the bakers are getting enriched by which I suppose he means they are advancing fast towards independency. I will ask the paragraphist—I will ask the Corporation of the city, or I will even ask the whole world to provide me one rich loaf-bread baker. Or let them even point out one that ever will grow rich in his trade, under any such regulation. In every other trade and profession, you will find some well engaged there, who have never been trained up to the particular profession, but who have entered into it with a vision of making a fortune. But search the globe (for I will not confine them to this city or even London) and shew me the man that engaged in the loaf-bread baking business, who was not brought up to it, and by thereat means compelled to follow it for want of a better.

The bakers have had several meetings lately, for the purpose of lowering the price of bread, as soon as their stock of 12 dollar flour is worked off, and though the public were not opposed to add 3 pence to the price of a loaf, when the price of flour made it absolutely necessary on the pain of inconvenience to make change; yet they will be again tried, to take 2 pence from the price of bread.

A BAKER

American Citizen, October 27, 1801

76. On the Necessity of Regulating the Bakers

A writer, in the *Daily Advertiser* of yesterday morning, in an address "to the Corporation of the City," censures the proceedings of the magistracy for the measures they have lately adopted to ensure to the citizens a supply of bread, made of proper materials and of a specific weight. He considers it "*impolite*," and "*arbitrary*," to "*limit a set of men, to a certain price, for a certain quantity of any article.*"

He has stated his reasons (if reasons they can be called) for his opinion; but we apprehend that both his opinion, and the reasons on which it is grounded, in the judgment of candid and well-disposed men, will be found to rest on the "baseless fabric" of prejudice.

"When bakers are unlimited," he says, "many compounds and qualities of bread will be made that are wholesome, as Indian meal, rice potatoes, &c. which would supply the poor cheaper than when the bakers are confined to wheat or rye."

But it does not occur to this writer that the bakers would ever *abuse this privilege*—that under the influence of *self-interest*, they would think of *accommodating themselves*, before they *accommodated the poor*.

In fact, the experiment has been sufficiently tried here, to open the eyes of those who are *willing to see*, and to justify the proceedings of the Corporation, and of those gentlemen who have associated under the name of the "Bread Company." In Charleston, S.C., in Baltimore, in Philadelphia and the West Indies, the bread is in general, far superior to that of this city. Strangers, who reside here, or who pass through our city, ask why our bread is of so inferior a quality, when we are able to command the best of materials.

To compound bread of various materials, may answer well enough in families, but is a dangerous privilege when extended to any *body of men*. It is setting private interest against the public duty—two principals, which the universal experience of civilized society has determined *ought* not to be put in opposition.

As to the "arbitrary" nature of the ordinance of the corporation; this writer seems to have formed a very incorrect idea of the true meaning of the word "arbitrary." Displacing a man from office, whose conduct has been faultless, or making an order, and revoking it again without a cause, may be said to be "arbitrary." But a *permanent regulation*, the result of *deliberate enquiry*—and aiming at the general good, can, with no propriety, be considered as "arbitrary." On the principles of this writer it might be alleged by the *millers* that is was "impolitic and arbitrary" to oblige them to make flour of a certain quality, subject to inspection, and to condemnation, if the flour were not of the quality required by law; by the importers of ardent spirits, that their liquors should be examined by a public officer and the quality of the spirits designated by a brand on the cask; and by the attornies and physicians, that their fees for services performed, should be "limited" by law. The truth is, *salus populi suprenta lex*—the public good is the first of laws. No one doubts the *authority* of the corporation to make the ordinance in question. Every dispassionate citizen must believe, they have been influenced by motives of the most laudable nature; every householder must be conscious that *already* the effects of their firmness and prudence are perceivable in the *quality* and *weight* of the bread—and the most interested should know and recollect, that resistance to the declared will of legal constituted authority is as contrary to the interest and happiness of the community, as it is to the principles of an enlightened policy and of good government.

Commercial Advertiser, November 12, 1801

77. New York City Artisans: Organize Against Monopoly

At a Meeting of MECHANICS, computed to be about 300 persons, the following resolutions were unanimously adopted – This meeting was held on the evening of the 8th inst. at Matheiu's Hotel agreeable to notice.

Wm. G. Miller, Chairman of the Meeting.

Resolved, That the Address read this evening, be published in the public papers of this city, for two days.

Resolved, That this meeting recommend to all the free Mechanics and Tradesmen of this city, the propriety and utility of uniting themselves in One Great Association, for the purpose of maintaining their general interests and equal Rights, as Mechanics.

Resolved, That it be recommended by this meeting to all the Mechanics and Tradesmen of this city, that they will not countenance any Monopolizing Speculators who embark in the pursuit of any mechanic branch whatever, by *employing* them, or be *employed* by them, while they are engaged in any mechanic branch or business, as the consequences of such monopoly may become fatal to every description of Tradesmen.

Resolved, That there be a Committee appointed this evening to draft a Memorial to the honorable Legislature of this state, praying that they will not grant any Charter of Incorporation to any set of men who work, either directly or indirectly, to monopolize any mechanic branch or business; which may be conveniently carried on by individuals; and likewise, that they will pass a resolve, recommending same to future Legislators.

Resolved, That this Committee chuse four persons from each Ward, to assist in procuring signature to the Memorial to be presented to honorable Legislature.

American Citizen, December 14, 1801

78. On Monopoly and the Destruction of Artisan Enterprise and Independence

For This Gazette

Fellow Citizens—No doubt you have long since heard of the attempt of certain monied men to establish in this city a Bread Company, in order, as they say, to alleviate the distresses of the poor; but, in fact, for no other purpose, than to establish a kind of banking system, and to monopolise by degrees all profitable mechanic branches, and at the same time to crush that independent spirit, which is so common among American mechanics, and so galling to the pride of most stockholders. The attempt is not only made, but even put in execution; and a greater addition to their capital is already subscribed, in order to secure the ruin and destruction of the Bakers, a class of citizens as respectable as any other branch of mechanics. Although this company has begun with the bakers, it will not stop there, but proceed gradually to the establishment of as many other branches as their capital will admit of. You must remember, fellow-citizens, that the Company are what is called monied men; 9 or 10 per cent is as much as they desire, or at least as much as they expect. But where is the mechanic that can make a living at such a percentage on his small capital? A company of this kind, if permitted to take place in one instance, will soon bring wretchedness and ruin to thousands of those who now least expect it. Do you not perceive, that from the vast amount of their capital, and numerous connections they possess advantages which you do not, witness the purchasing of large quantities of materials and very long credit, without the necessity of going to such expence for houses, in proportion to their capital, as you are obliged to. From the extent of the various pursuits you may enter into, they will find it to their advantage to keep hundreds of cartmen, masons, carpenters, and others, in their service, not as their workmen, as is not the practice, but as their servants. These will only receive common laborers' wages, the profits deriving therefrom going to the Company; they can save at least one third of your necessary expences; and should you try to oppose them, it will avail nothing, for while you must maintain your wives and children from the profits of that business, this company will not mind losing a year or two's interest for the sake of ruining a few obstinate mechanics, who from being masters, are unwilling to become servants. The consequence will be, that you must forget you have been a respectable mechanic, and now become a common labourer to some such company. It is the nature of mankind, to be always adding to what they already have; and you will find to your sorrow, that the company, after having ruined you in your business, and reduced you to the necessity of becoming one of their labourers, they will then reduce the small wages you may earn, to a mere nothing, and by that means effect the object of their desire, that of reducing mechanics to servants and labourers. Mechanics of every description, remember, that you form one class of citizens; remember that each of your professions is a link of that chain which united you altogether as a body; suffer one link to be broken, and you are disunited forever—therefore, use your influence to prevent the Company of Bakers from getting a charter.—An attempt is now making to break your chain and the link they are working on is the bakers; if no opposition is made, they succeed. The bakers are ruined first, shipbread bakers will be next, and in due time each of your professions will be monopolized by some such company. What will be the consequence they have established themselves in most branches, as to find employment for two, three or five thousand men? First they will screw down the wages to the last thread; next, that independent spirit, so distinguished at present in our mechanics, and so useful in public, will be entirely annihilated. The workmen will be servants and slaves, and their votes must be always at the command of their masters; and in a short time our elections would be, what they already are in England, a disgrace to any nation.

A MECHANIC

New York Gazette, November 14, 1801

79. In Defense of the New York Bread Company

To the Editor of the Mercantile Advertiser

Sir:

The late subject of the Bakers, although from the nature of it unconnected with politics, has afforded a proof how far people will endeavor to link everything with a spirit of Party. Although all parties are concerned, and it touches the interests of the whole; yet, in order to influence the passions, and give a fictitious weight to their favorite argument, much pain has been taken to make it a political controversy.

Let us, therefore, endeavour to take up the matter more coolly. The article of bread is an important one in all cities, and it is the concern of every inhabitant to be supplied with it on the best terms—the value of a loaf is easily reducible to a standard from the relative price of flour – It is therefore a great consequence to prevent imposition either in the weight or quality of our Bread. In order to guard this point, it has been thought necessary to establish by law an Assize – but here – the contest arises – shall bakers be restricted in their profits, while other manufacturers are left free? – It is tyrannical – it is unjust. This is very true, no man should be restrained in his profits by any power – it is fundamentally contrary to every principle of justice, and strikes at the root of industry.

If bakers impose on the public, let us remedy the abuse, but let us do it by just means – if they exact unreasonable profits, they do but teach us a lesson against themselves by inviting opposition. They should remember the old maxim that "trade will regulate itself." – Their complaints should not be directed to the Company lately established – as this was the natural effect of their own conduct and narrow policy, in wishing to make money too rapidly.

Opposition is the very spirit of trade, it is the regulator which never fails to regulate abuses; it is what every man in business must expect; and the bakers have no more reason to complain than tailors, shoemakers or Brokers – If the Bread Company can afford to supply the city on better terms than private individuals, it is just they should be encouraged; and if they should sell their loaves too high, the market is open to such as are willing to supply at a lower rate.

A BREAD EATER

Mercantile Advertiser, November 17, 1801

80. Mechanics Society Declines to Support Mayor Livingston's Public Workshop Proposal

To the Honourable EDWARD LIVINGSTON,[23]
Mayor of the City of New-York
New-York, February 3d, 1803

SIR,

Your communication to the General Society of Mechanics and Tradesmen, of the city of New-York, under date of the first ult., has been received and duly considered.

We beg leave to inform you, that we applaud your patriotism, in recommending the amelioration of human misery, and a restoration to the community of such as have been lost to it; and believe that each of us, as fellow-citizens and fellow men, are in duty bound to empart to others, a portion of the blessings afforded by a benevolent Providence, thereby alleviating the sorrows of the suffering poor, be the cause of their suffering what they may.

We therefore coincide with you in sentiment, that those who have suffered the penalties adjudged them for their crimes and would prefer honest labour to committing depredations on the public, ought to receive such encouragement, as to foster those principles, and make them useful to themselves, their friends, and to society.

But sir, we are impressed with a full conviction, that in the Situation in which we stand (could we approve of the measure) it would be extremely improper, for this society to enter into a work of the kind you have been pleased to propose.

When this society was incorporated, it was found necessary it should have for its primary object, that kind of charity the charter points out; while it was easy to be discovered, that any interference in the politics of the state – the police of the city – or other public concerns, would not only be wrong in itself, but would lead to discord among the members, and inevitably tend to impress the mind of the public with sentiments prejudicial to its institution, and consequently check its rising prosperity.

From these considerations this society has uniformly declined a cooperation, not having for its object the aid of the indigent members, their widows and children.

The propriety of this declining will be very obvious, when viewed in relation to the plan suggested.

First, because the members at present composing this society, make but an inconsiderable number, when compared to the mass of mechanics and tradesmen in this city and, therefore, our interference would be highly improper, inasmuch as our fellow mechanics would have reason to apprehend, we had lost sight of our original object, and would in time become an engine of oppression.

Secondly. It would be a vain attempt to persuade the mechanics of this city (*who suitably appreciate their weight within the community*) that an institution running counter to their interest, and which would converge to monopoly, could be beneficial to them, the public, itself patriotic, although it was conducted under the auspices of this society.

Thirdly, this society would act faithless, taking on itself the responsibility of a measure so degrading to mechanics by bringing them into a competition with men convicted of violations of the law . . . .

First, an institution of this kind, would not only have a tendency to keep convicts here, but to encourage others from other states and countries to resort to this city, where they might always be sure of employment till an opportunity offered for them to commit crimes . . . .

Secondly, such an institution would materially check a spirit of industry and enterprise, so essential to stimulate youth in acquiring a knowledge of the various branches, by which they could expect to get a livelihood in mature age – especially when it is considered that they must serve a seven year apprentice; while those who have forfeited the confidence of the public, will find ready employment, after having for a short time (*within the walls of a prison*) wrought at a trade of which they have but a partial knowledge.

But says the communication, "the rate of wages given by this institution should be _____ per cent less than is usually given to workmen of equal abilities." This arrangement, so far from preventing evil, would strike at the very vitals of the mechanic interest; and if the labour cost less, the manufactures would be vended at a cheaper rate, than those of the mechanic who works only on his own small capital; which must in the nature of things lend him to a competition proving ruinous to his business, while he has the mortification to reflect, that he must contribute by tax to the very funds that are pledged to sap his interest in society; and would in the issue, bring poverty to families that might otherwise have constant employment, and receive for their labour a suitable reward.

With respect to such other indigent as are mentioned in the plan, we only venture to presume, that in a city so famed for benevolence, the industrious poor will always be employed, in proportion to the quantum of business there is to be done; nor can we conclude that those who have atoned for their crimes and are reformed in their lives, will be left unemployed, when engaged in honest pursuits.

Under these impressions, and upright views, we are very adverse to the scheme laid before us; and are of the opinion, that the evils removed would be incomparably less than those it would create; and therefore believe that "industry may be left for the most part to its own direction," then "the people will divide themselves into different professions; their different skills will enable them to make a prudent choice, and lead them to pursuits, in which their private advantage, and that of the public, will concur."

We remain Sir,
With sentiments of esteem and respect
By order and in behalf of the General Society
of Mechanics and Tradesmen of the
City of New-York

James Warner, President
Wm. Whitehead, Sec'y.

American Citizen, February 12, 1803

LICENSED TRADESMEN

Municipal regulation of critical goods and services such as the price of bread was built and supported on a long tradition of British and American legislation that placed the good of the community before the interest of the private citizen. This dominance of the moral economy and just price, common to the pre-industrial economy and subject to enforcement by the strength of popular crowds, still held sway in early national New York in a number of critical professions. Along with the bakers, cartmen and butchers operated under strict municipal regulations and standards. To carry on their trades, these men were required to receive licenses; butchers were also required to be allotted one of the coveted stalls in the city's markets.[24]

Cartmen constituted the largest single group of tradesmen, numbering 1200 in 1800. Required by the city to own their own horse and cart, they provided the metropolis with its means of transport as well as garbage collection and wood delivery. City ordinances passed by the Common Council included published price lists for the haulage of various materials; standards of behavior for drivers while in the streets; and restrictions forbidding drivers themselves to buy or sell firewood. The latter rule was to prevent cartmen from cornering (fore-stalling) the market to drive up prices. Even more protests were filed against haulers who broke the law by buying up firewood and thus forcing up the price of fuel in winter—to the special detriment of the poor. Fines were imposed on those caught, but this was a difficult ordinance to enforce (Document 81).

In return for their submission to regulation and licensing, cartmen de-manded protection of their trade by the city fathers. They were particularly angry in 1818 when Irish immigrants who had been allowed temporary licenses during the labor shortage caused by the War of 1812 began to take away business from the regularly licensed drivers. The cartmen wanted the licenses of these aliens suspended, and when Mayor Cadwallader Colden refused this led to an angry exchange (Documents 82–83).

Butchers did not have their prices regulated, but their scales were closely watched, as was the quality of the meat they sold. The most important step in a butcher's early career was securing a license and stall in one of the city markets (Document 84).[25] A good location in a busy market could mean a very comfort-able profit, while no stall or one situated far from traffic could mean an income closer to subsistence level. Consequently the Common Council's Market Committee was subject to many strongly worded requests by the city's meathandlers. The Committee was also responsible for the discipline of miscreant butchers, for handling complaints from the public and butchers, and for deciding upon requests for market transfers (Document 85).

In its regulatory function, the city was also held responsible for ensuring that no artisan craft gravely endangered the well being of local inhabitants. Many pre-industrial trades, such as butchering, distilling, tanning, and tallow-chandling produced waste products ('effluvia') that were at worst noxious and at best distasteful and uncomfortable to the nearby population. It was the duty—long established by English common law—of the municipal government and courts to determine whether the good produced by the enterprise outweighed the danger and discomfort it created. The city community received complaints from unhappy residents such as the protest noted earlier about the slaughterhouse (see Document 18). A number of trials were held on this account, including the one presented here concerning the discharges and dangers produced by a carpentry shop (Document 86). The city took its responsibilities seriously; many craftsmen found themselves in difficulty because of infractions, including one petitioner who argued that he should not be held responsible for the behavior of a runaway apprentice (Document 87). However, defining the correct balance between the needs of the city and the rights of the mechanic entrepreneur was not an easy task. The Street Commissioner and Common Council spent many an hour considering which ordinances to enact.

Finally, in carrying out its regulatory duties, the Council hired many artisans. It received large numbers of petitions from disabled or otherwise incapacitated mechanics who sought a position as such bread inspector, measurer, or firewood inspector in order to stay clear of the ignominy of public relief. Many petitioners invoked prior Revolutionary military service as they asked that society now furnish them with a respectable livelihood, arguing that both their sacrifice and the obligations of a truly republican government entitled them to nothing less (Document 88).

81. On the Forestalling of Wood

To the Editor of the *Morning Post*

Sir,

It were much to be wished that the Dracos and Solons of this modern Athens, in their passion for Legislating, instead of making sage regulations, which do not harm, indeed, because nobody complies with them, would turn their attention to objects of more importance; wise Aldermen, who eat Turtle—ay, and digest it too—will, I hope, be able to digest what I am going to say; else there is not help for it, and they must be surfeited in spite of the whole *College of Physicians*. Let the Boys swim and the Dogs run, and the Horses trot, and the Cartmen drive full tilt over old women and little children *in spite of our Laws*—but let the Common Council listen to the detail of what is ten times worse than even all these together.

The price of Wood is now $4 per load, notwithstanding the present Summer weather. Is this owing to any scarcity in the country at large, or even in the city: I answer No. The landings on the river from Lunenburg to Dobbs' Ferry, exhibit huge piles of wood ready for our market. Why do not the boats bring it down, during the present fine weather, and in the dearth of all other freight? It is because this wood is forestalled by *humane city speculators*, who stand on tiptoe, waiting with eager impatience until the shrill winter winds—sweet the music to *their* ears, and the keen frosts that follow, shall enable them to wring from the hard hand of freezing poverty enormous and cruel profit. This is the primary evil; the next is, that the moment a vessel arrives with a cargo of wood, which has by miracle caught their attention, while prowling about the country, it is immediately forestalled, and deposited in yards, there to be hoarded until occasion offers to sell it at the price which the owner's greed dictates, or the bitter cold may *force* the wretched buyer to give. Our wharves swarm with these *righteous* speculators who haunt the docks to *filch* from the citizens an opportunity of imposing on *unsuspecting* simplicity of the boatmen, purchasing his wood at the *real market price*.

. . .

I have endeavoured briefly to point out the real causes of this evil, an evil which is felt by all, but more especially by those desolate beings whose natural and inevitable wants are at all times sufficient to excite our sympathy, without being aggravated by artificial rapacity. In the present state of all our maritime cities when the willing labourer is often without employment, and his family without bread—when honest industry is frequently involved in the common fate of profligate idleness; it is now time to attempt to add to their distresses by speculating upon the probable severity of the winter's cold; and the indignation of every honest mind ought to be roused at these attempts to make a market of the poor man's miseries. If, indeed, the forestallers of wood were actuated by the benevolent desire of supplying the poor with fuel at a reasonable rate, when the rivers should be shut, one might be brought at least to pardon this exertion of short sighted and mis-directed humanity—for mis-directed it is, because it enhances the price of the article during all the rest of the year. But when we reflect and *know* that this *infamous monopoly* is created for the sole purpose of *dirty gain*, to be drawn from those who in winter are too often *hungry* as well as *cold*, and whose hard alternative it sometimes is, to die of the *first*, or perish with the *latter*. When we know that this blessing is hoarded only for the purpose of making a commodity of distress, the trafficking with the miseries of

Poverty; I should like to hear by what extraordinary merits these men hope to make reparation to society; or by what strange immunity of obscurity or insignificance they expect to escape the public abhorrence?

. . .

> I am sir,
> A POOR MAN

Morning Post, November 21, 1811

82. Mayor Colden to Cartmen on the Licensing of Aliens

Gentlemen

I have attentively considered your communication of the 26th instant— Your reasoning with respect to the propriety of refusing licences to unnaturalised foreigners appears to me perfectly just;—Immediately after I came into office I perceived that if cartmens licences were granted to persons who were not liable to perform the same duties and bear the same burdens as our citizens, it would be gaining them an advantage which they ought not to have, and therefore I have uniformly refused to grant a licence to any one who was not a Citizen. I shall continue to observe this rule unless I am compelled to sway from it, by the Legislature, or Common Council. On the other I think it would be unjust to deprive a foreigner of a licence which he has heretofore obtained. This might in many cases produce great distress—If hereafter the course I now pursue is adhered to, the evil resulting from licencing foreigners will, in a little time, cure itself.—

No doubt there are many Violations of the law which relates to this subject, and it is obvious that they are as injurious to regular and respectable cartmen as they are to the community. You may be assured that I feel every disposition and will use every exertion to correct these abuses; but the magistrates can not do this, let them be ever so vigilant, without the assistance of those who have opportunities of knowing by whom the offences against the laws are committed. It is not sufficient to inform us that abuses exist—we must be informed of the persons who commit them, and the names of Witnesses by whom the facts can be proved. When ever this information is furnished prosecutions will be commenced and the event must, as in all other cases, depend on the decision of the proper tribunal—the Mayor, it is true, is authorised to take

A Cartman at work. These drivers did many tasks, including hauling of goods from the docks to stores and warehouses and vice-versa to street work and the collection of manure. ANDERSON COLLECTION, NYPL

away a licence, but as this summary proceeding deprives a Citizen of a trial by a jury of his country, it ought to be, and will be very cautiously exercised—

I can not approve of that part of your communication which seems to threaten that in certain events you will follow the example of those of whom you complain. This would be putting yourself on a footing with them and would lead to consequences in which I should be sorry to see you involved. I hope as good citizens you will think better on this subject—Let us unite in our endeavours to observe and to enforce the observance of the laws and we may hope that all parties will in a little time have reason to be satisfied—I am Gentlemen with respect your most humble serv.

> Cadwallader Colden[26]
> Mayors Office 27 May 1818

To Mr. John Butler Chairman & William Coquillet Secy. of
Committee of Cartmen—

City Clerk Filed Papers, NYCMA

83. Response of Cartmen on the Licensing of Aliens

New York June 1st 1818

To the honourable the Corporation of the City of New York in Common Council Convened,

      We the Committee that represents the great body of Licenced Cartmen of this City having sometime since present to your honourable body a petition praying for an Amendment in the present Law which was passed for the better regulation of the licenced Cartmen of the City of New York

      The Justness as well as the expediency of such a measure we Conceive to be fully Acknowledged by the honourable board in refering the petition to his honour the Mayor and thereby intended to answer the prayer of the petition, your petitioner conceives that it will not answer the purpose nor carry into effect the purposes for which our petition was presented. From the Just as well as the patriotick spirit that attends and marks your Deliberations in the Decisions made by your honourable Body we kneed but state that the Rights Liberties & privalages which we as a body of Citizens have prayed for are strictly and justly established upon the fact that our fathers having relinquished individual Interest & Substance with Spilling theire Blood & Laying down their Lives to obtain the Rights and privalages of free men and bequeathe the Inheritance to us theire offspring. This they did having Respect unto the Reward more than the Gold of Brittain. With this petition we present the decision of his honour the mayor in our Case and at the same time beg Leave to state wherein it will not answer the perpose desired and for which it is Intended. In reflecting upon this your honorable body cannot we trust but perceive that our Rights and Claims are founded upon the Broad Ground of Reason & Justice as may more clearly understood by refering to the first Sentance expressed in the polite and Liberal answer of his Honour the mayor to our Communication to him on this subject. The words are as follows, I have attentively Considered your Communication of the 26th Inst. your reasoning with respect to the propriety of refusing Licences to unnaturalised foreigners appears to me to be perfectly Just.

      Therefore after having fully established the principal that those rights and liberties privalages are ours as free Citizens who have to bare the Burden and expences upon the Grounds of reason and justice it remains with your honourable Body alone to say whether we shall enjoy them or whether those Disinterested shall divide them with us. Already have we been under the necessity of rallying around the standard of Liberty to maintain and support those very Laws and Constitution that guarrenties them to us while at the same time we have beheld those verry men Instead of Casting in theire Lot with us shrink back and Claim the privalages of Aliens and enter into bonds and security which was much more trouble than Swaring Alegance to a Contry which they profess to have adopted by Coming to it to reside. Your honourable body is not aware what material Injury we have sustained in these times of troubles by theire enjoying the privalages which as Citizens Could not and duty to our Contry should not in such a time that Claimed our Services in another way, we who was in employ by having to attend to the duties of a Soldiers Life had to relinquish our Imployment they having the opportunity offered thereby and from the Number of them have secured the principal part of the Merchants employ throughout this City your honourable body may rest assured that this fact is so well established that it needs no Comment. His honour having stated that the Course he had adopted to persue if after this should be strictly attended to (which we have no security for not knowing who may preside in time to come as Mayor) would Cease of Itselfe. To this we would most humbly reply that owing to the number and the privalages they enjoy being exempt from all duties both as Citizens and Soldiers is Clearly mannifest to us will take some forty or fifty years before it would accomplish the desired end. His honour having further stated that it would be unjust to deprive them of Licence who have them they having expanded all in establishing themselves in the Business. We would in answer to this Decision pray that it might be considered how much more unjust it is that we should Bare the Burden and pay of our hard earnt pittance to support them in such privalages and would venture to say that many of them Drives for men who follow other Business & Divide the proffit arising therefrom. To evade the Law under a fictitious sale of Both horse & Cart.[27]

We must acknowledge with no Small degree of gratitude and esteem it a great favour Confered upon us by his honour the mayor in his Candid Assurance of using every means to Check the evasions of the Law in which we pledge ourselves to render our cordial support. But the manner in which it is to be done will we feare exaust our patience for to Leave our daily employers whereby we obtain our Bread for our family and attend upon this part of our duty day after day while the Case is argued by Councill before a Jury is more than our Circumstances will allow of we had Better all be Aliens in this Case as well as many others if this is to be the end of our Informing against violation of the Sovereign Authority. The last part of his honours Communication we shall mention is respecting threatning. This we beg Leave to State is a misunderstanding in reading our Communication for we there state or ment to state that we the Committee have Been told by others the most wealthiest amongst us if others where not stoped from keeping a number of horses & carts Drove under a fictitious sale of the same that they themselves would persue the same Coarse and are only waiting to se the end of our petitioning.

For further Information we refer the Honbl. the Common Councill to the answer to his honour which accompany this petition and pray that the prayer of the original petition may be granted.

John Butler Chairm
Wm. Coquillet Sec.

By order of the Committee.

City Clerk Filed Papers, NYCMA

This drawing of the Fly Market reveals in the background the butchers in their stalls, and, in the foreground, female hucksters selling their wares, usually vegetables. The location of a stall within a certain market or the attainment of a stall in one of the more congested rather than one of the more isolated markets was a matter of the highest concern to applicants for butchers' licenses. There were more applications than the Market Committee could grant. The Committee also received many requests to relocate to different stalls. ABRAHAM VALENTINE ENGRAVING, MCNY

84. Petition of John Lyons for Butcher's Stall

To the Honorable the Mayor Aldermen and Commonalty of the City of New York in Common Council Convened

The Petition of John Lyons of the said City Butcher

Humbly Sheweth

That the Petitioner served a regular Apprenticeship to the Butchers trade in the said City with Messrs. John Hopkins and George Shep, and the term of his Apprenticeship having Exspired, he now wishes to set up his Business.

The Petitioner therefore humbly prays, that your Honours will be pleased to grant him a Licence, to follow his Trade, and that he may be favoured with a Grant of the Stand No. 9 in the Otswago Market, which Stand is vacant as the Petitioner is informed and as in duty bound the Petitioner will ever pray

John Lyons

New York April 30, 1803.

We the Subscribers recommend the above Petitioner John Lyons as a faithfull, Sober & industrious Man, Worthy of Your Honours Attention

George Ship
William Lawrence

Referred to Market Com.
Admitted provided the stall applyed is vacant.

City Clerk Filed Papers, NYCMA

A butcher in his stall. All weights and measures as well as the quality of the meat was carefully regulated by the Market Committee and their appointed inspectors. NICCOLINO CALYO, WATER-COLOR; NYHS

85. Petition of Butchers Against Forestalling of Livestock

To the Honorable, the Corporation of the City of New York in Common Council convened —

The Memorial of the Subscribers, respectfully sheweth —

That your Memorialists are Butchers, regularly licensed to sell Meats, in the Markets of this City —

That Henry Astor,[28] and certain others, who are also licenced Butchers, leaving the Care of their Stalls, and the selling of their Meats, to Journeymen, and others, who are not licenced Butchers, are in the constant practice of forestalling the Market, by riding into the Country to meet the drovers of Cattle, coming to the New York markets, and purchasing them up to sell again to other Butchers — That the said Henry Astor, is also in the constant practice of purchasing Cattle for other Stalls beside his own, and does not personally attend at any Stall —

That it is also become very customary for Drovers of Cattle from the Country, after selling their own Cattle, to purchase other Droves, and sell them out singly at an advanced price; thereby forestalling the market–That your Memorialists, by their regular, and constant attendance at their Stalls, have it not in their power to counteract these pernicious practices, but are thereby prevented from purchasing Cattle upon so good terms as they otherwise could, and are often obliged to purchase from the said forestallers, at an advanced price–That in consequence thereof the price of Butchers Meat is very considerably enhanced, to the great detriment of the City--

Your Memorialists therefore pray that your Honorable board would take the circumstances above mentioned, into the serious consideration and by such rules, regulations and active measures as they shall think fit and expedient, restrain the said Henry Astor, and others from forestalling the Markets, in manner aforesaid, and to do such other Acts and things in the premises as they in their wisdom shall think proper–

Dated New York June 2$^\text{d}$ 1801

Wm. Wright	John Forman
Wm. Cost	Alex Fink
Edward Patten	Joseph O. Bogart
Alex Peacock	Philip Fink
David Marsh	

City Clerk Filed Papers, NYCMA

Butchers in procession behind bull in front of the Bull's Head Inn, a watering hole for meat-handlers.
WILLIAM CHAPPEL, OIL ON CARDBOARD, EDWARD ARNOLD COLLECTION, MMNY

86. Prosecution of New York Carpentry Shop as a Nuisance

William Hamilton and James Latham's Cases

RODMAN, Counsel for the prosecution.

The Defendants in proper person.

To carry on and continue any particular branch of business, from which manifest danger, by fire, is reasonably apprehended by divers inhabitants, in a compact part of the city, is a nuisance at common law.

Where the decision, however, in a particular case may affect the interests of many citizens, exercising a particular branch of business, in such a city, the Jury, under the peculiar circumstances of the case, will judge of the law for themselves.

The defendants, during the term of December last, were indicted for a nuisance at common law, in keeping a shop or building in Stone-street, and exercising, and continuing to exercise therein, the carpenter's business, to the great danger of divers the inhabitants of this city.

It appeared in evidence, that the defendants, who were proved to be two coloured men, of sober, industrious habits, had occupied, since the first day of May last, an old wooden building, in a ruinous situation, in Stone-street, for a carpenter's shop. There was also considerable lumber, used in their business, in and about the building. Contiguous to, and within a short distance from this building, there are a number of buildings, of great value, adjoining to others. Being in a very compact part of the city, fears were entertained, by the owners, for the safety of their houses: and it appeared, that the exercise of that particular branch of business, in that place, was very dangerous; though no particular act of negligence, on the part of the defendants, appeared. The owner of the premises, occupied by the defendants, resided in Albany.

As no counsel was employed, Rodman did not press a conviction; and the court charged the Jury, that the decision of the question, to the generality of mechanics, exercising this particular branch of business, was interesting. The court, for this reason, approached the subject with much caution. Without expressing any opinion in the case, the court left to the decision of the Jury, this question: Whether the exercise of the business in which the defendants were engaged, was more dangerous, carried on in this particular place, than in other places within the city? The decision of this question could not affect the interests of those engaged in this business, in places less dangerous. Should the Jury decide this question in the affirmative, the defendants, in the opinion of the court, ought to be found guilty; if not, they should be acquitted.

The Jury acquitted the defendants.

The New-York City Hall Recorder, November 17, 1816

87. Petition for Remission of Fine for Illegal Discharge of Gun

To the Honorable the Mayor Aldermen and Commonalty of the City of New York.

The Petition of George Pye Respectfully Sheweth,

That your Petitioner has been prosecuted for discharging a pistol within the limits prescribed by an ordinance of your honorable body and in violation of the provisions of said ordinance.

Your petitioner has been informed by the Attorney of your honorable body that the fine incurred is twenty five dollars—

Your petitioner must solemnly aver that he is innocent of the charge alledged against him, and that if the offence whith which he is charged, has been committed at all on his premises, it was in his opinion, committed by an indented apprentice who has within about ten days past, absconded from your petitioner—That whether it was committed by said apprentice or by any other person, it was without the knowledge or privity of your Petitioner—Your Petitioner thus being innocent, and being unable without distressing his family, to pay said fine, humbly petitions your honorable body to remit the same—and as in duty will ever pray—

New York June 16th 1817   George Pye

🦢   🦢   🦢

The Attorney of the Board to whom was referred the annexed Petition of George Pye to report a statement of facts—respectfully states—that in the examination of several witnesses it appeared that the apprentice of the said Pye, about three weeks ago discharged a loaded gun, twice in the yard of the said Pye, and by his orders—That a day or two after he discharged a loaded Pistol, in said yard by the order of the said Pye—That the said gun was loaded with a ball at one time, and at the other time with shot—

That one of the neighbours was very much alarmed—and it also appeared that the said Pye had made use of some threats to one of the neighbours in conversation on the subject of discharging said guns—

June 30th 1817

Respectfully submitted,
A. Sherman

Leave to withdraw

City Clerk Filed Papers, NYCMA

88. Petition for Employment as Inspector of Bread

To the Honorable the Mayor
Alderman and Commonalty of the City of New York, in
Common Council Convened,
The Petition of Abraham Brevoort of the said City Baker Humbly Sheweth.

That the petitioner served a regular Apprenticeship to the Baker's Trade in the said City and for a number of Years has carried on the business in this City.

That several Years ago the petitioner had the misfortune to be run down by a Horse and was injured in one of his Arms thereby in such a manner so as not be able thereafter to carry on his business.

That the petitioner at the time of the American Revolution served as a Soldier during the whole of the War, and exerted himself to the utmost of his power in the defence of the liberty of his Country, and being at present advanced in Years and disabled from following his business he wishes to employ himself to the best advantage for the benefit of a large family, who are dependent upon him for support.

The Petitioner therefore humbly prays that Your Honors will be favorably pleased to appoint him to be Weigher and Inspector of Bread for the said City of New York.

And as in duty bound the petitioner will ever pray.

Abraham Brevoort

April 25ᵗʰ 1806

We the subscribers are readily acquainted with the petitioner Abraham Brevoort, who sustains a reputable character, do beg leave to recommend him as a person well qualified for and worthy of being favored with the appointment solicited by the within petition.

April 25ᵗʰ 1806

John Quackenboss	John Young
Beekman & Beekman	Geo. Arcularius
Mangle Minthorne	Rich. Smith
Henry Brevoort	Peter Wynkop
George Janeway	Ephr Brasher
Jacobus Bogert	Peter Ogilvie
Daniel D. Tompkins	

City Clerk Filed Papers, NYCMA

Petition of William Smith to be a City Measurer. Such offices were commonly given to disabled or unemployed artisans, usually in positions germane to their former trades. NYCMA

PART FOUR

Masters and Journeymen

*T*he early national era proved to be a formative period in American labor history. The major seaports became the focus of serious and sometimes protracted labor strife that threatened in some instances to seriously disrupt the local economy by cutting off needed food supplies or halting construction. Conflict took place largely within the mechanic community rather than between artisan and merchant. As masters struggled to prosper or even to survive in the marketplace, journeymen found themselves a set of skilled workmen with common interests more and more at odds with their employers. The means that they selected to defend their position and the means that masters used to thwart their actions have left a lasting imprint.

THE NEW
MARKETPLACE

W hile all craftsmen were touched by the new risks and opportunities of the growing economy and the "business revolution," profound changes took place in production and employer/employee relationships in a number of significant artisan trades. In these crafts, the greater demand for goods, the absence of British mercantile restrictions, improvements in communications and transportation, and available merchant capital provided mechanics with incentive to expand into national and international markets. Such entrepreneurship foresaw increased profits, but it also meant entry into a highly competitive economic universe in which success depended upon the ability to organize efficient and cost-effective production within the workshop.

Shoemakers, cabinetmakers, and tailors, sought expanded local and national markets together with foreign, particularly West Indian, outlets. In shoemaking, for example, adventurous masters, sometimes with mercantile assistance in procuring capital, credit, or markets, bought leather wholesale, distributed it to journeymen who converted the raw material to shoes, and then sold this footwear—much of it of low quality—to slave-oriented markets in the South or West Indies or to the less wealthy of New York. In the manufacture of these shoes, skill was less important than cost and speed.[1] The 1820 Manufacturing Census extract (Document 89) reveals the considerable capital needed in such a firm. This single establishment consumed $16,000 worth of leather; it employed thirty journeymen and around ten women and apprentices. The shoemaker advertisements point to the wide market expectations of the master shoemakers. Cabinetmaking, too, particularly with the popularity of windsor chairs, found large national and international markets, while tailoring saw a growing need for low-cost "slop" or ready-to-wear clothing. This, too, is readily seen in newspaper ads, with one chairmaker offering to ship as many as 5,000 chairs (Documents 90–92).[2]

The building trades, masonry and carpentry, were the largest of the city's crafts, employing two-fifths of the city's journeymen. While not directly involved in export markets, the building trades were also affected by the expanding economy. Merchants' inclination to invest in real estate and to erect elaborate homes and counting houses gave rise to a building boom. In constructing these sometimes complex dwellings, a new figure entered the business: the master builder. The duties of this individual were to procure supplies, hire journeymen, and oversee construction—all at the lowest possible cost. Printing outfits too, with elaborate and costly machinery, became more and more intricate businesses. Masters were less likely to work alongside their journeymen and more likely to spend their time overseeing shop operations, hiring hands, and procuring accounts.[3]

Masters working in these expanding trades faced the real prospect of losing some of their independence and status to their mercantile creditors by becoming foremen rather than proprietors. However, many did quite well in the new marketplace. While Duncan Phyfe's accumulated fortune of a half million dollars in the cabinetmaking profession may have been unusual, the fortunes of tailor Jonas Mapes (worth $15,900 in 1815) or builder Anthony Steenback (worth $49,500 by that year) were not uncommon, though most masters in 1815 possessed between $1,000 and $5,000 in assets.[4]

The situation of the city's journeymen, particularly the 60 percent who worked in one of these six trades, was much less bright. Working for set wages and hours, either according to finished piecework or a daily salary, they eked out only a subsistence living. According to the 1819 New York City Jury Lists, only a small proportion (8.4 percent) of journeymen owned even $150 worth of personal property, while most employers (72.4 percent) held at least that much. Too, over one-fourth of the masters (25.5 percent) owned a house or store as opposed to a small fraction of journeymen (2.1 percent). These disparities in wealth were compounded by the difficulties journeymen had in rising to independent standing. Wage earners outnumbered masters by between three and four to one. Since a number of masters still operated small stores where they worked by themselves or with one or two journeymen, the ratio in large shops where most journeymen worked was considerably higher. The age difference between masters and journeymen in these trades averaged only four to seven years, with many remaining dependent wage earners well into their forties and fifties. In the populous sixth ward, three-quarters of artisans less than fifty years old were still journeymen.[5]

89. Boot and Shoemaking Enterprises, 1820

A = Law & Butler, 127 Broadway
B = Boot & Shoe Manufactory, Seventh Ward

I. RAW MATERIALS EMPLOYED
    1. The Kind?
        A. Leather of various kinds
        B. Morocco red
    2. The Quantity annually consumed?
        A. Without a great deal of trouble this question can't be answered
        B. 1500 lb of soul leather 15 doz. uppers
    3. The cost of annual consumption?
        A. Somewhere about $16,000
        B. About four thousand dollars

Boots and shoes were made either bespoken (to order) as in this illustration, or wholesale for national and international markets. The trend in the early national era was toward quantity production.
ANDERSON COLLECTION, NYPL

II. NUMBER OF PERSONS EMPLOYED
    4. Men?
      A. Average 30
      B. 10 men
    5. Women?
      A. Average 5
      B. 5 women
    6. Boys and Girls?
      A. Average 4
      B. 3 boys

III. MACHINERY
    7. Whole Quantity and kind of Machinery
      A. None–properly so called
      B. None
    8. Quantity of Machinery in Operation?
      A. None
      B. None

IV. EXPENDITURES
    9. Amount of capital invested?
      A. Declines answering
      B. Two thousand five hundred dollars
    10. Amount paid annually in wages?
      A. Somewhere about $8000
      B. Eight hundred and fifty dollars
    11. Amount of Contingent Expenses?
      A. Somewhere about $1000
      B. None

V. PRODUCTION
    12. The nature and names of articles manufactured?
      A. Boots, Shoes, &c.
      B. Boots and Shoes of All kinds
    13. Market Value of the Articles to be annually manufactured?
      A. Somewhere about $28,000
      B. Boots from $5 to $8 Shoes 50% of Boots
    14. General remarks concerning the establishment, as to its actual and past condition, the demand for, and sale of its Manufactures
      A. From the year 1815 till 1819, the business was good, & paid well; from that date till midsummer last, (say 18 mos.) it paid almost nothing, but since midsummer last it has improved considerably.
      B. Sales very Dull

Federal Census, New York State Manufacturing, 1820, #1245, #1303

90. Shoemaker Trade and Supply

Joseph King's Boot and Shoe Warehouse Removed from No. 1 Golden Hill to No. 158 Queen Street, next door to Isaac Roosevelt Esq., where his friends and the public may be supplied, wholesale and retail, on very low terms. Boots from 44s. to 56s. per pair. Bootees 40s. Men's shoes from 6s. to 31s. Ladies silk and morocco shoes, Stuff Shoes from 5s. 6s to 11s. Leather do. 6s to 8s. Boys, girls and childrens black and morocco shoes of all sorts and sizes, English and American boot legs, Cordovan and calf skins, bend soles, morocco leather, silk binding &c. Merchants supplied with any quantity of coarse mens shoes. All orders from town and Country executed on shortest notice. Shopkeepers supplied with stuff shoes by the dozen or barrel, on shortest notice.—

New York Daily Advertiser, May 13, 1793

🐦 🐦 🐦

SHOE FACTORY RETAIL, WHOLESALE AND EXPORT

LADIES ELEGANT TEA and purple coloured Kid Slippers and a general assortment of Morocco and leather shoes of all descriptions, wholesale and retail, and for exportation, at very reduced prices by James Trivett, No. 72 Maiden-lane, corner of William-st. Where merchants and masters of vessels trading to the south-ward and West India Islands, will find a suitable supply on the most reasonable and accommodating terms, and all orders from town and country will be thankfully received and satisfactorily attended to. A number of good Workmen wanted at the factory at Corlaer's Hook, where comfortable accommodations are provided. Those who may wish to secure themselves a good sort of craft during the winter, will do well to apply without delay.

Republican Watch-Tower, November 3, 1802

91. Windsor Chairs: Domestic and Export Sale

JOHN DE WITT & CO., Windsor Chair Makers, Begs leave to inform their friends and the public in general, that they continue to carry on the above business at No. 38 White Hall Street, near the battery and at No. 450 Pearl Street, (formerly Queen Street).

Likewise, Windsor Chairs japann'd and neatly flowered. Also Settees of any size, made in the neatest manner. Masters of vessels or any other persons can be supplied with either of the above articles in large or small quantities, at the shortest notice. N.B. Punctuality and dispatch may be depended on.

New-York Weekly Chronicle, June 18, 1795

The large-scale manufacture of chairs. HAZEN, PANORAMA OF TRADES, NYHS

❧ ❧ ❧

JAMES HALLET Jr.—For sale 5,000 windsor chairs of various patterns, prepared for a Foreign market of the very best materials and workmanship, may be had on application at no. 8 John-street.

New-York Gazette and General Advertiser, October 22, 1801

92. Ready-Made Clothing: Every Description and Quality

George Thomson, Has constantly for Sale at his Store no. 52 Maiden-Lane, Gentlemen's ready made cloathing of every description and quality, of the latest fashion; surtouts, spencers and coats; Waistcoats, pantaloons and small-clothes; Under clothing and childrens dresses; Seaclothing and servants do. Slops of every denomination and quality, &c.

New-York Gazette and General Advertiser, November 2, 1804

❧ ❧ ❧

Weyman & Son, No. 41 Maiden-Lane, Have constantly on Hand, a variety of Ready Made Articles, Suitable for Ladies, Gentlemen, Children, and Servants' wear: Amongst which are Ladies Quilted Silk Coats and warm Travelling do. Gentlemens' superfine Body Coats and Frocks, Double milled Drab Driving Coats, Rough Bearskin, Princess Beaver and Frize do. Gentlemens' Spencers, Surtouts and Boat Cloaks, Fine Flannel Draws, Shirts & Powdering Gowns, Fine Linen Shirts, Fancy Waistcoats, Fancy Children's Dresses and Suits, An assortment of Boys and Servants' cheap Clothing And a general assortment of Sea ditto. Orders executed with care and on reasonable terms, for Cash.

New-York Gazette and General Advertiser, February 8, 1800

JOURNEYMEN AND
APPRENTICES

THE TRADITIONAL ROLE

The "business revolution" brought about fundamental changes in the American economy that would eventually touch all artisan crafts. However, as in any major economic transformation, progress was highly uneven. Many New York City trades such as blacksmithing and baking retained much of their eighteenth-century conduct of business, operating as family enterprises with but a few journeymen and apprentices.[6] Too, even in the six crafts most affected, some master craftsmen managed to run small-scale operations. Before describing the lasting alterations in the relations of journeymen and masters, it is necessary to examine the traditional role.

There are two significant sets of documents revealing the work of traditional journeymen. The first is the journal of cabinetmaker Elisha Blossom, who worked for small-scale masters from 1801 to 1815. The first entries find him just returned from Argentina. Finding it difficult to work on his own, Blossom labored as a highly skilled journeyman for various employers, though mostly for David Loring. Sometimes working for a piece rate and sometimes for a weekly wage of $8.25 (eleven shillings) per week, he made shelves, frames, and tables, including some very intricate construction that might involve gluing, mitering, fitting, veneering, banding, and carving. Blossom paid Mrs. Loring $3.31 a week for board and washing, but evidently was able to lead a comfortable life with the remaining part of his salary—he purchased a gold watch worth $75 in 1813. In 1814, he briefly quit Loring for a position as clerk to a bookseller for $375 per year, but soon left the job, stating that he "could not agree as it was too confining and quit." A solitary worker of fine skills, Blossom was quite independent and comfortable, isolated from the journeymen working in the larger shops (Document 93).

The other important figure is that of John Bradford, a journeyman bookbinder. Bradford was an amateur poet who took as his subject life at the bindery.[7] One of the most prominent themes in his poems, craft pride and independence, is evident in a verse in which this "Knight of the Folding Stick of Paste Castle" describes the apprentices' pride and possessiveness in obtaining his first tools (Document 94). Towards master craftsmen, Bradford displays a sense of assertiveness, particularly in a poem celebrating the journeymen's release from working nights by candlelight (Document 95). However, no serious antagonism is expressed. Moreover, one important poem—printed in the previous section—describes a sense of mutual support and interest within the trade, an important tenet of artisan republicanism. This is the curse directed at a master who, in striving to gain accounts has "injured the business" by charging less than the prices established by the masters (Document 65).

Traditional apprenticeships could also readily be found in early national New York. Under these, a boy was bound to work for a set number of years (usually to age twenty-one) in exchange for room, board, clothing and rudimentary education. As in the eighteenth century, runaways were a common problem, and ads either asking for their return or refusing any of their debts were commonly found in the daily papers (Document 96). Another traditional problem yet present was physical abuse of boys by masters (Document 97).

It must also be observed, however, that the early republic represented the twilight of traditional apprenticeships. As early as the eighteenth century, youths were leaving their indentures early to take advantage of the labor shortage in colonial America.[8] In the age of Jefferson the temptation of employers in the crafts oriented to the expanding marketplace to hire semi-skilled apprentices for a cheap wage was strong as was the desire of many of these boys to earn an immediate salary. By the mid-1820's, according to a correspondent in the *New York Observer*, "AN OLD APPRENTICE," the traditional apprenticeship was rare and society was much the worse for it. He blames the Jeffersonian republican spirit for this decline and, with it, a deterioration of craftsmanship. There is no doubt that the economic ambitions triggered by artisan republicanism caused many young boys to enter the marketplace early. But just as important, the changing economy and workforce had a large share in the changes he deplores (Document 98).

93. Day Book of Elisha Blossom

New York, February 27th, 1813

David Loring to making Breakfast

Table
Making Breakfast table Start	1 3 8
6 inches in length	3.
6 Do. [Ditto] width	2.
Shaping leaves double eliptic	3.
Reeding legs	8.
2 extra flys	2.4
Putting on castors	.10
Do. handle	.2
Veneering ends	1.
Banding rails	1.10
Beading and shamming front	2.7
Sawing 2 veneers	.4
	£2.9.9

Making Breakfast Table	1.3.0
9 inches in length	4.6
12 Do. width	4.
Shaping leaves	3.
Seeding legs	8.
2 extra flys	2.8
Putting on castors	.10
Do. handle	.2
Veneering ends	1.
Banding rails	2.
Pannelling legs	1.4
Beading and shamming fronts	2.7
	£2.13.1

3 joints in tops	19.
3 joints in bottom	9
	28 sh.

&ca; &ca; &ca;

Loring Blossom Creditor
Board Washing $3.50

John L. Dolan Creditor
By 3rd doz oil stone $4.21 ½

D. Loring Debtor
Making penhole table

Start	3.0
6 inches extra length	3.0
5 Do. width	1.8
Reeding legs	8.
Cutting top Do.	3.
Joint in top	0.9
In draw bottom	.3
Veneering ends	1.
6 feet banding	1.
Shamming front & beading	2.1

Day Book of Elisha Blossom, NYHS

94. An Apprentice's First Tools

The following lines were occasioned by the author's getting a small set of tools at his own expence while an apprentice.

Proclamation
Brother shopmates beware how ye handle these tools.
Whether journeyman, prentice or in whatever station
I charge ye henceforth to adhere to the rules
of Castle and mind too, this my PROCLAMATION from this
    day know ye,
    Henceforth it shall be:
All the tools in the cabinet belongs unto me,
And while I've my own, I will ne're trouble thine:
So ____ me if you shall 'er meddle with mine, of
Late in the bindery by all its well known

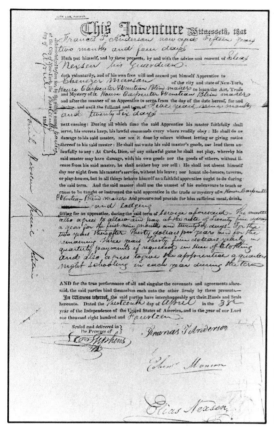

An 1814 apprentice's indenture to a carpenter. This form yet retains the traditional injunctions against licentiousness as well as demands on the master for education, religious training and decent treatment. Despite these words, such reciprocal obligations were in an increasingly weakened state.
NYCMA

Helter Skelter the tools were in constant confusion,
But now they've plac'd right and each one has his own
So I trust in my cabinet, there'll be no intrusion,
    If any there are
    who presumptuously dare,
To Finger one of them by the press pen I swear,
I'll tackle the genius besides sure I'll fine
Him a bumper of stingo for meddling with mine.
The tools I have stiled as my own are but few,
They are triangle, a knife, stabbing awl and a bodkin.
A hard hammer, baking and cutting boards too,
An oil stone, a cutting press, ploy and press pin.
    Plow knife, candlestick
    A tarbulum for Dick,
Needles, sewing keys, compasses and foldingstick;
Not one of these tools above mentioned are thine,
For while I work with them I stile them all mine.

John Bradford, *The Poetical Vagaries of a Knight of the Folding Stick of Paste Castle* . . . (New York, 1813), p. 9

A bookbinding shop. This was yet a traditional craft, not oriented to quantity production. HAZEN, PANORAMA OF TRADES, NYHS

95. A Song for the Tenth of March: The Night on Which Journeymen Mechanics Cease Working by Candlelight

Tune: Yankee Doodle

> The candle-light embargo we've
> Resolved to raise tonight, sirs,
> Until October from this eve,
> No more we'll strike a light, sirs.

Let the masters say what they may,
And look as grim as can be,
We'll do it in spite of what they say
To-it – Yankee Doodle Dandy.

For five months every night we were
Obliged to work till eight, sirs,
But lamp and candlesticks now are
Till October out of date, sirs.

Though if at night to work we stay
You know as well as can be,
For each hour we'll get the pay,
Yankee Doodle Dandy.

Now let's be jovial, douse the glim;
Extinguish every light, sir,
Tis seven months ere again we'll trim
Our lamps to work by night, sir.

Then lay your candle sticks away,
Where they'll be always handy,
And jovially we'll end the day,
With Yankee Doodle Dandy.

John Bradford, *Poetical Vagaries*, p. 50

96. Runaway Apprentices

25 DOLLARS REWARD

STOP THE TWO RUNAWAYS!!

RANAWAY from the subscriber, two apprentices to the Shoemaking Business, one named CORNELIUS VAN ALLEN, who went away about two weeks ago, the other named JOHN CARR, who went away on Sunday the 1st inst. had on when he went away, a cotton casimere olive colour coatee, thicksett pantaloons, and striped waistcoat; is between 17 and 18 years of age, 4 feet 10 inches high, full face, light complexion and dark brown hair. All persons are forbid trusting, harbouring or employing said apprentices at their peril. Any person or persons taking up said apprentices, and lodging them in any Gaol within the United States, or returning them to the subscriber, shall receive the above reward, and all reasonable charges paid.

Oliver Taylor
873 Pearl-Street

N.B. All masters of vessels are forbid carrying off said apprentices at their peril.
Evening Post, June 19, 1806

ONE HALF CENT REWARD.

SNEAKED away from the subscriber, on the morning of the 17th instant, Robert Bancker Saunders, an apprentice to the Printing business. A description of his dress is unnecessary; or of his person, save that he is a lazy full face lump of a fellow, about 4 feet 5 inches in height. His manners and habits are the most striking features in his description. He may be noted by a stupid unmeaning stare, as he drags his carcase along the streets—generally with his hands in his pockets. His countenance is expressive of nothing but carelessness, indolence and stupidity. There is scarcely a doubt that any one will harbor or trust him; but rather than benevolence should be misapplied, or goodness abused, this notice is given to the public, that they may not credit him on my account, as I will pay no debts thus contracted; or harbor him, under the penalty of the law.

GEO. ASBRIDGE.

Independent Mechanic, January 18, 1812

97. Assault and Battery Trial: Apprentice vs. Master

LAW INTELLIGENCE.

Court of Sessions, Tuesday, 12th May—Present, his honor Dewitt Clinton, mayor, alderman Douglass, and alderman Morse.

THE PEOPLE VS RICHARD T. LOWERY —

Assault and Battery upon Jesse Fash.

The complainant was an apprentice of the defendant. He stated, that his master had whipped him excessively on his return from dinner, alledging as a reason, that he had not been steady at work during his absence. It appeared, however, from the difference, that the lad was a bad boy, and very negligent; that Mr. Lowery had found fault with him; and that he had grumbled, and used impertinent language, in consequence of which he had given him a little *wholesome chastisement.* The mayor informed the jury, that they had only to decide whether the defendant used an improper weapon; or if a legal one, then, whether he had carried his chastisement too far.—In either case, he told them, they ought to convict the defendant; but if they thought otherwise, it was their duty to acquit. *Not Guilty.* J. W. Wyman, for defendant.

Independent Mechanic, May 16, 1812

98. On the Decline of Apprenticeship

. . . . it is of *mechanics'* apprentices, and the class who *should be* such that I would speak and lament their deterioration of character. The tendency of our laws, which give masters no control over their apprentices, or the manner in which these laws are enforced or abused, thus affording to unruly apprentices inducements to complain of, and to mortify and perplex their masters, has induced a resolution on the part of the most respectable master mechanics, not to take apprentices at all. It is a fact well known to many, that there are great numbers of poor and friendless boys in our streets, who are yet *honest*, and desirous to work, but who, in consequence of the state of disorganization, are unable to obtain the knowledge of a trade. These may be seen wandering about our docks, lounging at the Intelligence Office, until their scanty funds are exhausted, when to avoid starvation, they resort to pilfering, and are at length brought to the House of Refuge or in some other place of confinement less favorable to the reformation of character. I had occasion recently, to look at the form of an indenture; and presuming that I should find several in the first shop I entered, I stepped into my tailors, where to my surprise I found that, although one of the largest establishments in our city, the proprietors had not a single apprentice. I then went to several other tailors, jewelers, watchmakers, printers, and bootmakers before I could succeed. In enquiring the cause, I found that they all agreed, (with a single exception) in the reasons here assigned, *viz. the insufficiency of the existing laws to compel an apprentice to do his duty*, and the power given to an obstinant and exasperated boy, in case of even moderate punishment, to drag his masters before a court, exposing him to the degradation of unmerited punishment, or at least subjecting him to expense, loss of time and the mortifying experience of the rest of the boys that they may pursue the same course with impunity.

That apprentices' household be protected from the abuse of capricious or tyrannical conduct, is in accordance with the justice and spirit of government; but that a master should not have the power of compelling to the performance of his duty, an obstinant boy, who has been of little or no use in the early part of his apprenticeship, and who, when he has half learned his trade, will *court* the breaking of his indentures that he may be employed elsewhere as a journeyman, is a monstrous extension of Mr. Jefferson's "free and equal declaration." It is not only subversive of good order and government between masters and apprentices, but it is subversive also of these principles, in the exercise of which in their purity, we have the surest, indeed the *only* guarantee of the continuance of our boasted independence.

AN OLD APPRENTICE

New York Observor, October 7, 1826

❧ ❧ ❧

. . .

It is generally admitted, that intemperance among mechanics, and among the boys employed by them, has alarmingly increased of late; and it is, I conceive, a natural consequence of the present loose system of taking boys. In the course of my inquiries I saw four or five boys, from ten to fourteen years of age romping at their work; and upon asking, are not these boys apprenticed?" was answered, "Oh no! they are little journeymen; they are received upon the same footing, are paid their wages regularly, and know and feel that they are free men; and of course soon discover it by their conduct. If one of them should dislike a word of reproof, he will call for his wages and quit me instantly; and there are employers enough who will receive them, and care nothing for their moral character, or their steadiness or constancy of their work."

. . .

Masters will tell you that their journeymen repeatedly leave them, without a word of explanation, for several days together; and it is proverbial that during spring races, troops of them invariably drop the paint brush or the saw, for the racecourse; and the whole family is thus left in confusion til the races are past and the workmen are sobered. During last spring, I was hurrying to make some repairs for a tenant; three different mechanics undertook the job, and the workmen of each deserted for the racecourse. Several of my friends experienced the same treatment.

Now, I ask what is the cause of all these complaints? and why is a *punctual* mechanic so rare, as to induce the confession from one of the most worthy, "there is now no such thing as punctuality among them?" Is it not because the natural draw between master and apprentice has been rent asunder? As there is now no community of interest, so there is no community of feeling between them, master no longer lives among his apprentice, watches over their morals as well as mechanical improvement, accompanies them on Sunday to a place of worship, counsels them when in trouble, keeps them and comforts them in sickness, and when he is able, gives them, for their good name, some assistance to begin the world for themselves.

AN OLD APPRENTICE

New York Observor, October 14, 1826

🙋   🙋   🙋

. . .

As I have remarked, boys have *themselves* become the judges of the proper time to assume the character of journeymen; and it is lamentable, said my informant, to see men who profess to be respectable, countenance such a system. A stout boy lately applied to him for work, as a competent journeyman, and produced his credentials, viz. such as did for a respectable mechanic, the boy "*understood his business*, having worked for him during the space *of two years*." *Two* entire years! to acquire a complete knowledge of an art and *mystery*, which in England is now learned short of seven years! Surely our mechanics deceive themselves if they suppose that a plan which tends to reduce the perfection of their workmanship, and to degrade the moral character of boys, (the future mechanics of our city,) can in the end be profitable. If the present system is pursued, as it appears likely to be, ten years hence the names and relative duties of master and apprentice shall be virtually unknown, what is there to support the dignity and the wealth, the character and the skillfulness, of the mechanics of New-York?—a body of men who as a class, (I speak of the old regime) can number as much worth and wealth, as much public spirit and liberality, as any other class of our citizens. If the race who succeeds them are to be *bunglers* at their various crafts, and blots in the civil society, what is to prevent "the foe and the stranger" from taking at once their business and their bread? For let them rest assured, that although many people talk *loudly* of *patriotism*, there are *very, very* few who will consent to purchase at a nearly equal price, the clumsy American article, when foreigners shall bring to our shores, (assuredly as they will do,) their own manufactures, executed with all the cunning device and perfected skill. The decline and fall of mighty nations have been traced to slighter indications of decay than are here exhibited.

May we be wise today and so profit by experience that the future moralist shall not point us out, in classing us with Tyre, Bablyon and Rome, one may think of "Behold the glorious departed."

AN OLD APPRENTICE

New York Observor, October 28, 1826

JOURNEYMEN SOCIETIES AND CONSTITUTIONS

I f the process of economic expansion was uneven, for most journeymen working in shoemaking, building, printing, tailoring and cabinetmaking, the future was uncertain at best. Whatever their hopes of advancement, there was no guarantee of becoming a master craftsman, a status most journeymen in the colonial era might have expected. Instead there was the strong probability that they would become permanent wage earners, making subsistence salaries and struggling with their families to stay clear of poverty.

Attempting to attain a position in the new republic as skilled craftsmen and upstanding citizens who were entitled to adequate and secure compensation, many of these journeymen—and particularly the more highly accomplished— organized themselves into societies to protect their position in the marketplace. These organizations, like the benevolent societies, collected funds for the aid of sick members and for assistance to the families of deceased brothers. However, they also intended their associations to become a significant new economic force. For the journeymen were under siege to a new marketplace that was drawing an increased pool of labor to the city composed of immigrants, country craftsmen from the nearby hinterlands, and apprentices who left their indentures prior to age twenty-one for salaried work. These artisans did not have the fine craftsmanship of many of New York's veteran journeymen, but their abilities were suitable for the less refined work oriented to large national and international markets. Employers liked them, too, because they were often willing to labor for wages less than the prevailing norm.[9]

The constitution of the Society of Journeymen Cordwainers of the City of New York (Document 99), one of the more militant trade societies, serves as an example of how journeymen strived to gain leverage in the marketplace.[10] The Constitution forbade all members to work for masters who hired nonmember journeymen or apprentices, and provided for collective action against any master who lowered wages below those established by the Society. The New York Typographical Society had similar provisions, the important sections of which are printed (Document 100).

Rare excerpts from the minutes of a few of these societies give insight into the procedures they followed. The selection from the minutes of the shipwrights (a craft working in a business that involved large-scale capital expenditure and the combined work of numerous artisans) describes the society's efforts to enforce its by-law requiring members to refuse to work for any unqualified master or with fellow journeymen who were under twenty-one. In addition, the minutes illustrate the patriotic, republican spirit of these craftsmen in their effort to present themselves to the city with respect and esteem (Document 101). The selection from the New York Typographical Society illustrates a problem the societies had when a journeyman became an employer and yet refused to resign. The charges brought against this printer as well as a resolution adopted to deal with such situations in the future are printed (Document 102). Also included is an attempt by the Society through a "Committee of Vigilance" to increase its membership, to "compel" others working as journeymen to join the association, and to maintain members in the city's print shops (Document 103).

The journeymen preferred to negotiate with the masters and often were able to reach agreement. In 1809, for example, the printer employers, upon demands of the New York Typographical Society for increased wages, presented the newly formed association with a list of piece wages and salaries that, it contended, were a "maximum, beyond which it would be highly injurious, if not ruinous, to the interests of the trade to venture" (Document 103). The journeymen then assembled and considered carefully every item of the masters' proposal, then met with the masters and came to a final agreement that was satisfactory to a majority of the membership. Sections of the original proposal and final agreement are printed (Document 104). Similarly, in 1796, the Journeymen Cabinet and Chairmakers published a *Book of Prices* addressed to the masters stating the prices they would accept for the completion of various tasks (Document 105). It is significant to note in this document the contention that "every industrious mechanic" was owed a "comfortable subsistence," a concept in harmony with the producer ethic so common to artisan republicanism. There is, as well, a strong statement that the journeymen are not attempting to create antagonism with the masters who are also fellow producers, but only to "consiliate a mutual regard—to be treated as men professing an ingenious art."

❦

99. Constitution of the New York Cordwainers Society

Constitution

We, the Journeymen Cordwainers of the City of New-York, impressed with a sense of our just rights and to guard against the intrigues or artifices that may at any time be used by our employers to reduce our wages lower than what we deem an adequate reward for our labour, have unanimously agreed to the following articles as the Constitution of our Society.

ARTICLE I. That this Society shall consist of a President, Secretary, and three Trustees, to be elected annually; and a Committee of six members, to be chosen every six months.

ARTICLE II. The election for President, Secretary and Trustees, shall take place on the third Monday in January, annually, at the usual place of meeting, and they shall be respectively chosen by ballot, by a plurality of votes of the members present; and the Committee shall be chosen the third Monday in January, and the third Monday in July.

ARTICLE III. The President, in order to preserve regularity and decorum, is authorized to fine any member six cents, that is not silent, when order is called for by him, and all members are to address the chair, one at a time.

ARTICLE IV. Any person becoming a member of this Society, shall pay the sum of forty-three and a half cents on his admission, and six and a quarter cents as his monthly contribution; and should any member, leave the city at any time, and stay for the space of three months or upwards, if on his return it can be proved that he has been so absent, he shall still be deemed a lawful member, by paying one month's contribution.

ARTICLE V. All the money collected in this Society shall be delivered into the hands of the Trustees, and they shall hold an equal share till it amounts to fifty dollars; they shall then deposit it in the United States Bank, and it shall not be drawn on except in case of a stand out, and then left to a majority of the society.

ARTICLE VI. The secretary shall keep a regular account of all the proceedings of this Society, and he for his services, shall receive one dollar per month, and twelve and a half cents for each notice served on any member.

ARTICLE VII. The President, Secretary and Committee shall meet on the second Monday in each month, to consult and propose any measures they may think beneficial for the Society, who shall assemble on the third Monday in each month, at the hour of seven o'clock from September to March inclusive, and at the hour of eight o'clock from March to September, and for non-attendance of President and Secretary, to pay a fine of fifty cents, and any member of the Committee to pay a fine of twenty-five cents.

ARTICLE VIII. No member of this society shall work for an employer, that has any Journeyman Cordwainer, or his apprentice in his employment, that does not belong to this Society unless the Journeyman come and join the same and should any member work on the seat with any person or persons that has not joined this society and does not report the same to the President, the first meeting night after it comes to his knowledge, shall pay a fine of one dollar.

ARTICLE IX. If any employer should reduce his Journeyman's wages at any time, or should the same Journeyman find himself otherwise aggrieved, by reporting the same to the Committee at their next meeting, they shall lay the case before the society, who shall determine on what measures to take to redress the same.

ARTICLE X. The name of each member shall be regularly called over at every monthly meeting, and should any member be absent when his name has been called over three times successively, shall pay a fine of twelve and a half cents in the first night, twenty-five cents for the second, fifty cents for the third; and if absent three successive meeting nights, the Secretary shall deliver him a notice and if he does not make his appearance after being notified, on the following meeting night, (unless he can assign some just cause for staying away,) shall pay a fine of three dollars.

ARTICLE XI. Any Journeyman Cordwainer, coming into this city, that does not come forward and join this society in the space of one month, (as soon as it is known,) he shall be notified by the Secretary, and for such notification he shall pay twelve and a half cents; and if he does not come forward and join the same on the second meeting of the society, after receiving the notice, shall pay a fine of three dollars.

ARTICLE XII. Any member of this society having an apprentice or apprentices, shall, when he or they become free, report the same to the President, on the first monthly meeting following; and if the said apprentice or apprentices do not come forward and join the Society, in the space of one month from the time of the report, shall be notified by the Secretary, and if he does not come forward within two months after receiving the notification, shall pay a fine of three dollars.

ARTICLE XIII. There shall be delivered to the President at every monthly meeting, a sufficient sum of money to defray the necessary expenses of this society.

ARTICLE XIV. If any member should be guilty of giving a brother member any abusive language in the society-room, during the hours of meeting, who might have been excluded from this society by his misdemeanor, but by making concession have been reunited, he shall pay a fine of twenty-five cents.

ARTICLE XV. Every member of the society shall inform the Secretary of his place of residence, and should they at any time change their place of residence, they shall notify the same to the Secretary on the first monthly meeting following; not complying with this, shall pay a fine of twenty-five cents.

ARTICLE XVI. Any member may propose as amendments to this constitution, new articles, or alterations of those in force, which proposed amendments must be delivered to the Committee in writing, who shall present the same to the Society, at their next monthly meeting, and if two-thirds of the members present concur therein, such amendment shall become a part of the constitution.

ARTICLE XVII. It is the duty of the private members to attend the meetings and cooperate with its officers in promoting the welfare of the society, for in doing this, they will recollect they are promoting their own individual welfare.

People vs. Melvin, reprinted in John R. Commons et. al., ed., *A Documentary History of American Industrial Society*, 10 vol. (Cleveland, 1910–11), III, pp. 364–368

100. New York Typographical Society: Constitution and By-Laws

Article 1. This society shall be known and called by the name of the New York Typographical Society.

Article 2. The concerns of the society shall be managed by a board to consist of a president, vice-president, twelve directors, a treasurer and secretary, the two former of whom to be elected by ballot . . . .

Article 10. Duties of Officers. The board shall have power to pass by-laws for the government of themselves and of the society in general meeting, resolutions and acts not derogatory to the true interests and meaning of the constitution, and generally to transact all and every such business for the welfare of the society as is not in this constitution determined to be done in general meeting. It shall also keep a list of the prices of work, subject to revision and alteration as may become necessary, and if any member of this society shall be convicted of working for less than the established wages he shall be expelled and the secretary shall transmit his name with the nature of his offense to the other corresponding typographical societies in the United States.

Article 17. Sickness and Distressed Members. When the funds of the society shall have amounted to $100 the Board of Directors may award such sum to sickly and distressed members, their widows and children as to them may seem meet and proper. Provided, that such sum shall not exceed $3 per week. And in every case wherein a member may be thrown out of employ by reason of his refusing to take less than the established prices they shall advance, if required, on his own security, at their discretion, such a sum per week as is sufficient to defray his ordinary expenses. And if such member, by sickness or otherwise, shall be rendered unable to refund the amount, or part of the sum so advanced, the board may levy a tax upon every other member of the society which shall be sufficient, or in part sufficient to defray the amount advanced as aforesaid. And further, no person shall receive the benefit arising from this article until he shall have been six months a member of the society, unless he is a stranger and in absolute distress.

❧   ❧   ❧

By-Laws

Article 4. Every person immediately after being elected a member of this society and previous to his signing the constitution must give satisfactory answers to the following questions, and to such others as the president may deem proper: "Have you suffered yourself to be proposed as a member of this society with a view of supporting the interests thereof? "Do you promise to attend all meetings of this society when it shall be in your power so to do, provided it be not detrimental to yourself or family? "Do you hereby declare and affirm that you will support the constitution and by-laws of this society and hold

A Membership Certificate of the Hat Makers Society. There is no evidence of a strike by the hatters, although they were one of the larger crafts in the city. This society provided death and disability benefits and a fraternal outlet.

WINTERTHUR MUSEUM

yourself amenable to all legal acts and proceedings of the society and Board of Directors; that you, when thereunto required, keep all such matters and proceedings of the society or Board of Directors a profound secret, as shall be deemed necessary by a majority of either; and furthermore, do you declare that you will procure, or cause to be procured, if within your power, employment for all such members of this society as may be in want thereof, in preference to any other person or persons?"

Article 5. When a member speaks he shall rise and address the chair, and, avoiding desultory or irrelevant remarks, shall confine himself strictly to the merits of the question under consideration. He shall not be interrupted while speaking unless by the presiding officer when he shall think proper to call him to order, or admonish him to a closer adherence to the subject. Nor shall a member be allowed to speak oftener than twice on the same question without permission from the chair.

Article 12. Should any member of this society be detected in undermining or supplanting a brother member, or supplying the place of him who may be discharged by an employer in consequence of supporting the rules of this society, by refusing to work for less than the established prices, he shall be expelled therefrom and reported to the different typographical societies in the United States.

Article 13. No member of this society shall work for less than the wages which may be established; neither shall he engage or continue in any office where there is a journeyman working for less than the established prices.

George A. Stevens, *New York Typographical Union Number Six* (Albany, 1912), pp. 42–47

101. Minutes of the Union Society of Shipwrights and Caulkers

May 27, 1815

The minutes of the last meeting was read and approved. The following members was proposed and balloted for and duly elected: Abiah Higgins, William Banton, Charles Gordon. Afterwards

It was moved and seconded the society furnish a Banner by subscription for the purpose of walking in procession of the fourth of July next. It was then moved and seconded that a general meeting of shipwrights and caulkers would be published in the Mercantile, two days; Gazetteer, two days; Columbian two days – Friday and Saturday.

June 8, 1815

Thursday evening monthly meeting.

The society met at John Morris. The minutes of the last meeting was read and approved. No report from the standing commitee. The select committee that was appointed by the society to wait on the different portrait apointers of the city of New York for painting a Banner suitable for the union society of shipwrights and caulkers made the following report: that they had waited on the most emmenent portrate painters in the city to paint this Banner towit Mr. Tuffil, $65 Van der Pool, $90 Jarvis, the highest in the city Smith $100, Plum $80, Childs $80. But afterward considered that he could paint the same for $70. The society then agreed unanimously that the said Mr. Childs should paint the Banner afterwards proposed and balloted the following members, namely, Sanford, Manasseh Beckwith, Philip Doyer, John Dickey, William Williams, Joseph M. Beckwith. The Society then commenced balloting for a steward in the place of Peter Maalamar resigned, and William Martin was duly elected.

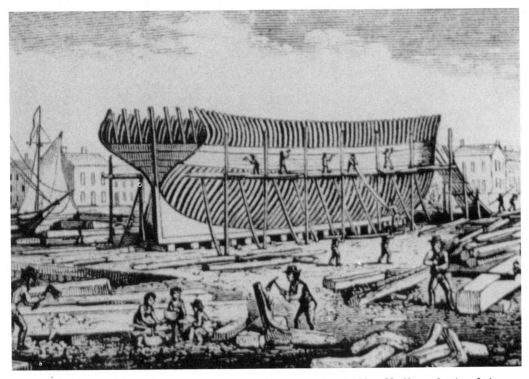

Shipbuilding was perhaps the most complex operation undertaken by New York's mechanics. It involved the coordinated efforts of shipwrights, caulkers, riggers, sailmakers, ropemakers, and others. Some shipyards were quite large, like the one depicted, while others were very small. Craftsmen would work in many shipyards depending on which shipbuilder received orders and the intensity of business. ANDERSON COLLECTION, NYPL

Sept. 14, 1815

The society met at John Morris. Being in order the minutes of the last meeting was read and approved. Monthly dues collected to the amount of $8. The standing committee reports that Daniel Read and Benjamin Basset members of the society went to work for Seaman & Kingsland in opposition to the first article of the constitution when by the unanimous voice of the society they were expelled.

It was moved and seconded and was unanimously carried that a committee of three be appointed to appoint three brothers to draw up a plan of the certificates for the society and offer to them for approbation on the next monthly meeting when the following brothers were chosen: John Dodge, Abraham Devere, Peter Turner, John Buel, Reuben Hoyt.

Sept. 21, 1815

An extra meeting of the society met at John Morris. Being in order the minutes of the last meeting was read and approved. Monthly dues received to the amount of $10.

The standing committee reports that Mr. Kingsland had waited on the chairman of the committee and also the president of the society. Know if he could bring sufficient vouchers that he had worked three years at the shipwright business whether or not the society would not work for him. If found so by the society that he had worked three years at the business they will go to work for Mr. Kingsland. The society then commenced balloting for candidates when the following member was unanimously elected, namely Reuben Miles.

Oct. 12, 1815

Being in order the minutes of the last meeting was read and approved. Monthly dues received to the amount of $12.06. The report of the second quarterly meeting by the treasurer and secretary was read and approved. The standing committee reports that Bennona Boss went to work for Seamond & Kingsland ignorantly and not knowing that he had violated the first article of the constitution. There was a motion made and seconded that he should be reinstated which was done by ballot and he was accepted unanimously. The chairman of the standing committee reports that Ichabod Avery went to work for Seamond & Kingsland and that he was acting in violation of the first article of the constitution. He says that he is sorry for all that he has done and hopes that the Society will forgive him. If so, he will come forward and pay his monthly dues: Several members waited on Mr. Ichabod Avery who was in the lower room and was in no way dezirous to come up when the secretary requested: unanimously agreed that Ichabod Avery should be expelled from the society.

It was unanimously agreed to by the society that the certificates be laid over till the next extra meeting held on Monday next for subscription. Received by subscription the sum of $9 for the widow Mills; brothers appointed to carry the money Donald Cutting, Abraham D. Mevine.

New York, Jan. 3, 1816

The society met at the house of John Morris. Being in order the minutes of the last meeting was read and approved. The society then commenced the proposition of candidates when the following was duly elected: Ichabod Avery was duly elected over again.

Minutes of the Union Society of Shipwrights and Caulkers, NYPL

102. New York Typographical Society: Resolution of Expulsion

1. For an attempt, in combination with a few employing printers, to lessen the established wages of journeymen.

2. For introducing into the printing business men wholly unacquainted with it, to the exclusion of regular bred workmen.

3. For refusing to give employment to a member of this society, and employing one not a member in preference – a direct violation of the solemn pledge he has repeatedly given us.

4. For divulging the proceedings of his brethren required by them to be kept secret – a second violation of the obligation he owes to this institution.

5. In direct violation of the most sacred pledge to the society, when initiated, for endeavoring to injure a brother member.

6. For suffering his name to be attached to an advertisement unbecoming a member of this society.

Experience teaches us that the actions of men are influenced almost wholly by their interests, and that it is almost impossible that a society can be well-regulated and useful when its members are actuated by opposite motives and separate interests. This is a society of journeymen printers, and as the interests of the journeymen are separate and in some respects opposite to those of the employers, we deem it improper that they should have any voice or influence in our deliberations; therefore, Resolved, that when any member of this society shall become an employing printer he shall be considered without the limits of this society, and not be allowed to vote on any question or pay any dues in the same. That all employing printers who hold seats in this society be considered under the regulations of the foregoing resolution after the first day of December next.

November 1, 1817 in Stevens, *New York Typographical Union Number Six*, pp. 73-74

103. New York Typographical Society: Help for the Unemployed

1. Let every member of this board volunteer his services with promptitude to procure the names of all those working as regular journeymen who are not members, and to report individually to the chairman; and that a Committee of Vigilance, to consist of five members of the board, be appointed, to whom these reports shall be handed over, and whose duty it shall be to communicate with those persons either by letter or personally, and induce them by every means to become members.

2. To find employment for those members who may occasionally want it. We do not conceive that anything at present can be done, other than by mutual exertion. We have noticed, and with the deepest regret and mortification, a relaxation on the part of some individuals, who, regardless and in violation of the solemn pledge they have given of assisting each other in obtaining employment, and with the utmost indifference, often give to strangers that preference which is pledged to a brother member. We do not point particularly to any individual, as no doubt some have done it inadvertently; we simply mention the fact that it may be guarded against in future. We take this opportunity to recommend a most rigid adherence to this principle, as containing the very vitals and spirit of the constitution, without which all the good effects intended by the formation of the institution are rendered nugatory.

March 30, 1814 in Stevens, *New York Typographical Union Number Six*, p. 71

104. New York Typographical Society: Counter Proposal of the New York Master Printers to the Society

New York, October 26, 1809

The master printers of the city of New York, having convened on the 25th instant, by public notice, to deliberate upon certain propositions which had been made to them by the journeymen for an increase of wages, unani-

Launching of the Battleship Ohio, 1820. Naval contracts provided employment for hundreds of crafts-men in the maritime trades at the naval shipyard in Brooklyn, just across the river. WILLIAM J. BENNETT, WATERCOLOR, NYHS

mously (except in two or three trifling instances) adopted the subsequent reso-lutions. In presenting them to the consideration of the Typographical Society, they think it proper to remark, that, although no circumstances have come to their knowledge which would justify on the part of the journeymen a demand for more than the customary wages; yet, desirous of meeting them in the spirit of conciliation and harmony, and to remove every obstacle that might have a tendency to interrupt a mutual good understanding, the master printers have made considerable advances on the prices hitherto given, and to as great an extent as the present state of the printing business would admit. The scale which is now offered may, therefore, be considered as a maximum, beyond which it would be highly injurious, if not ruinous, to the interests of the trade to venture.

In behalf of the meeting.
J. Swords.
J. Crookes.
G. Bruce.

George Barnett, "The Printers, A Study in Trade Unionism," *American Economic Quarterly*, 3d. ser. 10 (1909), 363

Composition

[Changes in Final Settlement in Brackets]

Article 1. That works done in common matter, on brevier or larger type, be paid for by ems at 24 cents [25 cents], on nonpareil 27 cents, on pearl 29 cents [30 cents] per 1,000 (except such as hereafter provided for), and those done in common matter on type larger than English be counted as English.

Article 2. That side, bottom, or cut-in notes, be each of them, whether occurring together or separately, paid for at the rate of 25 cents per sheet, and should they exceed what is considered as moderate, the price shall be struck by the journeymen of the office and the employer. No charge, however, be made for bottom or cut-in notes, unless they, in the course of the volume, exceed in folio or quarto one page, octavo or duodecimo one and one-half pages, and in eighteens or smaller works two pages.

By the early national era printing shops contained type and presses of considerable value and complexity. The cost of such capital made it increasingly difficult for journeymen to strike out on their own. HAZEN, PANORAMA OF TRADES

Article 3. That works done in a different language from the English (though common type) be paid 30 cents [31 cents] for minion and larger type, and 33 cents for smaller type.

Article 7. That broadsides, such as leases, deeds, etc., done on English or smaller type, be paid 30 cents per 1,000 ems. Play-bills, posting bills, etc., to be paid for as may be agreed upon between the journeymen and employer.

Article 10. That algebraical works, or those where characters of music are the principal part, and works containing physical, astronomical, or other signs, be paid for at a medium to be agreed upon by the journeymen and the employer.

Article 13. That no journeyman working at press on a morning daily paper shall receive a less sum than $8 [$9] for his weekly services; not those on an evening paper a less sum than $7 [$8]. If the quantity of work should exceed eight tokens per day, to be charged in a morning paper at 34 cents [37½ cents], if an evening paper at 31¼ cents [33⅓ cents] per token.

Stevens, *New York Typographical Union Number Six*, pp. 54–58

105. Journeymen Cabinet and Chairmakers
Book of Prices:
Introduction

TO THE

MASTER CABINET AND CHAIR MAKERS

OF NEW YORK

Gentlemen,

To you, who are materially concerned in the business for which the following work is intended as a regulation, little need be said in its support. The necessity of such a measure you cannot be ignorant of; and the recent improvements in the trade are sufficient to convince every reasonable man, that, without such a book of regulations, both employers and journeymen must labour under very great disadvantages; and, it is very probable, the greatest inconvenience is on our side: We therefore presume it is but justice to ourselves to endeavour to remedy the evil; and, should the plan we have suggested meet your approbation, we conceive there is little doubt but that it will be productive of the desired salutary effects.

The journeymen of New-York, desirous of shewing every possible degree of respect to their employers, have agreed to inscribe the following work to you; And, conscious of its meriting your attention hope it will be investigated with the candour which its importance to the trade requires; for such has been the disadvantage we have evidently laboured under many fears, that one man should get much more money than another, though of equal or superior abilities from the mere circumstance of his work being better paid for, and which is frequently the case, requiring less merit in the execution. To remove this inconvenience, and to regulate the whole as far as our judgments could lend us, our attention has been directed; and although some prices are raised, and others considerably reduced, yet, upon the whole, we hope the calculation will be found reasonable; and if a small advantage be given in our favour, we trust the increased price of every necessary of life will sufficiently justify the measure. We only wish to obtain a comfortable subsistence, so justly due to every industrious mechanic.

Whoever insinuates that our meetings, which we trust are legal, have been to concert measures hostile to your interests, are enemies to us both. To consiliate a mutual regard—to be treated as men professing an ingenious art—and to have your interests in view as well as our own, have ever been our aim; and for these ends have our labours been employed: In this, we hope, we have in a great measure succeeded; for when you consider the trouble and expense of such a publication, you will naturally suppose that nothing but a consciousness of its impartiality, recommending it to your approbation, could ever induce us to engage in such an undertaking.

> We are, Gentlemen,
>   With every degree of respect,
>   Your's, &c. &c. &c.
>   *The Journeymen Cabinet and Chair Makers of New-York.*

New York, February 15, 1796

Journeymen Cabinet and Chairmakers of New York, *Book of Prices* (New York, 1796), p. 3

COLLECTIVE ACTION

To gain and implement acceptable agreements, the journeymen societies resorted to collective actions of various sorts. These included appeals to employers, communications with societies in other cities, opening their own enterprises, appeals to the public, walk-outs against individual masters, and general turnouts against all the masters in the city in a particular trade. In taking these actions, the journeymen often published appeals and manifestos declaring their motives. There is in these documents, many of them elegant statements, no yearning for their lost hopes of financial independence. Rather, they describe a set of craftsmen with high regard for their abilities and standing and deeply fearful of losing their position as skilled working men a earning a decent wage. They argue that the American Revolution and the republic it produced demand that industrious craftsmen be treated with respect and given financial security in old age or infirmity. The documents reveal a sharp antagonism towards the master craftsmen, who are here portrayed as selfish and uncaring men bent on enriching themselves at the expense of their employees. By their actions these individuals had broken the bonds that unite mechanics as a producer class.

ﻉﻝ ﻉﻝ ﻉﻝ

PRINTERS

The journeymen printers generally relied on appeals to employers to act for the overall benefit of the trade, particularly with regard to the hiring of apprentices and unskilled journeymen (Document 106). Only in its initial year (1809) did the society have the unity and strength to successfully employ a walk-out against obstinant employers, as witnessed by the satirical message of one newspaper (Document 107). During this period of militancy, it corresponded with other societies in an attempt to prevent out-of-town journeymen from filling local jobs at salaries below those established by the Society (Document 108).

106. New York Typographical Society: Appeal to Masters vs. Half-Way Journeymen

To the Master Printers of the City of New York:

Gentlemen: Viewing with deep concern the improper practices in many of the printing offices in this city the journeymen composing the New York Typographical Society have appointed the undersigned a committee to address you on the subject and represent the many evil effects they have on the art of printing in general and the demoralizing effects on the professors.

The practice of employing what is usually styled "half-way journeymen" in preference to those who have served their time, while it holds encouragement to boys to elope from their masters as soon as they acquire sufficient knowledge of the art to be enabled to earn their bread, is a great grievance to the journeymen and almost certain ruin to the boys themselves. Becoming masters of their own conduct at a period of life when they are incapable of governing their passions and propensities they plunge headlong into every species of dissipation and are often debilitated by debauchery before they arrive at the age of manhood; and it also tends to an unnecessary multiplication of apprentices, inasmuch as the place of every boy who elopes from his master is usually supplied by another, while at the same time the runaway supplies after a manner the place of a regular journeyman and one who probably has a family dependent on his labor for support.

We also beg leave to call your attention to a practice as illiberal and unjust as the former and attended, perhaps, with evils of a more aggravated nature. We mean that of taking full-grown men (foreigners) when they are to be turned into the situations of men who are masters of their business, which men are to be turned out of their places by miserable botches because they will work for what they can get. By these means numbers of excellent workmen who ought to be ornaments to the profession are driven by necessity to seek some other means of support.

When a parent puts out a child to learn an art it is with the pleasing idea that a knowledge of that art will enable him when he becomes a man to provide for himself a comfortable subsistence. Did he know that after laboring from his youth to manhood to acquire an art he would be compelled to abandon it and resort to some business to which he was totally unacquainted to enable himself to live, he would certainly prefer that he should in the first instance seek a livelihood on the sea or by some other precarious calling than trust to the equally precarious success of a trade overstocked by its professors. Of the number that have completed their apprenticeship to the printing business within the last five years but few have been enabled to hold a situation for any length of time, and it is an incontrovertible fact that nearly one-half that learned the trade are obliged to relinquish it and follow some other calling for support.

Under the direful influence of these unwarranted practices the professors of the noblest art with which the world is blessed have become birds of passage, seeking a livelihood from Georgia to Maine. It is owing to such practices that to acknowledge yourself a printer is to awaken suspicion and cause distrust. It is owing to such practices that the professors of this noble art are sinking in the estimation of the community. And it is owing to such practices, if persisted, that to see a book correctly printed will after a few years be received as a phenomenon.

To render an art respectable it is indispensibly necessary that professors should be perfect masters of their calling, which can only be acquired by serving a proper apprenticeship. And in our art it is not always true that time will perfect the printer. Regard should always be paid to the capacity and requirements of a boy before he should be suffered to learn the art of printing; for it is too often the case that boys of little or no education are taken as apprentices, which the first services as devil frequently preclude the knowledge of, until they are bound, when the discovery is too late to be remedied. Owing to this deficiency they make sorry printers; whereas, had they learned some trade which does not particularly require a good education they might have been perfect masters of it and better able to gain a livelihood.

These are evils, gentlemen, which we sorely feel, and which it is in your power to remedy, and we sincerely hope that this appeal to your justice and your humanity may meet with that consideration which its importance demands.

D.H. Reins,
W. Burbidge
S. Johnston,
Committee

July 13, 1811 in Stevens, *New York Typographical Union Number Six,* pp. 67–69

107. Journeymen Printers on Strike

To Subscribers

Owing to journeymen *turning* themselves out of work, for increase of wages, the publication of this paper has been delayed. It is fully expected that the ensuing week will decide how much the journeymen *typos* expect for *imposition,* &c. And that afterwards, they will better mind their p's and q's. If their determination is put to the ballot, it is hoped they will handle their *balls* with judgment.

Washington Republican, November 4, 1809

108. Letter from the New York Society to the Philadelphia Society during the New York Strike of 1809

New York, November 13, 1809

Sir:

I received your letter of the 28th ultimo, acknowledging the receipt of mine of the 18th and 23rd; and thank you for the contents, which were peculiarly pleasing to the members of this society. But we have to regret that the communication of the 18th should have created so much trouble, upon a point evidently of little importance to either society. I must apologize for again troubling you. The Board of Directors, however, concerned for the honour of the members of this association, and in order to counteract the evil tendency of a report that this society had dissolved, and the members returned to their situations at the original prices (which we are told by persons arrived from Philadelphia have been circulated there) have directed me to inform you that they continue to persevere in the way they have begun. Most of the master printers have consented to give the prices, yet we have reason to believe that they only wait a favorable opportunity to destroy the society. Circular letters have been sent throughout this state, Connecticut, and Massachusetts, with a view to supply the daily papers with hands in the first instance, and afterwards the book offices. But we are rejoiced to say that as yet they have been defeated in their dishonorable designs. Several journeymen who arrived last week took the situations of those who had been discharged from one of the daily paper offices; but upon coming to a knowledge of their situation, immediately came forward and joined the society.

We know of no falling off yet, and believing that the society will eventually succeed in their "laudable Struggle", would thank you to correct any wrong information which may have been received on the subject.

With the highest respect I am,
Your obedient servant,
David H. Reins
Sec'y N.Y.T. Society

Barnett, "The Printers," p. 18

🕭 🕭 🕭

TAILORS

The journeymen tailors organized a trade society in 1804, whereupon many of the merchant tailors discharged those employees who were members of this incipient association. The society responded with a public appeal asking citizens to patronize only those merchants who were willing to employ its members (Document 109). In 1819 the journeymen tailors walked out on their employers and established their own shop in protest against merchant tailors' practice of hiring low-salaried women to do part of their work. Against charges of conspiracy and greed published by a detractor in the *Evening Post* (Document 110) the journeymen made a spirited if somewhat desperate reply, arguing that female labor degraded the profession and caused underemployment amounting to half a year's labor (Document 111). The author of this plea, describing himself as an "unlettered mechanic," is as much conscious of the deferential tradition of artisans as he is of the new respect and standing attained by republican government. In that line, women laborers, whose standing in the traditional hierarchy was considerably lower than artisans, are described in most contemptuous terms.

109. Organized Journeymen Tailors Appeal for Public Support

TO THE PUBLIC

The United Society of *Journeymen Taylors*, zealous to support that respectability in the eyes of their fellow citizens, which they have enjoyed since their institution, deem it not improper to acquaint the public with the objects of their Institution and the grounds of a difference which now exists between them and the Merchant Taylors Society.

The objects of our Society are, to unite men, whose interest are one, for the laudable purpose of preventing impositions from employers, or from each other, and for correcting those evils which too frequently occur, from various sources, in every mechanical branch; to relieve the necessities of our fellow members, who, through the dispensations of Providence, may be afflicted with sickness, and provide for the decent interment of such of our members as may fall victims to the natural laws of dissolution. We doubt not a humane and generous public will deem these objects worthy the attention of all mechanical bodies, and that the preservation of such an institution is not only praiseworthy to its members but, from its concomitant effects, of public utility, by ameliorating and lessening the sum of human misery.

But the Merchant Taylors Society have declared war against us without having any principle to establish. Our wages are granted, and our regulations, as a Society, have been complied with by them, contrary to the misrepresentations which have been frequently made by Merchant Taylors to reconcile customers to their disappointments.

The cause of this difference, by which the public are partially disappointed, is truly this: The Merchant Taylors have thought it very improper that we should exist as a Society, and have therefore resolved to dissolve us, by discharging our Members from their employ. Consequently, they are reduced to the necessity of serving these customers with the work of women, and unexperienced workmen from different parts of the country. The public will judge of the truth of our observations from their own experience.

A list of the Merchant Taylors in this city who employ Members of our Society.

Francis Davis	Robert Curtis	William Smilie
Frederick Garney	Ridgeway and Hawkins	William Day
Isaac Bloomfield	Wm. Williams	Thomas Ratcliff
Tucker and Allenson	Kenny & White	William Acheson
Joseph Tate	Robert Dunlap	Wm. Weyman
David Logan	Aaron Henry	M. Young
John McIntire	Wm. Arrowsmith	John Foote
Barnet Anderiese	Chesterman and Cheeseborough	Thos. McPherson
Hezekiah Peck	Peter Sutton	Smith & Thorp
Josua Parker	Charles Lee	P.B. Lloyd
Edward Parker	John Bowen	M. Culbert
Joshua Walsee	George Robertson	John McNab
	Robert Beatty	

Gentlemen and Ladies applying to any of the above Merchant Taylors may be supplied with any garment they may have occasion for on the shortest notice, and by the most experienced workmen in the city. By order of the committee.

JOHN BOYD, Secretary

Evening Post, November 23, 1804

110. Communication

The enclosed article from the *Aurora*[11], is, in my opinion, correct, liberal and manly. Not seeing it in the Evening Post, I have presumed that it had escaped your attention, and I therefore inclose it, that you may insert it, and shew yourself to be, what you always have been and, I am sure, always will be, the advocate of

WOMAN

"The Devil among the Tailors."–The journeymen tailors in New-York, it appears, have had what they call a *turn out*–that is, they have combined not to work, unless certain conditions, which they prescribe, are complied with. Every man has a right to determine what he can afford, or what wages he will give; the right to refuse is equal; but combinations of one class, to force another class into any measure against their free will, is an usurpation which violates the first law of society: but there is an aggravation in this case, of the tailors in New-York, which merits a particular and marked detestation: one of the avowed objects of their *turn out*, is to *compel the master tailors not to employ women in any part of the tailor's work.*–The stupidity and brutality of this unmanly conspiracy, requires no coloring to mark its odium; these wretched men, whose conduct almost justifies the contempt that has become proverbial on the occupation–would shut out a numerous class of females from industry and bread, in order to enhance their own wages, which is more than three times the wages that the same class of men receive in England; indifferent to humanity and to the equal rights which they possess, these wretches would consign women to indigence, that they might the more effectually impose upon the public.

"The original cause of casting odium on the occupation of a tailor, and making him the *butt of ridicule* as only the *ninth part of a man*, arose out of a similar occurrence; in about two centuries ago, this trade of a tailor was performed wholly by women; it was scandalous and effeminate, for *men* to work at the needle–this occurred in England, about the close of the fifteenth century; the period when the *doublett, tunic,* and *trunk hose*, began to give way to the *French* frock and skirted coat, with cape and collar, and the flapped breeches; when the name of a *male tailor* became as opprobrious as that of a male *milliner* in modern times. It is a curious instance of revolution in manners that the *men tailors* should now endeavour once more to injure women. If the master tailors are disposed to retrieve their trade from merited odium, they ought to resolve to employ women only; whose proper business it is."

Evening Post, April 20, 1819

❦

111. Journeymen Tailors: Appeal for Support Against the Use of Women

We are now called upon, by the imperative mandate of nature to develop to the world an act, unprecedented in its form, and intolerable in its oppression—I mean the unmanly and ungenerous conduct of the Merchant Tailors of New York, towards the Journeymen. It will be recollected that some two or three months ago the Journeymen Tailors were engaged in what mechanics call a turn out, by which is generally meant a contest with their employers for an increase in wages. This was not the object of the Journeymen Tailors in their then turn out so called; though stated as one of their objects by the pragmatical interference of a gentlemen from Philadelphia whose billingsgate production on the subject in question, made its appearance in the city through the vehicle of the *Evening Post*.

This is an egregious distortion of fact, founded on ignorance or malevolent mendacity. The Journeymen only contended for the privilege of making Vests and Pantaloons, a right which belong to them, and to them alone. The gentlemen in question after advancing the preposterous and truly ridiculous idea that garments of every description ought to be made by women, very categorically asserts, that an employer has a right to determine what he can afford or what wages he will give. We say not; such are the contracted views of men in common life, who, when fortune so propitiously smile upon them, as to enable them to commence and continue in, a profitable course of business; their only object is to accumulate money; in the aggregation of which, they were perfectly regardless of the wants of the Journeymen who they employ. The wretched helot is better qualified to feel the burden under which he labours than the merciless tyrant who inflicts it; hence the Journeyman is better able to decide upon the merit of his labour than his employer is for him. Believe me; in no part of America, are Journeymen Tailors so much oppressed as in New-York, and in no part of America are there so many wealthy Tailors, as their employers and oppressors. Not content with depriving them of a large portion of their work to complete the climax of their illiberality, they have even determined to reduce their wages one dollar upon each coat, already very insufficient indeed. The gentleman above alluded to states that the wages of Journeymen Tailors in this country is tergeminous to that of the same class of men in England. This is an evident mistake. A journeyman Tailor in this country only earns from $10 to

$12 per week, and that only about one half the year; the reason of which is that Vests and Pantaloons are made altogether by women in this country, (except in Philadelphia and Albany) whereas, in England, all habiliments worn by men are made by men, for which they receive 37 shillings sterling per week, and that too, almost through the year, which certainly gives the latter an infinite advantage over the former. It is truly astonishing that any man should be so limited in his judgement as to pretend to say, that the whole business of a Tailor ought to be performed by women, because the simple and formless dress of the doublett, tunic &c., worn by men, was made by women about the close of the 15th century. It is an indisputable fact that women are very inadequate to perform the work of a Tailor, which I shall endeavor to prove by the following syllogism. A Journeyman Tailor not above the level of mediocrity, cannot make a superfine plain coat to pass the ordeal of criticism, much less many

A gentleman's velvet embroidered suit, 1795. Handicraft skill of the highest level was required to produce fine men's wear. Even so, tailors often suffered contempt as one of the lower trades. MCNY

other garments that might be named; yet this very man can make waistcoats and pantaloons, and that too, with more judgement and solicitude than a woman can; hence we infer that women are incomplete, and if incomplete they ought to disclaim all right and title whatever to the avocation of a tailor–What right has any man to interfere to the prejudice of another, or any set of men and publicly pretend to decide upon a subject, the merit or demerit of which he is perfectly unacquainted with? Suppose that I, an unlettered mechanic, should endeavor to soar to the sublime and unmeasurable regions of astronomy, you would laught at my arrogance, and pity my ignorance. Hence it is reasonable to infer, that every man must be the sole judge of the nature of his peculiar avocation; Is it reasonable, I would ask, that the best of workmen should be unemployed half the year, and calmly submit to reiterated privations by the empiricism of women, many of whom have served but a few months at the business, aided by the mercenary support of their employers, merely because women work cheaper than men? Certainly not. Nothing can be offered in justification of women asking, or employers giving, work to women, other than the long continuance of an unwarrantable practice, which is, indeed but a very slender excuse. A man after having served a septenniel apprenticeship to a branch of business, (No matter what) has a right to all the profit accruing therefrom. In offering an address to the public, we necessarily appeal to all ranks of people, the rich and the learned, well as the poor and unlearned. We are well aware that many of the former disdain even the prospective of the concerns of common life; but let such remember, that in a grand theater of human action each one must perform the part allotted him, and that each is indispensible, and he whose humble lot it is to play a labourious, but inconspicuous part, ought nevertheless to be justly supported, or the whole drama would fall into a scene of chaotic confusion.

Much might be said on the this subject, but we forbear prolixity. We think, however, that we are entitled to public indulgence, so far as to make a public defence, to a public injury received–We feel extremely sorry, (especially at this glorious era) still glowing with the fond remembrance of liberty and emancipation, to have occasions to relate that the secret hand of oppression is still raising its ponderous force, endeavoring to shackle the feeble arm of poverty. Nevertheless, many of us are exotics, and can therefore duly appreciate the superiority of this above every other country, and proud in receiving it as the asylum of the oppressed of all, the guide to happiness and the landmark of freedom–Fully assured then, of the justice of our cause, we do not grovelingly beg, but manfully ask public support, which we feel confident will flow spontaneously from the hand of liberality. Resting safely on the approbation of the public, we anticipate a fortunate triumph over an ungenerous and dastardly attack against the feeble force of the now commencing dull season of the year. I must therefore conclude this article in behalf of the much injured journeymen tailors of New-

York, by inviting the public to pass at No. 88 Courtland-street where the very best of workmen perform their business in its great variety of parts. With due respect, I subscribe myself the public's most humble servant.

A JOURNEYMAN TAILOR

Evening Post, July 13, 1819

❧ ❧ ❧

CABINETMAKERS

The journeymen cabinetmakers, perhaps the most highly skilled of the city's craftsmen, were organized from the 1790s on. When in 1802 the masters unilaterally promulgated a new book of prices without negotiations, the journeymen walked out and opened their own store. The effort proved unsuccessful, and so a generally unsatisfactory pact was agreed to four months later and the journeymen's furniture auctioned off (Document 112). Again in 1805 the cabinetmakers walked out on their employers when they believed that they had been mistreated and deceived in negotiations to raise their prices in accord with the increase in the cost of provisions and rent (Document 113). During the Panic of 1819, the cabinetmakers working for Duncan Phyfe walked out and opened their own store when he insisted on lowering wages (Document 114).

112. Journeymen Cabinet Makers: Strike Appeal

TO THE PUBLIC

As the Journeymen Cabinet Makers of this city have deemed it expedient to leave off working for their employers a decent respect for the opinions of their fellow-citizens, points out the propriety of submitting to the public a few of those circumstances which have impelled them to take recourse to this measure.

With a view to prevent disputes between the employers and the journeymen there has existed in this city, for many years past, a *Book of Prices*, in which it is specified the precise sum to be paid by the master cabinetmaker to his journeymen, for every particular piece of workmanship in that line. Since the

This emblem, symbolizing both republicanism and usefulness to society, was displayed by the Chair makers at the Erie Canal Parade in 1825. Although masters and journeymen marched together at this parade, both still sharing pride in their craft, the divergent interests of the two groups were becoming more and more apparent as labor conflict intensified. NYPL

first establishment of this book, the rates have at different times, varied according to circumstances. On former occasions, however, an alteration was never attempted with respect to prices except at a meeting of a joint committee from the employers and journeymen, by whom, after the matter in dispute had been fully discussed, it was at last settled by the mutual consent of both parties.

In the present instance, however, the conduct of the employers has been exceedingly different:–They have associated by themselves, and, without deigning to have any consultation with us, have presented to us a *New Book of Prices*, which, on the average, will deduct at least 15 percent. from our former wages– and they have bound themselves under a considerable penalty to each other, that they will not employ any workmen except according to the prices which they themselves have laid down in their *new fashioned book*. Nor is that all:– They have by a variety of arts brought over to an acquiesence in their measures, such of the employers, as, being actuated by a love of justice and humanity, are still willing to employ and pay us according to the former established prices.

This being our present situation, we have no alternative but either to receive as a compensation for our labor what our employers may, from time to time, condescend to allow us, or to shift for ourselves. To the contemplated diminution of our wages, we cannot possibly agree, as that which we received previous to the intended imposition of our employers was barely sufficient to

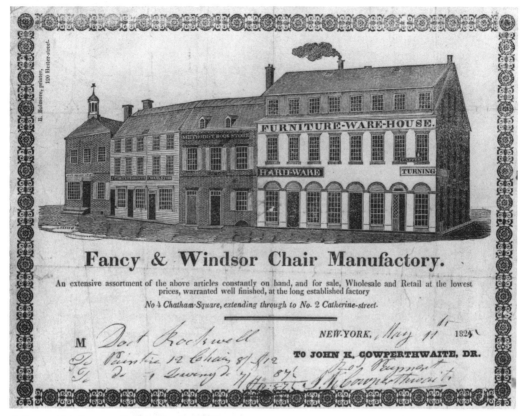

A large manufactory of chairs in the 1820s. LANDAUER COLLECTION, NYHS

maintain the most industrious mechanic, provided he had a family. For them,
therefore, we can work no longer. At the same time, as a hard winter is staring
us in the face, our circumstances will not admit to our remaining idle–Our
Society, therefore, have opened a WARE-ROOM, at No. 49 JOHN STREET, next door
to the Corner of William-street, where they will have ready, in a short time, a
quantity of as ELEGANT FURNITURE as has ever been exhibited for sale in this city–
and as they are determined to dispose of every article of their manufacture at
the LOWEST PRICES they have no doubt of being encouraged by the thinking part
of the community, who, by favouring them with their commands, will thus be
the means of rescuing a number of their fellow-citizens from the machinations
of an unjust combination to suppress them.

    P.S. We think it necessary to inform the public, that Messrs. McEvers
& Dolan, as also Mr. Thomas Tompson, and Mr. John T. Bull, do not belong
to the combination of Employers, but that they continue to pay their workmen
according to the former established rates. We would have mentioned the circumstance at the first insertion of our advertisement, had it not been generally
understood that the two last of these gentlemen would engage none to work for

them who had left their employers, and the two first, Messrs. McEvers & Dolan, had not commenced business at the time our dispute began. As, however, they have declared themselves altogether opposed to the combination, we wish to render them every tribute of respect to which they are justly entitled, for their *justice and humanity.*

American Citizen, December 22, 1802

113. Journeymen Cabinetmakers: Justification of Walk-Out

TO THE PUBLIC . . . The Journeymen Cabinet Makers having lately had a dispute with their Employers, and as they value the approbation of the public more then the object of their contention, they hope it will not be considered impertinent to lay before them the following letter, which contains the substance of their disagreement—

An eagle back Duncan Phyfe chair made in 1810. This is a fine example of a chair crafted in the Federalist style in the finest craft shop in New York. The eagle, of course, symbolized the new republic, a source of great pride for artisans.
MCNY

To the Society of Employing Cabinet Makers

"The high regard that the Journeymen Cabinet Makers ever evince for truth, candour and integrity, compels them to put you in remembrance of past facts, and the consequent resolution of their Society. You will recollect that in the year 1802 you published a book for the prices of their labor, about 8 per cent. lower than what they were accustomed to work for. The duty they owe themselves, their families and posterity, obliged them to resist it, but after a struggle of 6 months, when a few of the prices were advanced, and a promise of an advance on the whole book, in proportion to the increase of the price of provisions and other necessaries of life, the Journeymen returned to their employment.

"It is needless to tell you of the enormous rise of provision &c. but you will remember, about two months since the journeymen requested a meeting of your committee, at which meeting the promise was acknowledged and the journeymen desired an advance on the whole book of 10 per cent. which is far short of a proportionable advance. Your committee said they had not power from you to accede to it and desired a future meeting. At this meeting, however, (strange as it must appear to an honest heart) that very committee who on a former period acknowledged the existence of the promise, now defied the journeymen to produce a written document to prove it, and positively refused the advance requested. The journeymen, thus convinced that no trust or confidence can be placed in your committee, have resolved not to meet or consult with you as a body, or any committee appointed by you.

By order of Society
JOHN BLACK, Sec'y"

N.B. As it is not designed by publishing the above to irritate our late employers, but to prevent any prejudice that may arise through misrepresentations, we declare whenever they shall manifest a disposition to fulfil their former engagements, with us, we are ready to treat with them.

Evening Post, April 10, 1805

114. Journeymen Cabinet Makers: Walk-out Against Duncan Phyfe

The Journeymen Cabinet and Chair-Makers of New-York, being activated by motives truly honorable, (as we trust we shall not be considered by liberal minded men as acting unfairly toward our late employers) take the liberty of

The only known painting of Duncan Phyfe. A Federalist, Phyfe was a wealthy, conservative craftsman of strict moral habits. He was a demanding and perhaps occasionally parsimonious employer. AMERICAN COLLECTOR (MAY, 1942)

informing the public, and their friends in particular, that they have taken the old established Cabinet Warehouse, 61 Beekman Street, where all orders will be thankfully received and promptly attended to. They also inform the public, that most of the men at work at their Warehouse have been employed by Mr. Phyfe[13] for many years, and the reason of their leaving him is a demand for the reduction of our wages, which we cannot for a moment think of acceding to. We therefore pledge ourselves to all those who may honor us with their employ, as well as those employers who have not made a demand for a reduction of our wages, that their work shall be executed in a style equal to any in the continent, and on the most reasonable terms — our principle object being the maintaining of our wages and the support of our families, while these unhappy differences exist between the employers and journeymen.

P.S. All articles will be manufactured from good seasoned wood and the best of materials.

National Advocate, May 12, 1819

❧   ❧   ❧

CARPENTERS AND MASONS

Unlike the printers, tailors and cabinetmakers, journeymen in the populous building trades worked for daily wages ranging from nine to sixteen shillings per day (one shilling = 12½ cents). There is evidence that New York's carpenters had organized themselves as early as 1785 when they acted against masters'

The warehouse, workshop and showroom of Duncan Phyfe, 1814. At the height of his career the renowned cabinetmaker employed up to one hundred artisans. J.R. SMITH, WATERCOLOR, ROGERS FUND, MMNY

attempts to reduce their wages while at the same time raising the charges asked of builders. In this instance the journeymen attempted to establish their own hiring hall where builders could employ them directly. They continued this attempt to control their terms of employment as late as 1800 (Document 115). In 1810, the carpenters turned to much more militant actions when, during the height of the building season, they went on strike demanding an increase in wages. Their eloquent statement, echoing the Declaration of Independence, is representative of the meaning that artisan republicanism held for this generation of skilled journeymen (Document 116). Further declarations condemn the business methods of charging customers high prices while cutting wage costs and of threatening to bring in out-of-town laborers to break their strike (Documents 117–118). The masons, who went on strike in 1809 and 1819 over wages, exhibited similar zeal and unity (Documents 119–120).

Indoor carpentry workshops. ANDERSON COLLECTION, NYPL

115. Carpenters Establish Employment Agency

Notification–The Public are hereby informed that at a respectable Meeting of House-Carpenters, Held on the 6th day of December 1799, it was taken into consideration and agreed, that the present mode of employing Carpenters is attended with many inconveniences   both to Employees and Carpenters. First. Arising from the impossibility of certainly determining the ability of the Person taken into employ.

Secondly. From the negligence or indifference or many of those concerned in employing of Workmen to perform the business for which they are employed. These observations contain in their Bosom thousands of others, which no attentive Employer can be entirely ignorant of, and which might be improper to insert in a public advertisement.

It was therefore agreed that a House be appointed to be known by the Name of a House of Call for Carpenters, and that Employers and others concerned in Building, by applying there shall be served without favor to any, agreeable to the above Resolution.–The House hereby appointed is at Hatfield's Tavern, opposite the Fields in the Front Room Upstairs.

The Abilities of the Body of Workman need not be told, since the Public will be more competent Judges of their qualifications than they have hitherto been.–

Mercantile Advertiser, April 25, 1800

116. Carpenters' Strike Manifesto

TO THE PUBLIC

At a general meeting of the journeymen House Carpenters, convened at Harmony Hall on Tuesday, the 4th of April, it was unanimously resolved, that on mature consideration of their rights, and the necessity of their situation, to work no longer than April the 10th inst. for less than eleven shillings per day.

When one class of society find it necessary to act in any manner that concerns the general interest, justice to themselves and respect for the public require that the reasons of such actions should be signed.

Among the unalienable rights of man are life, liberty, and the pursuit of happiness. By the social compact every class of society ought to be entitled to benefit in proportion to its usefulness, and the time and expense necessary to its qualification. Among the duties which individuals owe to society are single men to marry and married men to educate their children. Among the duties which society owes to individuals is to grant them compensation for services sufficient not only for the current expenses of livelihood, but to the formation of a fund for the support of that time of life when nature requires a cessation from labor. We will now revert to the particulars of our own situation, to show the justice and necessity of our demand. We have only to give a statement of our annual income and expenses. The year is composed of 365 days, 52 of which are Sundays, which leaves 313 days of labour. Deducting from this amount those days of which custom and labor deprive us of pursuing our avocation, we will find that 300 is the aggregate amount of the days a mechanic can call his own for pursuing the means necessary to the support of himself and family. Calculating from the 10th of March to the 10th of November which is two thirds of the year, (that is 200 days according to our calculation, at eleven shillings per day) the amount is $275.

From the 10th of November to the 10th of March, at 10sh. per day, $125. Total amount of our income is $400.

These items of expense will be:

House rent	$ 55	
Fire wood	50	
Victualling a family at the average of 50 cents per day	162	50
Our own wearing apparel	60	
Expense of wear & loss of tool, unavoidable in our branch	10	
Contingent expenses	20	
Total amount of these items	$357	50
Balance	$ 42	50

Leaving for wife's clothing, expenses of family sickness, and the clothing and education of children, the sum of 42 dollars 50 cents. And now let us ask those that are fathers of families to judge what will be the amount of the surplus for the maintenance of old age?

ROBT. TOWNSEND Jun.
RICHARDSON RYAN
BENJ. HOGHLAND
Committee appointed by and behalf of the Journeymen House-Carpenters

American Citizen, April 10, 1809

117. Journeymen House Carpenters: On the Conduct of the Masters

JOURNEYMEN HOUSE CARPENTERS of the City of New-York, convened at Harmony Hall on Thursday evening, 17th inst.—when the advertisement of those *men* calling themselves Master Builders having been read and considered, *It was unanimously resolved*, that as we have received twelve shillings per day we will not work for any Master Carpenter whatever, until the wages shall be established at 12 s. per day.

ROBT TOWNSEND Jr. Chairman,
GEO. HANSEN Secretary.

When we published the reasons which induced us to require 12 s. per day for our labour, we trusted we should engage in our favor men of generous feelings, which we did. They gave us our just demand—after having enjoyed it for three weeks we are suddenly deprived of it, and by whom? By men some of whom but yesterday were Journeymen, some are master builders but in name, some, who if they were to pay journeymen what they owe them, would do better than sending their names to curtail our wages. There are some among them whom we respect for their abilities as workmen—But the haughtiness and overbearance of whose conduct better fits them to give laws to slaves, than assume the prerogative of depriving freemen of their just rights. There are a few among them whom we never did or can respect for their abilities as workmen or their conduct as men towards us. Employers may perhaps believe (as most of these would wish them to believe) that it is for their interest alone that has induced them to oppose us contrary to their late assurances of giving us the wages thro' the season.

Is it for the interest of employers that they should be charged with full wages for men working below wages—Or that one employer should be charged with the wages of a journeyman working at another's employ? Is it within such conduct that master builders would be able after being in business two or three years, either to glide in their Carriages, or build brick houses for themselves? When we require just compensation for our labour, such are the first men to cry out against it as an imposition. That such things may be done away, employers have justice done them, and we a sufficient compensation for our labour we offer to work under the superintendence of men of our own choice, who shall be competent thereto either by the day, or by book of prices which the master builders of this city framed, and by which several buildings have been built, a copy of which book the employer may obtain when he engages with us, that he may know whether or not the surveyors do them justice. Those employers who may wish to have work done may be served by applying at Harmony Hall, corner of William and Duane streets, where proper persons are appointed to attend.[13]

N.B. At a meeting of the above, on Saturday afternoon, the 19th Inst. it was unanimously resolved, That the resolution of the meeting on Friday evening be published, viz. That when any new hand comes to work for any Master Carpenter, the *workmen* in his employ shall examine his abilities and whether or not he is worth the full wages, and if not, endeavour to find out what he receives per day, and what the employer charged for him, and if there is any imposition to inform the employer thereof.

American Citizen, May 23, 1810

118. Journeymen House Carpenters: On the Use of Strikebreakers

Wanted from one to three hundred Journeymen Carpenters for which immediate employment will be given at $1. 37½ per day by the master carpenters of this city.[14]

New York June 2

TO MASTER CARPENTERS

Three hundred journeymen carpenters wishes immediate employment at a fair price for their services. N. York June 4

TO THE PUBLIC

If there is sincerity in the above notice of the master carpenters, why, we ask, are they now willing to give country hands eleven shillings per day, when it is a well known fact that the only arguments made use of by them to the journeymen have been that they would not subscribe to any stated prices, whereby they would be obliged to give country hands 11s. per day, or any stated sum a day; that but one green hand out of twenty (meaning country carpenters) were capable of earning one dollar per day. — And now with these assertions staring them in the face, they come forward in an advertisement, headed in staring capitals, indiscriminately offering 11s. per day to country carpenters, particularly inviting them from the Eastern states, (and the Back Woods) where it is known not one man out of twenty has half a knowledge of his business; and such are the men whom master carpenters are going to set to work to finish off a gentleman's house in taste and elegance; and this too at 11s. per day, while they at the same time refuse one shilling more to the competent workman, whom they themselves (the master carpenters) have acknowledged are worth two green hands; and yet these men talk of consistency. The fact is, in the above advertisement the master carpenters have completely exposed themselves to the ridicule of every journeyman and have given us stronger grounds to hold out for our just rights than before. Feeling fully persuaded that if country carpenters (Green Hands) are worth eleven shillings per day, the city carpenters (experienced workmen) are worth twenty; all which is fully submitted to the discerning public.

JOURNEYMEN CARPENTERS

To Boss Carpenters in the country from every section of the union, particularly from the Eastern states.

Wanted instantaneously from five hundred to one thousand Country Bosses, particularly such as have been employed in building Log Houses and Indian WIGWAMS[15] for the purpose of instructing the drove of country carpenters who are now on their way by forced marches to the city of New York.

N.B. No monopolising Bosses will be employed, but such as are willing that journeymen should have an existance as well as themselves.

American Citizen, June 6, 1810

119. Journeymen Masons: On Unity in Action

At a numerous meeting of the Journeymen Mason's Society, held at Menley's Long Room, on the 26th inst. the resolutions of the master masons, passed on the 21st inst. were read, whereupon it was

Resolved, that if the object of the said resolution should be acquiesced in and the journeymen's wages reduced, that it would be impossible for many to support themselves and families.

Resolved, That Journeymen Masons do not work after this meeting until their wages are established and allowed by the master masons, at the rate of fifteen shillings per day.

Resolved, That it is but justice to state to those other masons and employers who are willing at this time to pay the usual wages, that it is with great reluctance that they have left their employ, as they consider that it will be impossible to establish the wages at any price unless they stand to the foregoing resolution unanimous, until the question is decided.

> JOHN C. MATTHIAS, Chairman.
> JOHN M. DEMAREST, Sec'ry.

Evening Post, May 27, 1819

120. Journeymen Masons: Economic Justification for Walk-Out

TO THE PUBLIC

The journeymen masons of the city of New-York, being desirous as possible to convince a candid public of the peculiarity of their situation, when contrasted with that of other mechanics, submit the following statement for their consideration, which it is presumed will show sufficient cause why they at present refuse to work, at the price established by the master masons.

The number of days which masons usually work will not exceed 213, which at 15 shillings per day amounts to $399 37½; whereas, could they work every day, Sundays excepted, the amount would be $536 87½; which makes a difference of $187.50.

We now ask, how it is possible for a journeyman who has a family of five persons, and numbers have more, to support them as they should be, when a tenement, in the suburbs of the city, cannot be rented for less than $60; fuel will cost at least $13; clothing for five, $100; provision $195; which will leave a balance of $26 37½, for schooling, physician's bills, &c. &c.

After thus candidly making the foregoing statement, it is hoped no redeeming person will accuse them of being extravagant in their demands.

Evening Post, May 31, 1819

SHOEMAKERS

Shoemakers were as miltant as any group of journeymen. In 1809 they went on strike against employer Charles Aimes because he hired first a non-member and then an illegal apprentice. When the other masters came to Aimes's aid, the Society called a general strike against all master shoemakers. The mas-

Masons at work. ANDERSON COLLECTION, NYPL

ters then took the journeymen to court where they were indicted and convicted for conspiracy under English Common Law (See Documents 127–131). This did not deter them as they again went on strike in 1811 and were again indicted for conspiracy. Affidavits extant from that trial (Documents 121–122) indicate the strength and methods of the Society.[16] In 1815 and 1816 there are further records of walk-outs, the latter coupled with the opening of a journeymen-operated store (Document 123).

121. Cause and Consequences of Expulsion from the Cordwainers Society

City of New York: William Dougherty of No. 4 Albany Bason being duly sworn deposeth and saith that he is a Cordwainer by trade and has followed that trade for a livelihood for himself & family a number of years last past and for a considerable time in this City—That he has for some time worked for Messr. Tucker and Lockwood as a Journeyman—That on or about the fourteenth day of October

Last Mr. Lockwood called at the House of the Deponent and left him the Materials whereof to make a pair of boots – That afternoon, towit on the same day Henry Bogert, Moses Deane and Henry Van called upon the Deponent and informed the Deponent that the Journeymen Shoe Makers – had made a Strike, or turn out to raise their wages and requested the Deponent not to take out any more work until that business should be settled. The Deponent promised to conform to their wishes and accordingly finished what he had on hand and took out no more until the Bauses had consented to give the wages demanded – The Deponent after the raising of the wages as aforesaid went and procured work of a Mr. Norris in Broadway and had done some thing for him when the regular time of the meeting of the Journeyman Cordwainers Society came around towit the third Monday of the month of October and knowing that there was a Difficulty in obtaining work without being a Member of the said Society he called at the place of meeting and as he conceived had become a member by paying the fee to Mr. James Melvin the President of said Society such as he demanded therefore – That after he had so as aforesaid become a member of said Society Valentine and George Holman and Moses Deane and perhaps thirty or forty more of said Society asserted that this Deponent had worked during the time that the Society or the Journeyman Cordwainers were standing out for wages and that according to the rules of their Society this Deponent was Subject to a fine of three Dollars nothwithstanding he was not a Member at that time, and because the deponent refused to pay the said fine his initiation fee was returned to him by the said President and he was removed from the said Society – That about a couple of Days after the Deponent called upon Mr. Norris whom he then worked for for more work but was informed by said Norris that some of the society had called upon him and had told him that if he gave the deponent any more work to do that they would Strike against him or would quit him and not work for him in consequence of which the said Norris said he could not give the Deponent any work whereby the Deponent was much injured in his business – Since which he has applyed also to L & W Burton Cordwainers in Broadway and W. Frond in Pearl Street who all have refused him work on account of the Society's rules not to work for any Bause who gives work to any Journeyman Cordwainer under like circumstances wherefore the Deponent prays that the said President and Members of said Society may be constrained to answer the said offence.

Sworn before me on this 4th day of Nov. 1811
$50

William Dougherty
James Warner
special Justice

Court of General Sessions, Indictment Papers, NYCMA

122. Experience of a Scab: The Power of the Cordwainers Society

City of New York: William Benton of No. 82 Broadway Cordwainer and Thomas Benton being duly Sworn depose and say that about two or three weeks ago a person said to be named Dougherty called at the shop for work. That one of the Deponents gave him work but after he had the work the said Dougherty addressing himself to these Deponents or one of them said Do you know I am what they call a Scab, meaning as these Deponents believe that he was excommunicated the Cordwainers Society. Thereupon he was told it was not worth while to make a Disturbance in the Society Whereupon the said man left the work and went off—

Sworn before me this 6th day of Nov 1811

> Wm Benton
> Th Benton
> James Warner special Justice

Court of General Sessions, Indictment Papers, NYCMA

123. Journeymen Boot and Shoe Makers: Opening of a Journeymen's Store

TAKE NOTICE

The publick are respectfully informed, that owing to the differences existing between the journeymen boot and shoe makers and their employer occasioned by an ungenerous attempt on the part of the employers to reduce the journeymen's wages at this inclement season of the year, then they had good reason to believe their necessaries could compel them to submit to whatever reduction of prices the employers might think proud to offer—considering such treatment too harsh to be borne, the journeymen have been induced to open a store, where the public may be supplied at a few hours notice with gentlemen's boots and shoes of every description. The above articles shall be manufactured with the very best of materials; and as it is an association of the journeymen the public will really see that they have it fully in their power to furnish all articles in the above line at the first rate worksmanship, which they promise faithfully to perform—and they trust that the well known liberality of the citizens of New York will not be backward in support of an establishment which has for its object to do justice to the laboring mechanic and honestly to serve the public. Application to be made at the number 32 Maiden-Lane. The business will be conducted under the firm of MELVIN and MOREHOUSE.

Evening Post, February 14, 1816

THE MASTER'S RESPONSE

Master craftsmen were resourceful at meeting the challenge posed by the journeymen. Like the journeymen, they formed associations to allow a collective response and to promote the interests of their professions. Although no constitutions of these societies are extant, their existence is revealed in notices that they issued annually announcing the wages that they would pay to journeymen in the oncoming year. These rates may have at times been agreed to by negotiation, but it is apparent that often they were unilateral manifestos (Document 124). According to charges made by the journeymen, the associations were willing to urge or coerce suppliers of raw materials not to furnish recalcitrant journeymen shoemakers with leather, and carvers and upholsterers not to deal with rebellious journeymen cabinet and chairmakers (Document 125). Too, the masters could bring in new hands or lock out and wait out the journeyment as "Candour," a spokesman for master builders, advised in 1810 during a carpenters' strike (Document 126).

A final and potentially powerful weapon was court action. In 1809, the master shoemakers took the journeymen to court, charging that their attempt to enforce a closed shop through a constitution that prohibited members from working with nonmembers or unqualified apprentices was an illegal conspiracy under the common law (Document 127). Through their noted counsel, city recorder Richard Riker and Irish emigre Thomas A. Emmet,[17] along with attorney Griffin, the masters argued that the shoemakers' practices constituted a monopolistic conspiracy harmful to society, a violation of a "tacit compact" of artisans to follow their trades towards the general good. Too, they reasoned, it was a violation of the rights of journeymen not wishing to join the society and of masters who wished to employ hands of their own choice (Documents 128–129). Through their eloquent advocate William Sampson,[18] the journeymen replied that English common law on which the indictment was based was invalid in this case because it was contrary to human rights and to the United States Constitution. Furthermore, he argued, the journeymen, like others in society, should have the right to organize and create market leverage (Documents 130–131).

In its charge to the jury, the court clearly thought otherwise and the journeymen were quickly convicted, this verdict casting a shadow over future labor actions.[19]

It should be noted that in the contrasting arguments, each group of artisans contended for a conception of artisan republicanism. The masters argued for the concept of civic humanism and collectivity that put public interest ahead of private gain, while the journeymen argued for the right to compete freely in the marketplace, or the Lockean conception of private right. (The masters, of course, were benefitting from the open market.) This is a dramatic example of how the two very different strands of republicanism became directly entwined in artisan conflict within the community.

The master craftsmen saw themselves as the protectors of their trades, believing that they alone had the knowledge and foresight to set proper compensation and the limits of permissible employee conduct. This is apparent in a letter by John McComb, a master builder and architect of the new City Hall in reply to a request for increased wages (Document 132). This paternal attitude was no small cause of the considerable labor strife in this era.

124. Master Carpenters and Masons Assert Wage Scales

At a meeting of Master Carpenters of this City, held at Crook's Inn, 12th November 1800; Andrew Durham, in the Chair, Resolved unanimously – that from the 10th instant to the 10th of March next, our wages shall be One Shilling per day lower than last summer regulations. And that in future old work, repairing, and what is commonly called jobbing, shall be allowed one shilling per day more than the established wages for the time being. By order of the meeting. Isaac Sharpless. sec.

Daily Advertiser, November 11, 1800

&.   &.   &.

At a meeting of the Master Masons of the city of New-York, held on Friday evening the 21st, at St. John's Hall, agreeable to public notice – Wm. Westerfield was appointed chairman, and H. Wicks secretary – the following resolution was unanimously adopted:

Whereas those employers who are at this time engaged in building in this city, feeling much dissatisfied at the present high wages given to the mechanics under their employ, considering the great depression[20] on almost every article of merchandize and provisions in general – We, therefore, the master masons in this city, after having duly considered the reasons in favor of reducing the wages at this time, are of the opinion that it is neither politic nor right for the mechanics to insist on the present high wages: We, therefore, for the benefit of those under our employ, as well as for our own advantage, do *resolve*, that we will give no more than *fourteen shillings per day*, after the 22d of this month, to the journeymen under our employ.

> WM. WESTERFIELD, chairman.
> H. WICKS, secretary.

Evening Post, May 12, 1819

125. Journeymen's Complaint of Masters' Tactics

. . . . Thus far, however, we can vouch for, that individuals belonging to their association, whether acting as a committee, or in their own private capacity, we know not, have run about with much zeal from shop to shop, dissuading those gentlemen who seemed disposed to allow our former wages from employing us on any other terms than those laid down in the new book. With respect to their having used no endeavours to force us into an acceptance of the new prices, the statement of one solitary fact will afford sufficient conviction to the contrary to every thinking mind: they have waited upon different carvers and upholsterers, whom they have endeavoured to prevail on both by threats and caresses, to have no connection with us, hoping that by thus preventing us from earning a subsistence by ourselves, we should be glad to return to them, and work on their own terms . . . .

Morning Chronicle, January 1, 1803

126. In Defense of the Master Builders

A Hint to the Industrious Mechanic

It cannot be denied that the present standing out for wages is becoming no small evil on that class of people who now are rallying around the standard of impropriety at *Harmony Hall*.

I will read with attention their names if they will publish them, and believe that six out of ten of that number, who are constant attenders of that Tavern and who are the first to stand out for wages, never in their time, and I doubt if ever they will, do justice to the wages offered by the Master Workmen; there are some among them that has obtained information, and are very useful members in Society, that exert themselves to do justice to the employers to the master workmen, that credit so necessary in this improving city. Such are the men the most able and the least willing to stand out in the present contest, others cannot without contracting debts, they must work hard to discharge in the ensuing season.

Each day a Journeyman does not work is a loss to him, (amounting nearly to the advance should they succeed) of two weeks work, and should the journeymen contend for one week more, and get the wages they ask, on about next November they will have profited by their labor (taking no notice of the money they spend during the time they are not at work) nearly the same sum they would have made had they not deserted their employers on the 15th, should they not succeed in getting the wages it must be a great loss–I boldly assert they will not.

The unanimity of the meeting [of master workmen] at Hodgkinson's and the increase of the names of those who did not know of the meeting, or from other engagements could not attend, the support given by the employers to the resolution of the Master builders, together with the unwarrantable conduct of those journeymen who parade on the streets, must induce every reasonable person to believe they cannot succeed.

There are many useful journeymen in this city who do not attend the meetings at *Harmony Hall,* but are working for their friends, others working for themselves, much to their credit, and I pledge myself that at the close of the season they will find that it has been much to their advantage.

There are master workmen who attended the meeting at Hodgkinson's that have acted contrary to their promise. I mean Messrs. Brittan and Ludlow, there are also some master workmen who did not attend the meeting, for causes being known only to themselves, perhaps in order to select good workmen, are giving the wages required by the Journeymen. *All* this will not cause the major part of the master workmen to consent *altho' they have contracted for buildings.*

I say it is out of the power of many to give the wages, and for this reason the employer says I *will not*; if they will not work for the wages you offer them, cover up my walls–I will suspend building for the season. And much to the credit of many employers is the generous manner in which they have come forward to those who have *contracted* for buildings. They say altho' you are limited to time, I will take no advantage of it–from the extraordinary exertions of the master workmen, and the support given to that exertion by the employers, it is impossible for the Journeymen to establish any other wages than that offered by the master workmen in their resolution on Tuesday last at Hodgkinson's. The advice to them is to do their work, and make the best of a bad promise; all informed men say, a bad promise is better broken than kept.

Candour

WHEREAS experience has shewn that much irregularity and confusion has taken place for want of a uniform regulation, pointing out the proper time to be observed by Carpenters and Masons, so as to suit the different seasons, and the wages from time to time established, to enable them to work ten hours in the long, and nine hours in the short days,—

IT was therefore, after due deliberation, Resolved, by the Company of MASTER BUILDERS, at their Stated Meeting, held on the 11th of March 1805, That in future the following regulations should be observed as nearly as well may be.

	To begin in the Morning.	Time at Breakfast.	Time at Noon.	Time to quit Work.	Working Hours.
	Hours.	Hours.	Hours.	Hours.	
1. From Second Monday in March to First Day of April, ...	6	1	1	6'	10
2. From First of April to First of May, ...	6	1	1½	6' 30"	10
3. From First of May to First of September, . .	6	1	2	7'	10
4. From First of September to Second Monday in October, ...	6	1	1½	6' 30"	10
5. From Second Monday in October to Second Monday in November, ...	7		1	6'	10
6. From Second Monday in November to First Day of March, ...	7		1	5'	9
7. From First of March to Second Monday in do.	6' 30"	1	1	6' 30"	9

ANDREW MORRELL, President.

THOMAS HEWITT, Secretary.

Printed by Isaac Collins & Son, New-York.

In order to compete in the more competitive market, masters, ever cost-conscious, were demanding that journeymen comply strictly to hours of work. This broadside is typical of this demand, which was contrary to many of the traditional journeyman practices and prerogatives common to a pre-industrial order. NYPL

It is to be regretted that master workmen employed in the public works of the city and state are so lukewarm in that small exertion necessary to establish the wages, according to the resolution of so great a majority of employers and master builders.

American Citizen, May 28, 1810

127. Indictment of Journeymen Shoemakers for Conspiracy

Case of the Journeymen Cordwainers of the City of New-York

THE PEOPLE OF THE STATE OF NEW-YORK against James Melvin, William Abernathy, Thomas Baker, Henry Vane, James Glass, Daniel Allen, John Gibson, Samuel Browning, Henry Bogert, Robert Baird, John Newland, William Cosack, Robert Lambert, Terence Murray, Patrick M'Laughlin, James M'Ninch,

Wright M'Farland, William Beach, James Read, John Daly, George Read, John Morehouse, John Gillen, and Nehemiah Bradford.

The first count states that the defendants, being workmen and journeymen in the art, mystery, and manual occupation of cordwainers, on the 18th October, 1809, &c. unlawfully, perniciously and deceitfully designing and intending to form and unite themselves into an unlawful club and combination, and to make and ordain unlawful by-laws, rules and orders among themselves, and thereby to govern themselves and other workmen in the said art, and unlawfully and unjustly to extort great sums of money by means thereof, on the day and year aforesaid, with force and arms, at, &c. together with divers other workmen and journeymen in the same art, &c (whose names to the jurors are yet unknown,) did unlawfully assemble and meet together, and being so, &c. did then and there, unjustly and corruptly conspire, combine, confederate and agree together, that none of them, the said conspirators, after the said 18th October, would work for any master or person, whatsoever, in the said art, mystery and occupation, who should employ any workman or journeyman, or other person in the said art, not being a member of the said club or combination, after notice given, &c. to discharge such workman, &c. from the employ of such master, &c. to their great damage and oppression not only of their said masters, employing them in said art, &c. but also of divers other workmen and journeymen in the said art, mystery and occupation, to the evil example, &c. and against the peace, &c.

. . .

4th Count. That they (the defendants) wickedly, and intending unjustly, unlawfully, and by indirect means, to impoverish the said Edward Whitess, and hinder him from following his trade, did confederate, conspire, &c. by wrongful and indirect means, to impoverish the said E. W. and to deprive and hinder him from following his said art, &c. and that they, according to the said unlawful, &c. conspiracy, &c. indirectly, unlawfully, &c. did prevent, &c. the said E. W. from following his said art, &c. and did greatly impoverish him.

5th Count. That the defendants did conspire and agree, by indirect means, to prejudice and impoverish the said E. W. and prevent him from exercising his trade.

6th Count. That the defendants, not being content to work at the usual rates and prices for which they and other workmen and journeymen were wont and accustomed to work, but falsely and fraudulently conspiring, unjustly and oppressively to augment the wages of the other workmen, &c. and unjustly to exact and extort great sums of money for their labour and hire in the said art, mystery, &c. and did meet, &c. and being so met, &c. did unjustly and corruptly conspire, &c. that none of them should, after the said 18th October, work at any lower rate than $3.75 for making every pair of back-strap boots, $2.00 Suwarrow laced boots, full clammed, $1.75 for laced boots in front, $2.37½ for footing back-strap boots, $3.25 for footing Suwarrows, $1.25 for booting old boots.

. . .

7th Count. That the defendants falsely and fraudulently conspired, &c. unjustly and oppressively to increase and augment the wages of themselves and other workmen, &c. and unjustly to exact and extort great sums for their labour and hire, &c. from their masters who employ them, did assemble, and being so assembled, did conspire, &c. that they, and each of them, &c. would endeavour to prevent, by threats, and other unlawful means, other artificers, &c. in the said art, &c. from working, &c. at any lower rate than, &c. (setting out the prices in the preceding count, and concluding likewise.)

People vs. Melvin in Commons, *Documentary History*, III, pp. 252–256

128. Prosecution: Strike vs. the Good of the Community

. . . . Suppose the bakers of this city were to combine not to bake a loaf of bread till some demands, as to the assize, were complied with; and that the butchers were at the same time to combine not to sell a pound of meat till some object of theirs should be gained, what would be the consequence? A misfortune worse than pestilence would instantly befall the city. And are we to be told, that not only the individuals of those classes of men, to whom, in the general distribution of employment, society has confided the care of providing for its most important wants, may singly abandon their duty; but that those classes *en masse*, without any intention of permanently relinquishing or changing their occupations, but merely as a measure of extortion from the necessities of others, for private interest, may lawfully conspire together to inflict the most terrible calamities on the community; and this is called the mere exercise of individual rights, and the toleration of it is considered as sound political economy! But no. Individual rights are sufficiently secured by letting every man, according to his own will, follow his own pursuits, while public welfare forbids that combinations should be entered into for private benefit, by the persons concerned in any employment connected with the general welfare; in which combinations they would make common cause against the community at large; and in which the individual rights of those in the combining classes, who may wish to be industrious, are most grievously violated; because, if they were permitted to follow their pursuits, it would tend to relieve society from the extortions of the conspirators. These combinations are an infringement of that tacit compact which all classes reciprocally enter into, that when they have partitioned and distributed among them the different occupations conducive to general prosperity, they will pursue those occupations so as to contribute to the general happiness; and they are therefore at war with public policy. But when it is further considered that they are always accompanied with compulsory measures against those of the same class or trade, who would willingly pursue their occupation with industry and tranquillity, they are most tyrannical violations of private right, and inevitably tend to the unjust impoverishment of multitudes, either of those against whom the confederacy is directed, or of those who are forced into it, or devoted by it, for exercising their own individual rights, and refusing to cooperate with the unlawful association.

People vs. Melvin in Commons, *Documentary History*, III, 328–329

129. Prosecution: The Aristocratic and Tyrannical Power of the Journeymen's Society

. . . . Mr. Griffin then argued upon the evidence, and admitted that there had been no personal violence, no outrage or disorder, but asked if the coercive measures of the society were less cruel or oppressive for that reason. He made strong remarks upon the imperious and tyrannical edicts of the constitution and by-laws of the society, and asked whether it was possible for any workmen to enjoy without molestation, the indisputable rights of peace, neutrality, and self-government, in his own private and particular concerns. A journeyman was neither free to refuse entering into the society, nor at liberty, having done so, to leave it, without incurring ruin or unmerited disgrace; and to the real impoverishment which he must undergo, and to the evils heaped upon all who befriend him; to all this was added, the opprobrious epithet of scab. If an individual master refused obedience to their laws, or fell under the displeasure of the society, a stroke was directed against him. And, though this stroke was not a corporal wound, it was a cruel and ruinous infliction, from which he could have no relief, unless the law provides one. He was proscribed without remorse, and outlawed without mercy.

If the master workmen in general happened to offend this society, a general cessation of labour amongst the members of their own body was decreed, to which obedience was rigorously enforced; however much the necessities of their families might require their work, idleness was enjoined upon them. They were commanded to do no manner of work; but it was a sabbath not of rest, but of vengence, of desolation, and of suffering. Mr. Griffin urged then a variety of other topics with great strength and effect, and concluded by what might be understood as a summary of his argument. He did not complain of the defendants for forming themselves into a society, but for compelling others to become members. He did not accuse them of having advanced the price of their own labour, but of conspiring to regulate, by measures of rigour and coercion, the wages and the will of others; his charge against them was not that they chose and determined for what employers they would or would not work, but that they had exercised an aristocratic and tyrannical control over third persons, to whom they left neither free will nor choice; and that they employed, to effect this purpose, means of interference in their concerns to which it was impossible for the sufferers to oppose any resistance.

. . .

People vs. Melvin in Commons, *Documentary History*, III, pp. 377–379

130. Journeymen's Defense: Plight of the Shoemakers

. . . . Those who framed the constitution under which we live did not abolish all the common law, and they did right, because in that, as in other systems, there is always something to approve, and use had sanctioned it. They did not pursue it through all its complex details, for that would have been endless and impossible: but they abolished all the English statutes, and by a general clause, abrogated all of the common law that should prove in contrariety with the constitution they established. In Philadelphia, the recorder says, you shall not even inquire whether the act in judgement is or is not an attack upon the rights of man.[21] But the constitution of this state is founded on the equal rights of men, and whatever is an attack upon those rights is contrary to the constitution. Whether it is or is not an attack upon the rights of man, is, therefore, more fitting to be inquired into, than whether or not it is comfortable to the usages of Picts, Romans, Britons, Danes, Jutes, Angles, Saxons, Normans, or other barbarians, who lived in the night of human intelligence. – Away with all such notions.

Shall all others, except only the industrious mechanic, be allowed to meet and plot, merchants to determine their prices current, or settle the markets, politicians to electioneer, sportsmen for balls, parties and bouquets; and yet those poor men be indicted for combining against starvation? I ask again, is this repugnant to the rights of man? If it be, is it not repugnant to our constitution? If it be repugnant to our constitution, is it law? And if it is not law, shall we be put to answer to it?

If it be said, they have wages enough, or too much already, I do not think any man a good witness to that point but one who has himself laboured. If either of the gentlemen opposed to us will take his station in the garret or cellar of one of these industrious men, get a leather apron and a strap, a last, a lap-stone and a hammer, and peg and stitch from five in the morning till eight in the evening, and feed and educate his family with what he so earns, then if he will come into court, and say upon his corporal oath that he was, during that probation, too much pampered or indulged, I will consider whether these men may not be extortioners.

People vs. Melvin in Commons, *Documentary History*, III, pp. 279–280

131. Journeymen's Defense: The Right to Countervailing Force

. . . . But to examine the substances of the charges in these respective counts more particularly. So far from having been anything illegal or immoral in the conspiracy or agreement to which these defendants were parties, the court will find that their confederacy, and the rules which they adopted, were not only legal but highly meritorious. Like most other societies of the same nature, the journeymen shoemakers' society is a charitable institution.

They raise a fund, which is sacred to the use of their helpless or unfortunate members, and to the relief of the widows and orphans of their departed brethren. Their by-laws are, each member shall contribute to this fund. And to induce every one to join the society, while by his labour he may make something to spare for their fund, they refuse to work with any one who is so wanting in charity as not to join them. And as a sanction to their laws, they have also declared that they will not work with any who shall break their by-laws, that is, who shall refuse to pay his dues, till he has paid a fine. Who will say that an association of this nature is illegal? What human laws can presume to punish acts, which, according to the laws of God are deserving of rewards even in heaven? or can it be said that the resolution not to work for a master who employed more than two apprentices, was unpraiseworthy? The masters were in the habit of crowding their shops with more apprentices than they could instruct. Two was thought as many as one man could do justice by. The journeymen shoemakers therefore determined to set their faces against the rapacity of the masters, and refused to work for those who were so unjust as to delude with the promise of instruction which it was impossible they could give. In England, the legislature has interfered on this point, and has by statute limited the number of apprentices which certain tradesman may take.

It is to be observed, that neither of these counts charge that the design of the defendants was to raise their wages. And though it should be admitted that a conspiracy to raise their wages would subject the defendants to an indictment, yet I doubt if any authority can be found to support an indictment for charges like these . . . .

The 4th count charges, that these defendants, intending to injure E. W. conspired, by wrongful and indirect means to impoverish him, and hinder him from following his trade, and that they did in pursuance of their conspiracy, indirectly hinder him from following his trade . . . .

Now it may well have been that the defendants intended to injure the persons named in these counts, by indirect, yet by perfectly lawful means. If they had agreed that they would work better or cheaper than the persons named, this would have been an indirect, means of injuring them. If they had combined in the invention of some improvement of the cordwainer's art, which should have entitled them to a patent, this would have have given the defendants a monopoly which could not fail of being an indirect means of injuring all who were not sharers in it. If they agreed to increase the number of master workmen in our city by inducing those who are now settled elsewhere to take their abode with us; or, if the defendants had agreed that they would no longer work as journeymen, but establish themselves as masters. All these would have been indirect means of impoverishing and injuring other persons engaged in the trade. But will it be said that indirect means like these would be unlawful means? I am sure it will not. It follows, then, that the defendants are not charged by either of these counts, with a conspiracy to do an unlawful act.

But if we should say that by the terms wrongful, wicked, and indirect means, are to be intended unlawful means, then there remains the important objection, that the indictment does not specify the necessary circumstances to show that the intended means were unlawful.

People vs. Melvin in Commons, *Documentary History*, III, pp. 299–302

132. John McComb, On Holding Wages Down (New City Hall)

Gentlemen:—

Agreeable to your direction, I have made the requisite inquiries respecting the propriety of complying with the applications for the Junnymen S. Cutters, Cartmen for an increase of pay.

As it respects the application from the Stone Cutters I find on inquiry of Mr. Campble, that they are not correct in stating that ¾ of their body get higher wages at the different shops that very few of them get 13 per day, and from the quality of work to be done at the shops, it is not likely that there will be a great demand for workman.

It is admitted that the markets and House Rent is high but we deem it impossible to regulate the wages so as always to be equal to them, as the stone Cutters already receive a higher price for their labor than either Masons or Carpenters, we are of the opinion that the wages ought [not] to be raised for when we consider that this is a steady job, and that they receive their money regularly, we believe they cannot better themselves, it would answer no good purpose, we will not be able to get a man the more fit for it, as the price at the shops would of course raise also, and it would be the means of raising the wages of masons, carpenters, laborers and of all persons connected with the building line.

As to the application from the cartmen, Mr. Smith is of opinion that the price ought to be allowed them, but Mr. Stunback and myself think it is a reasonable price, that 1/9 [one shilling, nine pence] is fully as good as the price they get of individuals and they taking it altogether it is a much better job than there ordinary business of carting for private buildings, which is respectfully submitted by,

April 20, 1806

Jn. M. C. [John McComb Jr.]

Letter of John McComb to Building Committee of the New York City Hall, John McComb Mss., NYHS

NOTES

Introduction

1. Extensive population figures as well as a great deal of other valuable statistical detail is to be found in David T. Gilchrist, ed., *The Growth of the Seaport Cities, 1790–1825* (Charlottesville, 1967), pp. 34–34, 41 and *infra*.

2. John Lambert, *Travels Through Canada and the United States* (London, 1814), pp. 82, 91, 102–103. See also Frank Monaghan and Marvin Lowenthal, *This was New York: The Nation's Capital in 1789* (New York, 1943); Franklin Scott, ed., *Baron Klinkowstrom's America* (Evanston, 1952), ch. 13; D. R. Fox and J. A. Krout, *The Completion of Independence* (New York, 1944), pp. 29–40.

3. Housing conditions were determined from the New York City Jury Lists for 1816 and 1819. For further detail see Howard B. Rock, *Artisans of the New Republic: The Tradesmen of New York City in the Age of Jefferson* (New York, 1979), pp. 253–257, 265–268. During the yellow fever epidemic of 1803, between seven and nine out of ten of the inhabitants of the elite first and second wards moved out of the city. In the poorer outer wards only one or two out of ten had the means to leave. *Ibid.*, p. 3; *Morning Chronicle*, October 29, 1803. Further discussion on public health and epidemic is found in John Duffy, *A History of Public Health in New York City, 1625–1866* (New York, 1968). The problem of poverty is thoroughly discussed in Raymond A. Mohl, *Poverty in New York, 1783–1825* (New York, 1971).

4. Lambert, *Travels through Canada and the United States*, p. 103; Jackson Turner Main, *The Social Structure of Revolutionary America* (Princeton, 1965), p. 288; Billy G. Smith, "The Material Lives of Laboring Philadelphians, 1750–1800," *William and Mary Quarterly* 38 (April, 1981), 163–202; "New York City in the Nineteenth Century," *American History Magazine* 32 (1906), 203.

5. The Terms "craftsman", "mechanic", "tradesman", and "artisan" were used interchangeably by the early national period, although they did have more specialized meanings in England and in earlier periods. For a discussion of terminology see Charles S. Olton, *Artisans for Independence: Philadelphia Mechanics and the American Revolution* (Syracuse, 1975), p. 7.

6. For an analysis of population figures for the mechanic population of New York see Rock, *Artisans of the New Republic*, pp. 14 and 15–16, n. 13. and Sean Wilentz, *Chants Democratic: New York City and the Rise of the American Working Class: 1789–1850* (New York, 1986), p. 27, n. 13.

7. Rock, *Artisans of the New Republic*, pp. 4–8; Samuel Johnson., comp., *A Dictionary of the English Language* (London, 1730); the *Compact Edition of the Oxford English Dictionary* (New York, 1971), p. 1756; Stephen Botein, "Meer Mechanics and an Open Press: The Business and Political Strategies of American Printers," *Perspectives in American History*, 9 (1975), 136, 157–158, 222; Roger J. Champagne, *Alexander McDougall and the American Revolution in New York* (Syracuse, 1975), p. 136.

8. Wilentz, *Chants Democratic*, ch. 1; Rock, *Artisans of the New Republic*, chs. 1–5.

9. Joyce Appleby, *Capitalism and a New Social Order: The Republican Vision of the 1790s* (New York, 1984).

10. Among the important works for this discussion are J.G.A. Pocock, *The Machiavellian Movement: Florentine Political Thought and the Atlantic Republican Tradition* (Princeton, 1976) and "Virtue and Commerce in the Eighteenth Century," *Journal of Interdisciplinary History* 3 (1972), 119–134; Lance Banning, *The Jeffersonian Persuasion: Evolution of a Party Ideology* (Ithaca, 1978); *idem.*, "Jefferson Ideology Revisited: Liberal and Classical Ideas in the New American Republic," *William and Mary Quarterly* 43 (1986), pp. 3–19; Joyce Appleby, *Capitalism and a New Social Order; idem.*, "Republicanism in Old and New Concepts," *William and Mary Quarterly* 43 (1986), pp. 20–34; *idem.*, "The Social Origins of American Revolutionary Ideology," *Journal of American History* 64 (1978), 935–978; Isaac Kramnick, "Republican Revision Revisited," *American Historical Review* 87 (1982), 629–664.

11. Wilentz, *Chants Democratic*, ch. 3.

Part One: Citizenship

1. On artisan ideology, see Rock, *Artisans of the New Republic*, ch. 5; Wilentz, *Chants Democratic*, ch. 2; and Edward Countryman, *A People in Revolution: The American Revolution and Political Society in New York, 1760–1790* (Baltimore, 1981).

2. Sean Wilentz, "Artisan Republican Festivals and the Rise of Class Conflict in New York City, 1788–1837," in Michael H. Frisch and Daniel J. Walkowitz, eds., *Working Class America: Essays on Labor, Community and American Society* (Urbana, 1982), pp. 37–79.

3. On the Democratic Societies, see Eugene P. Link, *Democratic-Republican Societies, 1790–1800* (New York, 1942) and, more recently, Philip S. Foner, *The Democratic-Republican Societies, 1790–1800* (Westport, 1976), ch. 4. On the impact of the French Revolution, see Alan Blau, "New York City and the French Revolution, 1789–1797: A Study of French Revolutionary Influence," Ph.D. dissertation (CUNY, 1973).

4. William Godwin, 1756–1836, a radical reformer and husband of feminist Mary Wollstonecraft. In his writings, especially *An Enquiry Concerning Political Justice,* he argues that the perfectibility of man through social reform and engendered by reason and discussion was possible and that institutions of the time were organized by the wealthy for legal oppression of the poor.

5. Duncan Phyfe, the City's most prominent cabinetmaker.

6. Thomas Muir, a Scottish reformer and defender of the French Revolution and Thomas Paine's *Rights of Man*, was sentenced in 1793 to Botany Bay for sedition. He was rescued and brought to Paris in 1796.

7. On the battle for incorporation, see Sidney I. Pomerantz, *New York, An American City: 1783–1803* (New York, 1983), pp. 95–97, 214–215.

8. The best description of the Mechanics Society is to be found in Thomas Earle and Charles T. Congdon, eds., *Annals of the General Society of Mechanics and Tradesmen, 1775–1880* (New York, 1882). See also, Edward Countryman, *A People in Revolution, The American Revolution and Political Society in New York, 1760–1790* (Baltimore, 1981), pp. 223, 242, 244.

9. Carl F. Kaestle, *The Evolution of an Urban School System* (Cambridge, 1973), pp. 41–55.

10. The Municipal Archives holds material on Hook and Ladder Company Number 2 (1812), No. 1 and No. 36 (n.d.). The New York Historical Society holds the Minutes and By-Laws of Fire Company No. 11 (1791–1797, 1807–1809). These companies could accumulate considerable assets for its members. Number 11, for example held $8,456.57, mostly in stock from such institutions as the Manhattan and New Jersey Banks and the Eagle Fire Insurance Company along with mortgages. Minutes, December 11, 1809. See also Augustine E. Costello, *Our Firemen: A History of the New York City Fire Department* (New York, 1887).

11. Manure was a very valuable commodity and cartmen vied for the right to collect and sell it. On the other hand, other tradesmen living in the outer wards where it was often stored protested when it was placed too near them. This was a constant problem for the city. See Rock, *Artisans of the New Republic*, pp. 227–228.

12. This issue is discussed in detail in Howard B. Rock, "A Delicate Balance: The Mechanics and the City in the Age of Jefferson," *New York Historical Society Quarterly* 63 (1979), 101–111.

13. Nightmen were laborers, usually black, who emptied the privies at night.

14. The phrase "industrious part" was a common term artisans used when referring to their part of the population.

15. This school was for the children of French and Spanish colonial immigrants.

16. Bruce Laurie, "Nothing on Impulse: Life Styles of Philadelphia Artisans, 1820–1850," *Labor History*, 15 (1974), 337–366; and *Working People of Philadelphia, 1800–1850* (Philadelphia, 1980); Faul Faler, "Cultural Aspects of the Industrial Revolution: Lynn, Massachusetts Shoemakers and the Industrial Morality, 1826–1860," *Labor History* 15 (1974), 367–394; Faler and Alan Dawley, "Working Class Culture and Politics in the Industrial Revolution: Sources of and Loyalism and Rebellion," *Journal of Social History*, 9 (1976), 466–471. See also Wilentz, *Chants Democratic*.

17. For a discussion of pre-industrial work culture see Laurie, "Nothing on Impulse;" Eric Foner, *Tom Paine and Revolutionary America* (New York, 1976), pp. 48–56; Herbert G. Gutman, "Work, Culture and Society in Industrializing America, 1815–1919," *American Historical Review* 78 (1973), 533–588.

18. *Evening Post*, January 9, 1810; Report of Committee of the Common Council, City Clerk Filed Papers, March 8, 1816; Michael and Ariane Battenberg, *On the Town: A History of Eating, Drinking and Entertainments from 1776 to the Present* (New

York, 1973), p. 43; Rocellus Guernsey, *New York City During the War of 1812* (New York, 1889), p. 73. For an overview, see W. J. Rorabaugh, *The Alcoholic Republic: An American Tradition* (New York, 1979).

19. Pomerantz, *New York, An American City,* pp. 488–489; bull-baiting consisted of dogs engaged against a bull.

20. E. P. Thompson, "Time, Work-Discipline and Industrial Capitalism", *Past and Present,* 38 (1967), 58–97; Douglas Reid, "The Decline of Saint Monday," *Ibid.,* 71 (1976), 75–101.

21. See Rock, *Artisans of the New Republic,* pp. 317–319.

22. The opening issue of the *Independent Mechanic* appeared April 6, 1811. In February the paper was sold to George Asbridge, a former president of the Franklin Typographical Society. The paper lasted for eighteen months, the last issue appearing in October, 1812.

23. Articles on the danger of drink appeared on April 6, August 10, 17, 31, September 7, 1811 and February 29, 1812.

24. See issues of the *Independent Mechanic,* April 6, May 11, June 1, 15, November 9, 23, 30, September 7, 14, October 12, 1811, March 21 and April 11, 1812.

25. For other examples, see Rock, *Artisans of the New Republic,* pp. 312–316

26. The Urus was a type of wild ox.

27. For a further discussion of the three documents as well as reprints of the articles that stimulated these female responses, see Howard B. Rock, ed., "A Woman's Place in Jeffersonian New York: The View from the *Independent Mechanic,*" *New York History* 63 (1982), 435–459. There are two fine books that cover women in the Jeffersonian era and are of value in understanding female interests and ambitions: Mary Beth Norton, *Liberty's Daughters: The Revolutionary Experience of American Women* (Boston, 1980) and Linda K. Kerber, *Women of the Republic: Intellect and Ideology in Revolutionary America* (Chapel Hill, 1980).

28. Miss Mackaboy was the trade name of a popular brand of snuff.

Part Two: Politics

1. For an analysis of mechanic voter impact, see Staughton Lynd and Alfred F. Young, "The Mechanics in New York Politics, 1774–1788," *Labor History* V (1964), and Young, "The Mechanics and the Jeffersonians, 1789–1801," *Ibid.,* 247–276, and Rock, *Artisans of the New Republic,* pp. 33–35.

2. Important studies of colonial and revolutionary New York politics include Patricia Bonomi, *A Factious People: Politics and Society in Colonial New York* (New York, 1971); Gary Nash, *The Urban Crucible: Social Change, Political Consciousness, and the Origins of the American Revolution* (Cambridge, 1979); and Countryman, *A People in Revolution.* The work that spawned much of this research is Carl Becker, *The History of Political Parties in the State of New York* (Madison, 1909). On New York mechanics in the American Revolution, see Lynd and Young, "The Mechanics in New York Politics;" Philip S. Foner, *Labor and the American Revolution* (Westport, Conn.,

1976); Roger J. Champagne, "The Liberty Boys and the Mechanics of New York City," *Labor History* 8 (1967); and Bernard Mason, *The Road to Independence, The Revolutionary Movement in New York, 1773-1777* (Lexington, 1977).

3. For a description of the importance of the 1790s in American politics, see John R. Howe, "Republican Thought and the Political Violence of the 1790s," *American Quarterly* 29 (1967), 147-165.

4. Young, "Mechanics and Jeffersonians," 247-249.

5. *Ibid.*, and see also, Alfred F. Young, *The Democratic Republicans of New York: The Origins, 1763-1797* (Durham, 1967), pp. 207-230.

6. For assembly and congressional elections only evidence of payment of a minimal rent was required. The restrictive requirements for charter elections were considerably lessened in 1804. For a discussion of suffrage requirements and legislation, see Pomerantz, *New York, An American City*, pp. 26-27, 64-75, 134-146; see also, Edmund P. Willis, "Social Origins of Political Leadership in New York City from the Revolution to 1815," Ph.D. dissertation (Berkeley, 1967), ch. 2.

7. Young, *Democratic-Republicans of New York*, Ch. 17.

8. "Yesterday" refers to the Federalist victory in the aldermanic election, allowing that party to retain control of the Common Council. In the 1790s a model guillotine was exhibited at the Tontine Coffee House. Hundreds of New Yorkers crowded in to see the clay head of an aristocrat severed from the rest of his body. James Cheetham (New York) and William Duane (Philadelphia) were emigre English Jacobin editors.

9. King George III of Great Britain, whose ships were at the time seizing American vessels and impressing American sailors as part of the struggle with France.

10. A law requiring tallow chandlers (candle makers) to remove their businesses beyond the city limits. It was argued that the fumes of their manufactories were harmful to the health of residents. The Democratic-Republicans backed the tallow chandlers.

11. Roman god of Medicine. A reference to doctors testifying against the tallow chandlers.

12. A London marketplace.

13. Willis, "Social Origins," pp. 285-286, finds a slightly higher percentage of Federalist officeholders with loyalist backgrounds (9.2) than Republican (5.6), though the corresponding difference in patriot backgrounds was greater (Republican–40.7; Federalist–26.7).

14. A 'freeman' was the technical term for a municipally licensed craftsman. The holding of a freemanship entitled a citizen to vote, but Federalists had long since ceased granting such licenses and the status was obsolete. This was a reply to a Federalist statement defending current restrictions.

15. The Democratic-Republicans consistently nominated far more artisans for public office than the Federalists. Between 1801 and 1811, 38.9 percent of Republican assembly candidates were artisans, while the corresponding Federalist figure was 12.5 percent.

16. Robert Lenox, John B. Church, and Robert Bowne were prominent, wealthy Federalist merchants. General Hamilton is Alexander Hamilton.

17. In an address to Irish citizens, Rudd, a Federalist spokesman attempting to reach artisans, described the excesses of the French Revolution: "murder, assassination, rapine and plunder . . ., parents murdering children and children murdering

parents," and compared it to Democratic-Republican designs to gain suffrage merely for "place of profit and emolument." "American Ticket" was the name the Federalists devised for their banner, hoping it would be more acceptable among the middling and lower orders. *Evening Post*, April 22, 1807. For Rudd's response, see pp. 89–90.

18. William Coleman, Federalist Editor of the *Evening Post* and close associate of Alexander Hamilton. He later became a supporter of Andrew Jackson.

19. James Cheetham, the Jacobin editor of the strongly partisan Democratic-Republican newspaper, the *American Citizen*. Perhaps the most radical and most outspoken Jeffersonian, subject to numerous lawsuits, he had formerly been an English hatter and was a political emigre. An active proponent of suffrage reform.

20. These included the Non-Intercourse bill (actually signed by Jefferson) that forbade trade only with France and England and Macon's Bill Number 2 that offered to open trade with France or England and stipulated that if either country removed its trade barriers before March 3, 1811, the Non-Intercourse Act would be invoked against the other.

21. Among the provisions of the law passed January 18 and February 27, 1815, aside from the tax, were items requiring artisans owning machinery to state the purpose of the machinery; to make a complete inventory of tools, machines and utensils upon penalty of forfeiture of such equipment and a $500 fine; and allowing a collector to enter any building or vessel without a search warrant to examine the goods produced and tools and machinery employed under penalty of $500 for refusal. *Columbian*, April 18, 1816.

22. The Federalists captured the city-wide Assembly elections in 1811, 1812, 1813 and 1815 with 57.5, 52.5, 50.7 and 50.5 percent of the vote respectively. The Republicans won in 1814 with 49.8 percent of the vote with a few percent going to dissident factions. Rock, *Artisans of the New Republic*, p. 33.

23. The Hartford Convention, called by the Massachusetts Legislature, was an assemblage of Federalist representatives from Connecticut, Rhode Island, Massachusetts, New Hampshire, and Vermont to discuss revision of the Constitution in order to prevent national dominance by one sector of the country. Although controlled by moderates, it did threaten disunion and, with the American victory at New Orleans, was looked at as an act of treason.

24. Imposed by the Federalist administration preparing for a possible war with France.

25. Madison's message to Congress calling for a Declaration of war against Great Britain was printed next to this message. This was a most unusual statement for this newspaper, whose general stance was militantly apolitical.

26. Headquarters of Tammany Hall, the Madisonian wing of the Democratic-Republican Party.

27. *The Examiner* was a weekly journal founded by Barent Gardenier, formerly a Federalist leader and congressman from Ulster County.

28. The major divisions were between the Burrites and Jeffersonians in 1804 when Burr ran for Governor; between the Livingstonians and Clintonians in the 1807 gubernatorial election; and the long running feud between the Clintonians (led by DeWitt Clinton) and the Madisonians. After 1815 Clinton remained at the center of politics, pitted against the Van Buren bucktails upstate and Tammany Hall in

New York City, a political club whose leaders had been at the center of Madisonian support. Federalists continued to hold some influence making occasional alliances, usually with the Clintonians. See Jerome Mushkat, *Tammany: The Evolution of a Political Machine* (Syracuse, 1971), chs. 1–4.

29. For an analysis of voter apathy, see Rock, *Artisans of the New Republic*, pp. 126–182.

30. Morgan Lewis, governor of New York (1804–1807), was a leader of the Livingstonian faction, now at odds with the Clintonians who defeated him in 1807.

31. Noah Brown (1770–1827?), a prominent Republican shipwright elected first to the Common Council in 1815. He was running in 1820 on the Clintonian ticket against the Tammany candidates.

32. "Timoleon" was Tunis Wortman (d. 1821), formerly a brilliant secretary of the Democratic-Republican Society of New York and later a Clintonian and clerk of the City of New York. Perhaps the Clintonian disillusionment with Madisonian policies led to this essay. Identification courtesy of Professor Alfred F. Young.

Part Three: The Marketplace

1. On colonial craftsmen's ambitions, see Carl Bridenbaugh, *The Colonial Craftsmen* (New York, 1950); on artisans, the American Revolution and entrepreneurial release, the finest work is by Joyce Appleby, "The Social Origins of American Revolutionary Ideology," 935–958, and *Capitalism and a New Social Order;* see also Thomas C. Cochran, *Frontiers of Change: Early Industrialism in America* (New York, 1981).

2. Thomas C. Cochran, "The Business Revolution," *American Historical Review* 79 (1974), 1449–1466 and *Frontiers of Change*, ch. 1–4, 6–8; Alan R. Pred, *Urban Growth and the Circulation of Information: The United States System of Cities, 1790–1840* (Cambridge, 1973); Gilchrist, ed. *The Growth of the Seaport Cities 1790–1815*, pp. 41, 56, 68–78, 113, 119, 199; Pomerantz, *New York, An American City: 1783–1803*, pp. 149–166.

3. Willis, "Social Origins and Political Leadership," 123, 130, appendix.

4. John F. Kasson, *Civilizing the Machine: Technology and Republican Values in America, 1776–1900* (New York, 1976), ch. 1.

5. This document was presented as an affidavit submitted by three New York City bankers, Christian Nestell, George Arcularious, and Jacob Beekman, sworn before Mayor Edward Livingston during an impassioned debate over the rights of bakers to free themselves of price regulation (See pp. 151–158). The declaration of a daily loss is to be taken in this light, and may not be accurate. The breakdown of general expenses is no doubt very close to reality.

6. It was common on May 1 for renters to move or be removed. This was the date for new leases. *Poor Richard's Almanac*, published by Benjamin Franklin, contained many sayings that were popular at the time.

7. Allen was the exception in owning real estate. In 1801, 22.8 percent of adult males

owned real property. The percentage of artisans is likely less than half this number. See Willis, "Social Origins," p. 51, and Rock, *Artisans of the New Republic*, p. 266.

8. This was written by journeyman bookbinder John Bradford. Other of his poems may be found in Documents 94–95.

9. A reference to J.D.H. Huggins, a New York hairdresser famed for his advertisements. See Rock, *Artisans of the New Republic*, pp. 160–163.

10. On Manhattan Bank, see Young, "The Mechanics and the Jeffersonians," 266.

11. Those allowed entry into the Mechanics Society included real estate broker Samuel St. John, insurance broker Gabriel Furman, and auctioneer Naphtali Judah. The latter, once a bookbinder and bookseller, had long been out of artisan ranks. The slightest relationship with the mechanic arts in one's background or parentage was used as an excuse for membership. The orginal directors represented the elite of the artisan community. They included Jacob Sherred, a German painter and glazier whose fortune skyrocketed between 1795 and 1815 (from $430 to $120,300); Anthony Steenback, mason and builder also upwardly mobile ($1100 in 1795, $49,500 in 1815); Francis Cooper, prominent coppersmith ($4500 in 1808, $37,500 in 1815); John Slidell, soapmaker ($19,600 in 1808, $72,500 in 1815); Matthew Davis, former printer, in 1810 leader of Burrite political faction; Samuel St. John, real estate broker, Naphtali Judah, former bookbinder, in 1810 a wealthy auctioneer, George Warner, sailmaker ($8400 in 1795, $41,100 in 1815); John R. Murray, merchant, Jonathan Lawrence, Jr., bank clerk and merchant ($15,900 in 1815). For more detail, see Rock *Artisans of the New Republic*, pp. 165–69.

12. F. W. Taussig, *A Tariff History of the United States* (New York, 1892), p. 15; Victor S. Clark, *History of Manufactures in the United States,* 2 vol. (New York, 1949), I, pp. 270, 288; Curtis Nettels, *The Emergence of a National Economy, 1775–1815* (New York, 1962), pp. 69–70.

13. On the new protectionist spirit after the War of 1812, see George Dangerfield, *The Awakening of American Nationalism, 1815–1828,* (New York, 1965), pp. 12–16, 204–207.

14. The report outlines drawbacks and tariffs already implemented by the federal government.

15. While issuing a rather negative response to the petitioners, the Committee did recommend a number of adjustments. Among these, it recommended freely admitting such products as rags of linen, cotton, woolen and hemp, saltpetre, and swine bristles; admitting imported brushes subject to a 25 percent duty (previously 12.5 percent); raising furs and hats from 10 to 15 percent; raising duties on stone ware and window glass and cannon balls from 15 to 25 percent; and imposing small duty increases on hair powder, glue, dried fish, tarred cordage, and printed calicoes, gunpowder, umbrellas, soap, candles, anchors and spikes, and bolts of iron.

16. The Jeffersonian concern with the effects of commercialization and large-scale manufacturing is brilliantly expounded in Drew R. McCoy, *The Elusive Republic: Political Economy in Jeffersonian America* (Chapel Hill, 1980).

17. For a detailed discussion of the assize, see Howard B. Rock, "The Perils of Laissez-faire: The Aftermath of the New York Bakers' Strike of 1801," *Labor History* 17 (1976), 374. For traditional English roots, see E. P. Thompson, "The Moral Economy of the English Crowd in the Eighteenth Century," *Past and Present* 50 (1971).

18. The Board of Directors included merchants Henry Rutgers, Jonathan Lawrence, David Lewis, William Bayard, Walter Borne, John B. Church (brother-in-law of Alexander Hamilton), auctioneer David Dickson, and former congressional candidate Gordon Mumford. This included both Federalists and Democratic-Republicans.

19. The fire is described in Augustine E. Costello, *Our Firemen: A History of the New York Fire Departments,* (New York, 1887), pp. 206–207.

20. The assize was finally discontinued in 1821.

21. The Workshop Proposal is discussed in detail in Raymond A. Mohl, *Poverty in New York, 1785–1825* (New York, 1971), pp. 230–233, and Rock, *Artisans of the New Republic,* pp. 197–199.

22. Federal Census, 1820, New York State Manufactures, 1260, 1782.

23. Edward Livingston, member of the famed Livingston family so prominent in colonial and early national politics was the first Republican governor of New York. Forced to leave because of a scandal in the city's finances, he became governor of Louisiana and Secretary of State under Andrew Jackson.

24. The various regulations governing these trades together with other city ordinances can be found in *Laws and Ordinances Ordained and Established by the Mayor, Alderman, and Commonality of the City of New York,* published every three years by the City. For further discussion, see Rock, *Artisans of the New Republic,* ch. 8; Pomerantz, *New York, An American City: 1783–1803,* pp. 172–78; and Thomas DeVoe, *The Market Book* (New York, 1862).

25. The most important market in New York was the Fly Market in the First Ward on the East River at the foot of Maiden Lane in the heart of the commercial district. Others included the smaller Exchange Market on Broad Street, also in the lower part of the city. In the Third Ward, the Bear Market stood on the Hudson River near Partition Street, and the Oswego Market – not situated on a dock but convenient for farmers bringing their animals in overland. Further out stood the Catherine Market on the East River in the Seventh Ward and the Spring Street Market in the Eighth Ward, serving many of the artisans who lived in these distant wards.

26. Cadwallader Colden, scion of a famous New York loyalist family headed by the former Lieutenant Governor Cadwallader Colden, was a prominent Federalist and then a close associate of DeWitt Clinton.

27. Cartmen were required to own their own horse and cart. Thus a merchant or entrepreneur might make a 'fictitious sale' transferring ownership of a horse and cart, but in reality requiring a large percentage of the driver's profit.

28. Henry Astor, one of the wealthiest butchers in New York, was brother of the noted fur trader and real estate mogul John Jacob Astor.

Part Four: Masters and Journeymen

1. There has been no detailed study of market relationships of artisan trades in the port cities. For shoemakers, John R. Commons states that masters did their own retailing including travel to other ports, while David Saposs argues that merchant

capitalists were lending shoemakers and others considerable sums, doing much of the marketing and often using the masters as foremen. Studies of Lynn, Massachusetts for this period reveal how commission merchants worked as both wholesalers and retailers to some masters while acting only as creditors to others. John R. Commons, et. al., eds., *A Documentary History of American Industrial Society,* 10 vols. (Cleveland, 1909–11), III, pp. 34–39; David Saposs in John R. Commons, et. al., eds, *History of Labor in the United States,* 4 vols. (New York, 1926–35), I, pp. 88–107; Paul Faler, *Mechanics and Manufacturers in the Early Industrial Revolution* (Albany, 1981), chs. 1–2; see also Alan Dawley, *Class and Community: The Industrial Revolution in Lynn* (Cambridge, 1976), chs. 1–2.

2. Charles F. Montgomery, *American Furniture: The Federal Period, 1788–1825* (New York, 1966) pp. 13–14; Wendell P. Garrett, "The Matter of Consumers' Tastes," in John D. Morse, ed. *Country Cabinetwork and Simple City Furniture* (Charlottesville, 1969), pp. 205–233; Egal Feldman, "New York Men's Clothing Trade, 1800–1860," Ph.D. dissertation (New York University, 1959), pp. 5–7, 35–37, 65–75, 143–158, 168.

3. Robert Christie, *Empire in Wood* (Ithaca, 1956), pp. 10–12; Pred, *Urban Growth,* p. 193; *Evening Post,* June 19, 1810; Rock, *Artisans of the New Republic,* pp. 239–240; Rollos G. Silver, *The American Printer, 1787–1825* (Charlottesville, 1967), pp. 1–96; Richard P. Brief, "The Philadelphia Printer: A Study of an Eighteenth-Century Businessman," *Business History Review* 40, (1968), 46.

4. Willis, "Social Origins and Political Leadership in New York City," Appendix, pp. 123, 130.

5. Rock, *Artisans of the New Republic,* pp. 265–268.

6. In a sample taken from the 1819 Jury Lists and composed of residents of the fourth, sixth, and eighth wards of New York City, journeymen working in the nonconflict trades composed 35 percent of the journeymen population and worked in over sixty different trades. Rock, *Artisans of the New Republic,* p. 268.

7. A collection of Bradford's poems was published in New York in 1813 under the title *The Poetical Vagaries of a Knight of the Folding Stick of* PASTE CASTLE, *to which is annexed the History of the Garett, & Co. Translated from the Hieroglyphics of the Society by a Member of the Order of the Blue String.* It is available at the New York Public Library, Rare Book Room.

8. The decline of apprenticeships in the eighteenth century is traced by Ian M. G. Quimby, "Apprenticeship in Colonial Philadelphia," M. A. thesis (University of Delaware, 1963); and Sharon V. Salinger, "Artisans, Journeymen and the Transformation of Labor in late Eighteenth Century Philadelphia," *William and Mary Quarterly* 40 (1983), 62–84. For the early national era, see W. J. Rorabaugh, *The Craft Apprentice* (New York, 1985).

9. The origins of the mechanics have been traced from New York City Watch Lists that gave place of birth. Rock, *Artisans of the New Republic,* p. 243. On immigration, see Carol Groneman Pernicone, "The 'Bloody Ould Sixth': A Social Analysis of a New York City Working Class Community in the Mid-Nineteenth Century," Ph.D. dissertation (University of Rochester, 1973), pp. 29–35; Pomerantz, New York, *An American City,* pp. 201–209.

10. A discussion of the role of European shoemakers in trade union organizations as well as in politics may be found in Joan Scott and E. J. Hobsbawm, "Political Shoemakers," *Past and Present* 89 (1980), 86–114.

11. A Philadelphia newspaper.

12. Duncan Phyfe, the best and wealthiest known of New York's cabinetmakers, enjoyed a worldwide reputation for his elegant furniture. He owned an elaborate warehouse and workshop and employed some of the finest journeymen in New York City. He was known for his conservative Calvinist habits, while politically he belonged to the Federalist Washington Benevolent Society. This strike was triggered when he attempted to lower wages in response to the general deflation triggered by the Panic of 1819, a general business depression lasting until 1822.

13. "Employers" refers to those hiring master builders to erect structures. The journeymen were attempting to deal directly with these employers.

14. Reprint of an ad published by the master builders.

15. "WIGWAMS" is a reference to the Tammany Society, the prominent Democratic-Republican club, in 1810 part of the Madisonian camp. Many noteworthy artisans belonged to this society, and the journeymen's view of them as adversary is an indication of the difficulty the Democratic-Republicans had in building a coalition of mechanics when the artisans were split.

16. In this instance, the journeymen were acquitted. The case is analyzed in Sean Wilentz, "Conspiracy, Power, and the Early Labor Movement: The People vs. James Melvin, et. al., 1811," *Labor History* 24 (1983), pp. 572–579.

17. Richard Riker was the first Democratic-Republican to hold the office of the City District Attorney (Recorder). He had been a strong supporter of Governor George Clinton. Thomas A. Emmett was a prominent Irish attorney active in the United Irishmen cause and forced to emigrate as a Jacobin after the failed invasion of Ireland. He became an active Democratic-Republican, engaging in a spirited if low-level newspaper debate with Rufus King in 1810. Clearly the Democratic-Republican party, a loyal ally of artisans' objectives in politics were not behind the journeymen's militant actions in the marketplace. For an analysis of the relation between journeymen and Republican Jacobins, see Richard Twomey, "Jacobins and Jeffersonians: Anglo-American Radicalism in the United States, 1790–1820," Ph.D. dissertation (Northern Illinois University, 1974), ch. 6.

18. Also an Irish emigre, he was a radical Jacobin with a wide reputation in Ireland and America.

19. On the meaning of the conspiracy cases in labor history, see Marjorie S. Turner, *The Early American Conspiracy Cases, Their Place in Labor Law: A Reinterpretation* (San Diego, 1967) and Leonard W. Levy, *The Law of the Commonwealth and Chief Justice Shaw* (Cambridge, 1957).

20. Reference to the general deflation brought on by the Panic of 1819.

21. Reference to the trial of nine Philadelphia cordwainers on similar conspiracy charges in 1806 in which Recorder Moses Levy argued that any contention that application of the common law constituted an attack on the "rights of man" was "unnecessary and improper." Commons, *Documentary History*, III, p. 225.

SELECT
BIBLIOGRAPHY

Albion, Robert. *The Rise of the New York Post, 1815–1860*. New York, 1939.

Appleby, Joyce. "The Social Origins of American Revolutionary Ideology." *Journal of American History* 64 (1978), pp. 935–958.

———. *Capitalism and a New Social Order: The Republican Vision of the 1790's*. New York, 1984.

Baker, Mary Roys. "Anglo-Massachusetts Trade Roots, 1730–1790." *Labor History* 14 (1973), pp. 352–396.

Barnett, George. "The Printers, A Study in Trade Unionism." *American Economic Association Quarterly*, 3rd ser. 10 (1909).

Bridenbaugh, Carl. *The Colonial Craftsman*. New York, 1950.

Champagne, Roger J. *Alexander McDougall and the American Revolution*. Syracuse, 1975.

Christie, Robert. *Empire in Wood*. Ithaca, 1956.

Commons, John R., et. al. *History of Labor in the United States*, Vol. I. New York, 1926.

Commons, John R., ed. *A Documentary History of American Industrial Society*, 10 vols. Cleveland, 1909–1911.

Countryman, Edward. *A People in Revolution: The American Revolution and Political Society in New York, 1760–1790*. Baltimore, 1981.

DeVoe, Thomas. *The Market Book*. New York, 1862.

D'Innocenzo, Michael. "The Popularization of Politics in Irving's New York." In Andrew B. Myers, ed., *The Knickerbocker Tradition: Washington Irving's New York*. Tarrytown, 1974.

Earle, Thomas and Charles Congdon, eds. *Annals of the General Society of Mechanics and Tradesmen of the City of New York, 1775–1880*. New York, 1882.

Feldman, Egal. "New York Men's Clothing Trade, 1800–1861." Ph.D. dissertation. New York University, 1959.

Foner, Eric. *Tom Paine and Revolutionary America*. New York, 1976.

Gilchrist, David T., ed. *The Growth of the Seaport Cities, 1790–1815*. Charlottesville, 1967.

Gilje, Paul. *The Road to Mobocracy: Popular Disorder in New York City, 1763–1834*. Chapel Hill, 1987.

Gottesman, Rita Suswein. *The Arts and Crafts in New York, 1800–1804, New York Historical Society Collections, 1949*. New York, 1965.

———. *The Arts and Crafts in New York, 1777–1799, New York Historical Society Collections*. New York, 1984.

Hindle, Brooke. *Technology in Early America*. Chapel Hill, 1966.

Hodges, Graham. *The Cartmen of New York City, 1667–1850*. New York, 1986.

Kaestle, Carl E. *The Evolution of an Urban School System: New York City, 1750–1850.* Cambridge, 1973.

McCoy, Drew R. *The Elusive Republic: Political Economy in Jeffersonian America.* Chapel Hill, 1980.

Mohl, Raymond A. *Poverty in New York, 1783–1825.* New York, 1971.

Morgan, Charlotte. "The Origin and History of the New York Employer Printers Organization." In *Columbia University Studies in History, Economics and Public Law.* New York, 1930.

Morris, Richard B. *Government and Labor in Early America.* New York, 1946.

Mushkat, Jerome. *Tammany: The Evolution of a Political Machine, 1789–1865.* Syracuse, 1971.

Nash, Gary B. *The Urban Crucible: Social Change, Political Consciousness, and the Origins of the American Revolution.* Cambridge, 1979.

Pomerantz, Sidney I. *New York, An American City: 1783–1803.* New York, 1938.

Pred, Alan R. *Urban Growth and the Circulation of Information: The United States System of Cities, 1800–1840.* Cambridge, 1973.

Rock, Howard B. "The Perils of Laissez-faire: The Aftermath of the New York Bakers Strike of 1801." *Labor History* 17 (1976), pp. 372–387.

——. *Artisans of the New Republic: The Tradesmen of New York City in the Age of Jefferson.* New York, 1979.

Rorabaugh, W. J. *The Alcoholic Republic: An American Tradition.* New York, 1979.

——. *The Craft Apprentice: From Franklin to the Machine Age in America.* New York, 1985.

Silver, Rollo. *The American Printer, 1787–1825.* Charlottesville, 1967.

Stansell, Christine. *City of Women: Sex and Class in New York, 1789–1860.* New York, 1986.

Steffen, Charles. *The Mechanics of Baltimore, 1762–1812: Workers and Politics in the Age of the Revolution.* Urbana, 1984.

Stevens, George A. *New York Typographical Union Number Six.* Albany, 1912.

Turner, Marjorie S. *The Early American Conspiracy Cases, Their Place in Labor Law: A Reinterpretation.* San Diego, 1967.

Willis, Edmund P. "Social Origins and Political Leadership in New York City from the Revolution to 1815." Ph.D. dissertation. Berkeley, 1967.

Wilentz, Sean. "Artisan Republican Festivals and the Rise of Class Conflict in New York City, 1788–1837." In Michael H. Frisch and Daniel J. Walkowitz, eds. *Working Class America: Essays on Labor, Community and American Society.* Urbana, 1982, pp. 37–79.

——. *Chants Democratic: New York City and the Rise of the American Working Class, 1790–1865.* New York, 1984.

Young, Alfred F. *The Democratic-Republicans of New York: The Origins, 1763–1797.* Chapel Hill, 1967.

——. "The Mechanics and the Jeffersonians: New York, 1789–1801." *Labor History* 5 (1964), 247–276.

INDEX

V

Vagrancy, 53–54
Van, Henry, 240
Van Allen, 193
Varick, Richard, 84

W

Wages, 210–12, 222–23, 225–27, 229, 230–31, 234–38, 248
Warner, George James, 3, 6–11, 109, 160, 240–41
War of 1812, 15–16, 161
Washington, George, 13, 110
Washington Republican, 80
Watson, James, 83

Westerfield, William, 244
Whitehead, William, 160
Whitess, Edward, 238
Wicks, H., 245
Wilentz, Sean, xxv
Willett, Marinus, 106
Willis, Edmund P., 111
Women, 182; marital problems, 61–63; right to snuff, 67–68; taking infants to church, 64–67; used to replace male tailors, 221–25
Workshop proposal, 149, 158–60
Wright, Augustus, 122

Y

Yellow Fever, xxi